THE GIRL
ON THE WALL

THE GIRL
ON THE WALL

ONE LIFE'S RICH TAPESTRY

JEAN BAGGOTT

Icon Books

Published in the UK in 2009 by
Icon Books Ltd, Omnibus Business Centre,
39–41 North Road, London N7 9DP
email: info@iconbooks.co.uk
www.iconbooks.co.uk

Sold in the UK, Europe, South Africa and Asia
by Faber & Faber Ltd, Bloomsbury House,
74–77 Great Russell Street,
London WC1B 3DA or their agents

Distributed in the UK, Europe, South Africa and Asia
by TBS Ltd, TBS Distribution Centre, Colchester Road,
Frating Green, Colchester CO7 7DW

Published in Australia in 2009
by Allen & Unwin Pty Ltd,
PO Box 8500, 83 Alexander Street,
Crows Nest, NSW 2065

ISBN: 978-184831-126-8

Book design by Simmons Pugh

Printed and bound by 1010 Printing

To Angela for her skill at keeping my memory bank open and for inspired suggestions such as 'Z' for Zaire; and to Jim for giving me the rugby ball together with the benefit of his vast knowledge of many things.

CONTENTS

FOREWORD

I first met Jean when she took one of my courses on twentieth-century American history, and was immediately impressed by her enthusiastic embrace of her subject. I admired Jean's willingness to participate in class discussions with students much younger than herself, as well as her love of music – as evidenced by her iPod. Several discussions resulted and we discovered a shared love of various acts, including the magnificent Pink Floyd. Jean is a great conversationalist, and it also came to light that she had grown up during the 1940s in West Bromwich, a town which is often described in less than flattering terms.

Some time later Jean, rather tentatively, brought in her tapestry to show me. As she explained the autobiographical rationale behind her work, my eyes were drawn to the detail in each of the circles, and the story that they told. There was no doubt that this was something very special, something that demanded a wider audience. The visual representation of a life in this form was innovative and intriguing. However, it was the way that the circles captured the experience of an 'ordinary' life in a period of such historical change that made the greatest impact. The circles mix the personal, social, cultural and political, avoiding a straight narrative in favour of a thematic representation of a life. And they reveal that the 'ordinary' is quite frequently extraordinary; that it can contain imagination, courage, humour and personal discovery. In our celebrity-obsessed culture, this is something that is all too often forgotten; Jean's work serves as a timely reminder.

Roger Fagge
Department of History, University of Warwick

The Girl on the Wall: The school portrait of
me aged eleven, in 1948, that started it all

PREFACE

At the stroke of midnight on 31 December 1999, I stood in my sitting room and looked long and hard at the girl on the wall. This is a school photograph of me taken when I was eleven which I have re-created in needlework.

When I looked at her that night I saw a girl full of promise, eager to embrace the future. But, in truth, even at the tender age of eleven I was destined never to do anything remarkable. I was a product of 'her' time, and had always known my place: the pinnacle of my achievements would come from being a wife and mother. Although I tried hard to find fulfilment in other ways, I had never quite found what I was looking for.

I was born in 1937 in a heavily industrialised area known as the Black Country, which spilled through three counties: Staffordshire, Warwickshire and Worcestershire. Many towns in these counties looked the same: they consisted of cramped living conditions and factories all covered with a layer of grime. This doesn't mean I was born on the side of a slag heap or that we kept coal in the bath. Indeed, having a bath to keep the coal in would have been a luxury. Our bath hung on a nail in the yard by the back door.

I have never been able to forget my life of that time and have no desire to. My recollections of the area, our street and the people are still very clear but it is the house which holds the most memories. I was born there and lived with my parents and two brothers, Ted and Jim. We led very simple lives and many of my most treasured memories come from this simplicity. Through-out the country there were millions of families who struggled through the war to keep what was theirs, and who struggled after the war in an attempt to get back to some semblance of normality. My parents moved into the house in 1931 and left in 1962, during a massive campaign of so-called slum clearance when the houses were demolished.

By this time only my younger brother Jim was still living at home with Mom and Dad, and they were re-housed in a flat. Neither parent was ever the same after that. The masses were manipulated into believing that being slotted into high-rise blocks of flats was for their own good. It was the same throughout the country as millions of people were transplanted. It was declared that these moves were all part of the great plan which would culminate in the creation of the New Jerusalem and would lead to better lives.

When my parents left the house Britannia no longer ruled: the Suez crisis in 1956 had put Britain well and truly in its place. Things we had known all our lives began to disappear. The fields had gone. Factories had been built on the land and expressways ensured that traffic could flow freely. Keeping the traffic flowing has always come at a terrible cost. In bulldozing all of these little streets the authorities robbed many who had lived in them of community spirit, as they were scattered in all directions.

But I and others of my age, and younger, saw it all as progress. It became normal to want to own your own house, with a garden and a nice family car. It became normal for the woman of the house to work to help pay for it all. Going to work and still having the responsibilities of a wife and mother would mean that she also needed a car. Technology and the new 'must have' gadgets would ensure that she became enslaved in the process.

By the end of the last millennium I could look back on a life spent putting everyone before myself. Most people do, and there is nothing wrong with self-sacrifice. But there does come a point when it is necessary to think about yourself. I reached this point as the twentieth century was becoming history. By then, I had already developed the habit of discussing my problems with the girl on the wall and would share bits of news with her, much as I had done with my husband Ray before he died. As I stood there, eye to eye with my younger self while the clock struck midnight on the eve of the new millennium, I promised her that from then on my life would be dedicated to making her happy. At that moment my life took on a new meaning. I moved forward and have never looked back. Everything I have done since I've done for her, for the girl I was then.

In the late nineties I had finally begun the arduous task of getting the education that had been denied to the girl on the wall. After spending four years at Warwickshire College doing, among other things, a university access course, I was rewarded with a place at the University of Warwick. I began work on a history degree and will hopefully graduate in 2010. While it would be rather conceited of me to be proud of myself, I feel I am allowed to be proud of her.

The course at Warwick has helped me to put all my memories into the context of world history. From being an old woman with a habit of keeping her head down and her mouth shut, lest her naïve opinions betray her ignorance, I've learned how to think about history and express myself with confidence. I've learned that many of my opinions are valid, and that they might even be of interest to others. It's been hard work but I do it for the girl on the wall who was destined to live through a slice of history whose significance is already being deliberated.

When it comes to life stories I have always thought that mine is as interesting as anyone else's. From about the age of 25, I would spend a couple of months every year writing feverishly away, attempting to capture for posterity the finer details of a working-class life. But, as nobody showed any real interest in what I was doing, my efforts always ended up in the bin. This went on for 40 years. At the turn of the century I decided that if I did not record now how I had lived my life it would be the greatest loss to world history, ever! I felt much better after that and was able to concentrate on my studies again.

Inspiration struck after I saw the ceiling in the billiard room at Burghley House in Lincolnshire in May 2006. It had been created in an ornate plasterwork design of interlocking circles that looked like a perfect template for a piece of needlework. When the idea for the 'circles of life' came to me the next morning (see Circle 2) I rubbed my hands together with glee, and nodded happily in the direction of the girl on the wall. This was more like it.

I threaded my first needle on 1 June 2006 and completed the last stitch on 8 October 2007. By the time the tapestry was finished I was amazed at the journey it had taken me on. It made me realise that, although I've lived a very ordinary life, it has not lacked richness. I was also impressed by the effect the tapestry had on others, especially my son-in-law Mark and his colleague Harry, who would drop by occasionally when in Warwick on business. They had watched its progress with interest, something I had not expected from men. I became aware that they and others who saw it wanted to know more about the meanings of its symbols. I started to write short pieces to accompany each circle, although as you will see I did not explain every single detail on the tapestry for the simple reason that there are so many of them. Before too long, I was wondering if this wouldn't make an interesting book.

The book you now hold in your hands would not have amounted to much without the efforts of all those who taught me the things I know, from Miss Cook with her pink thread to Roger Fagge at the University of Warwick, whose words have influenced me greatly. Throughout the needlework and the writing it was reassuring to know I could always bank on my daughter Angela's thoughts on any subject. I must also thank Ann Hume who allowed me to be excited when she herself had so much to be excited about. I'm grateful to Betty Warner and all my friends at Leek Wootton who have supported me through my education and continue to do so. My sincerest regards go to Joyce James who can always find wise words when I need them most. I would like to thank Margaret Minty and Marian Bennett who, I hope, will understand, and of course, Ethel Skerratt.

I am deeply indebted to my son Jim, without whose help my life notes would again have ended up in the bin. I have appreciated so much his editorial advice and support and for introducing me to the team at Icon Books. I'm grateful to Kate Agnew and Sarah Higgins, Andrew Furlow, Najma Finlay and Simon Flynn at Icon for their faith in the project and for making me feel so warmly welcome. The book has greatly benefited from the photography of Scott Wishart, the cover design by Rose Cooper and the design and typesetting skills of Oliver Pugh.

I am grateful to everyone I have mentioned here. Their wisdom, expertise and abilities have given me support that have made the book possible. I am deeply aware that the girl and I could not have done it alone.

The circles that can be seen in the following chapters are reproduced at their actual size.

MEMORIES BEGIN

It has been said that everyone has two births: their natural birth and the birth of their conscious life. The birth of my conscious life came in 1940 when my ability to remember began. Some of my memories are just to do with family but many are about the world in which I have lived. There are good memories and bad. They begin in a very humble house in a very humble street which represented a way of life for millions.

The street was just one of thousands that made up an area known as the Black Country. In those days it belonged to another world compared to today. There was a public house on the right-hand corner and the Bentley family lived in the house on the other corner. A little further down the street on the left-hand side was a terrace of six houses with an arched entry, rather like a narrow tunnel, which ran through the middle and led to the party yard* at the back. At the top of the yard were three lavatories and three wash houses which were shared between the houses. The first three houses had a cellar but water had to be fetched from one of the wash houses. The other three houses each had a tap in the kitchen but no cellar.

Our house had a tap. By the end of the 1940s the rent for a house with a tap was eleven shillings (55p) a week and the rent for a house with a cellar was eight shillings (40p) a week. In the early fifties one family was re-housed and the landlord put their house up for sale. It was snapped up for £450. Mother commented at the time that she 'didn't know who had bought it, but they must have wanted some oil in their lamp paying for a house like that.'

Opposite our house was a double-fronted cottage where a Mrs Jenkins lived with her two grown-up daughters. The rest of the street, on both sides, was made up of seven large factories. My elder brother Ted, younger brother Jim and I enjoyed a great deal of freedom. For example, we could go for miles in search of adventure. If we intended to go off to some distant area we were given a bag of emergency rations, usually bread and scrape† and a bottle of water, with the reminder to be sensible. We could be gone all day and Mother didn't have to worry about us. We were told not to take risks. Now, when I look back, I realise that we were surrounded by risks and we didn't always see them.

---

*A party yard was an area shared by all the houses and could not in any respect be called a garden (see circle 40). Children were not allowed to play in this area because it would annoy the neighbours.

† Scrape, familiar to most people my age, was margarine that had been put on a slice of bread and then scraped off again.

Next door to our house was a factory which made caterpillar tracks for tanks during the war. The street at that time was in a bad state. The war department would regularly send a tank so that tracks could be tested. There was no road surface and no pavement – just mud, potholes and small rocks. We never had street lights. During bad weather we would step out from the front door straight into a quagmire. After the war the factory was taken over by another company, the road was surfaced and a pavement put in. After this, by six o'clock every evening – when all the factories had closed for the day and there was no traffic – the street became our playground and we were joined by youngsters from other streets. With no houses at the bottom end of the street we could make as much noise as we wanted and disturbed no one.

Everyone in the area and beyond lived in streets made up of two-up-two-down houses and was working class, so you knew where you stood. There were the odd one or two families who thought they were a cut above the rest of us but, as Mother said: 'You can tell them a mile off. The men are full of their own importance while the women walk as if their knees have been welded together. In their primness they're old beyond their years and always look as if they've just sucked a lemon.'

I remained in the street until I married in 1955. I had lived there through a period of great change. There had been the hustle and bustle of wartime with its attendant misery, shortages, making do and pulling together. However, this was always accompanied by hope and, for the children, the certain knowledge that God was on our side and we would win the war. With the end of the war came the realisation that things would have to get worse before they could get better. And they did. By the time I left the house there had been another war, this time in Korea, which lasted from 1950 to 1953, and several skirmishes worldwide. However, rationing had come to an end at last, ballpoint pens had been invented and we now had plastic washing-up bowls and buckets. I was led to believe that things were now back to 'normal'.

What a let-down. After all that misery we had a plastic bowl, a bucket and a biro. While the children might have been optimistic and free throughout the period, the adults had not. They had suffered twelve to fourteen years of strife, hard work and worry. For many of them what should have been the best years of their lives had gone. These days, when I hear people going on about the grim state of the world we live in today, I remind them that it cannot possibly be worse than the one I was born into.

– CIRCLE 2 –

BURGHLEY HOUSE

It was in the billiard room at Burghley House in Lincolnshire that the idea for the tapestry began. It was 17 May 2006 and I was on an outing for the day with my friend Betty. In the billiard room other people were looking at the furnishings and paintings, but my eyes were drawn to the ceiling and stayed there. It was designed with an intricate plasterwork pattern of interlocking circles. I knew I could create something using its outline in needlework but what could I possibly make? The walls of my home were already crowded with various samplers and floral scenes and I had no room for any more cushions.

The following day, while drinking my early morning cup of tea at the table in my sitting room, an idea began to form in my mind. What about a table cover? I imagined this as something that would fit only the top of the table without overhanging on any side. The subject would have to be interesting and something that one could associate with circles. The idea that was more prominent than any other in my mind was 'the circles of life'; and so it was decided. I would sew circles, containing details of my life. Then I would be able to sit every morning and contemplate what I had lived through.

I have been a needlewoman from childhood and eventually became capable of doing everything from delicate needlework to re-upholstering a sofa. To create the circles the basis of the pattern consists of ovals and squares which took 36,992 stitches to form; only then could the serious work begin.

Each circle is three and three eights of an inch in diameter and the whole piece measures 44 inches by sixteen. I started in the middle, with the circle about Parks (Circle 37) and then completed the first set of circles that surround this. I carried on like this until the circle on the Lord of the Rings (Circle 35), which I consider to be one of the best. Then I began completing circles first to the left and then to the right. It all became something of an obsession. During this time, apart from looking after myself and my home, I was also studying for a history degree, writing essays and sitting exams. By the time I finished this piece of work on 8 October 2007 I had had 63 years of immense pleasure from threading a needle, but nothing gave me the satisfaction that I found in doing this.

In the tapestry there are 73 circles representing people, places and events in my lifetime, taken from between January

1940 and December 2006. The four corners serve as reminders of my education and my pride in being British. Around the edges of the tapestry you will find 22 half-circles which represent people I simply would not like to forget. Two are memorials to friends I have lost. One shows the men who tramped to work every day to the factories in the street. Others remind me of friends from my earlier years. Some are representative of my friends at Leek Wootton. All of these people are remembered with pleasure. And there is one, the girl on the wall, who has become essential.

'The girl on the wall' refers to a black-and-white photograph of me taken at school when I was eleven. A few years ago I produced an enlarged version of this picture in needlework, and this now hangs in my living room. I can remember exactly what the girl was thinking when the photo was taken, and know just what made her happy and what made her sad.

She had always been part of my life but since the first day of January 2000, the day I decided to think more about the things that matter to her, she has given my life balance and a reason to be kinder to myself. Having lived most of my life for others, at the beginning of the new millennium, at the age of 63, I decided to live more for myself.

In giving consideration to her I am finally putting myself first, and she makes it easier to do things for me rather than always doing things for other people. Ours is a relationship with tremendous advantages: it is impossible to talk about her behind her back. Not only is she the sort of friend I can berate to her face without fear of offence, but I can also overcome my feelings of regret at a frivolous yet expensive purchase by deciding that I'm buying it for the girl on the wall. Special treats do us the world of good and even an occasional guilt-laden, toffee-flavoured ice cream can be eaten without remorse, because I am eating it for her. We have our good days and our bad days but, given a nice cup of tea, we can cope with anything.

HAWKERS, DEALERS AND PEDDLERS

Handcarts and horse-drawn carts were still an important method of selling goods when I was a child. In fact handcarts had many uses. A man in the lane owned two which he kept by the front of his house and rented out to those who needed them. They were used by people who were flitting (moving from one set of rooms to another) or those moving to a new house. Both of these might involve several journeys and I would imagine that the charge for these would have depended on how long you needed them for.

Periodically, a man would come to sharpen knives and scissors using a foot-controlled, battery-driven grindstone. This would be mounted on a small handcart together with other tools, and I believe he did small repairs and other jobs with these tools which the layman was incapable of doing.

While everyone relied on coal for heating the home many, including Mom, also used it for cooking and baking. There were several coal merchants and they did varying degrees of trade in summer and winter. One of them still used a heavy horse-drawn cart for his deliveries; the horse was the most docile of creatures who, while the men ran up and down the entry to the yard doing their work, would stand unmoving while we made a fuss of him. When the work was finished one of the men would reach into a paper bag on the cart, tell us to stand back, and then hold what-ever was in his hand to the horse's mouth. As the horse started munching, they would pull away.

The fish man came round with his handcart on a regular basis. On the cart were three or four enormous slabs of ice on which would be displayed pieces of fish. In the warm weather you could smell him both coming and long after he had gone because of the drips from his cart as he arrived, the puddle that he left in the road and the drips as he left.

The salt man also used a handcart in which he carried very large blocks of salt. Using a large knife, which was similar to a small machete, he would chop a chunk from one of the blocks and then, by guesswork, decide what it was worth and sell it to you. Having made your purchase you would take it home and, using a grater, reduce it to a usable condiment. He would come round every three or four months and on one of these visits Mom decided to buy some salt from him. On this occasion he had much difficulty breaking a chunk from the block and could only do so in the end by using a saw. Even then it was not an easy task. At this point Mom should have given some consideration as to why he had thought it necessary to bring a saw with him, but she didn't. Having got the salt home I was given the task of grating it but, no matter how hard I tried, I had no effect on it. It was the same for Mom. She then decided that the rogue must have kept the main block somewhere damp and it had dried like concrete. The next time she heard his cry of 'salt', Mom was ready for him and, after much deliberation and threat, she got her money back.

The pig man arrived on a horse-drawn trap to collect everybody's waste food to be used as pig swill. He would be seated quite high at the front and behind him were dustbins without lids for the waste collection. He was always accompanied by a cloud of flies and, in today's parlance, the smell was gross.

The rag and bone man would also do his rounds on a horse and cart, and a bundle of old rags would buy you either three clothes pegs or a balloon. The women were allowed to rummage through the rags on his cart and if they found anything that they could use he would sell it to them. Eventually he made enough money to buy a small lorry and gave up collecting rags in favour of scrap metal. He became a very rich man.

Mom was not happy with the gypsies who displayed what they had to sell in a basket hung over their arm. She didn't like them because she knew that the bits of ribbon and elastic and haberdashery items in the basket were greatly overpriced, but she felt obliged to buy from them because, if she didn't, they would give her the 'evil eye', and she had enough trouble coping with life without bringing more misfortune down on herself. She saw it as a form of terrorism on her own doorstep.

THE FAMILY

When I began work on the tapestry I did not give a moment's thought to the notion that I would eventually write about each circle or that the writing would be published. The tapestry was intended for my own pleasure, and I naturally composed circles devoted to my immediate family because family has always been a powerful force in my life.

These family circles are as laden with meaning as any of the others. The individual designs captured in each family circle refer to memories of events in our shared lives and achievements of theirs of which I am especially proud. However, not only are many of these memories intimate and personal, they are also rather domestic, and I fear that my writing about them would become the thinly-disguised boastings of a very proud woman. I have therefore chosen not to write about these circles and hope that the reader will understand. Circles number 4, 7 and 25 to 28 reflect the lives of my son Jim and daughter Angela and their families, who all feature briefly in some of my yarns.

I have made an exception for Mom and Dad in circles 47 and 48 because they loomed too large in my childhood for me to be able to exclude them. My brothers Ted and Jim also feature in many of the stories behind other circles. Brother Ted died in 1993 so I have checked with brother Jim that he is comfortable with me telling stories of our childhood together, even though in Circle 30 I quote Mother's reference to him as 'a miserable little bugger', which at the time he was.

All of which leads me to my lovely Ray, who could always be relied upon to say the right thing. I filled two circles with memories of him – Circles 5 and 6 – and you will also find them in the place where he was always at his happiest – in the cinema – in Circle 65.

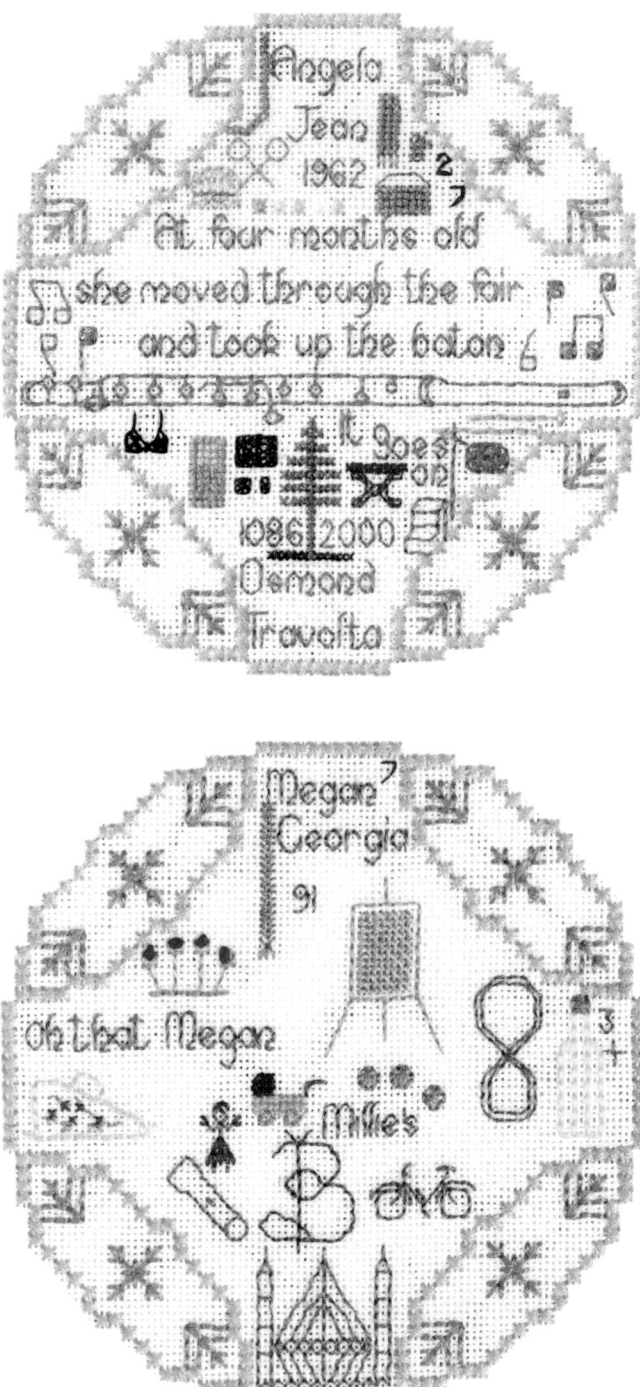

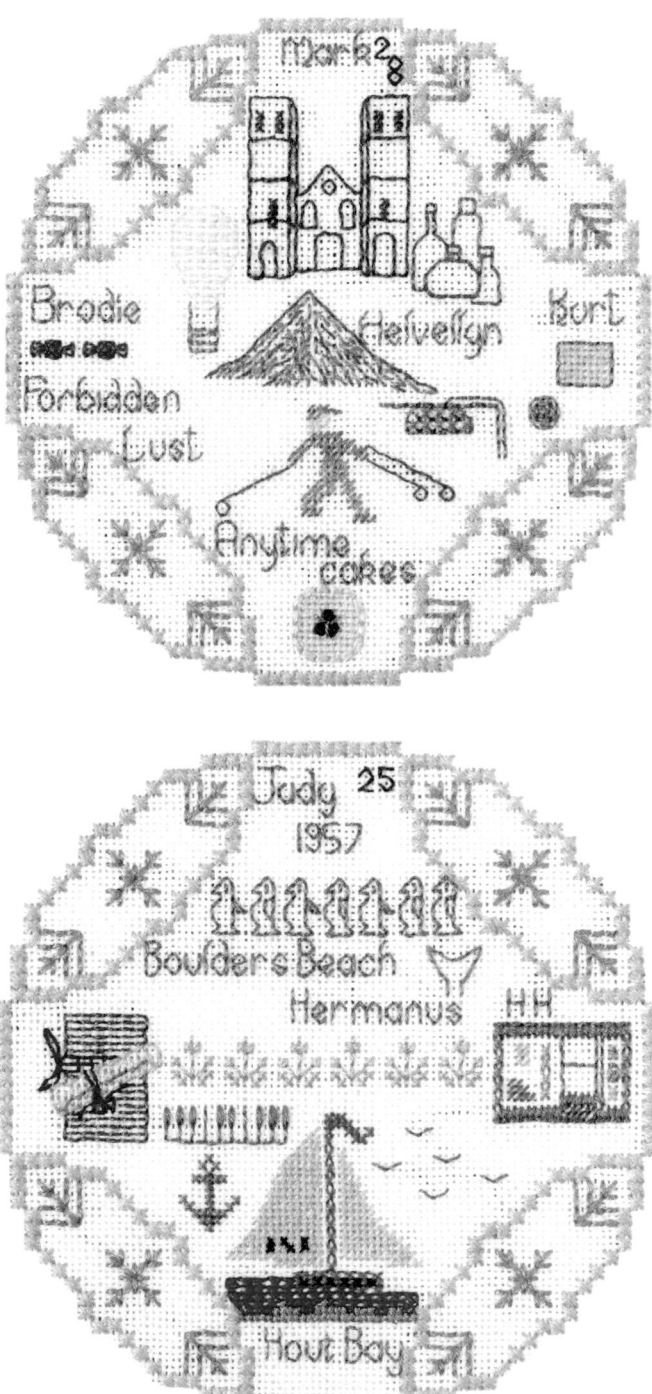

PINK FLOYD

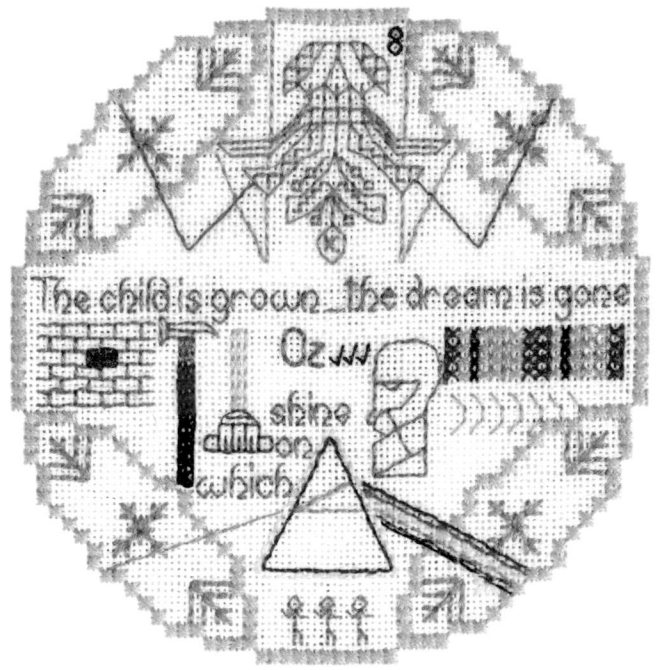

It was in the seventies that I first heard the music of Pink Floyd. I was in a record shop and heard something extraordinary playing in the background. I asked at the counter what it was and, after finding out more about the group, I bought it. The album was *Meddle* and the track that had done it for me was called 'One of These Days'. After playing the album at home I was also impressed with the 28-minute track 'Echoes', and I have been a committed fan ever since.

This was a time when progressive rock music was at its peak

and I was already familiar with the work of Led Zeppelin, Emerson, Lake and Palmer, King Crimson and other groups. However Pink Floyd, as far as I was concerned, had the edge by then. Ray could not hear in them what I did but I was not surprised. His taste never extended beyond Frankie Laine. While I could also appreciate Mr Laine I have always believed a little variety never hurt anyone. Ray had always been tone deaf and when Pink Floyd was playing would always ask: 'What do they have to keep singing for?' But over the years he gradually got used to them.

They had been around since the early sixties using a number of names such as The Abdabs and The Megadeaths. All of these names seemed to reflect the flippant mood of the sixties. Syd Barrett, a founder member of the group, thought up the name Pink Floyd after seeing the names of blues singers Pink Anderson and Floyd Council in a descriptive piece on the back of an album sleeve. The Pink Floyd of that time are remembered for being a prominent group in the London underground scene; they were a very popular house band at the Roundhouse in Camden and featured prominently in the 'psychedelic' period. They had had some success in 1967 with the singles 'Arnold Lane' and 'See Emily Play', but this stuff was not for me.

I can listen to any sort of music, be it classical, middle of the road, heavy metal or pop (see Circle 46), but the work of this group has a hold over me like no other. In world rankings their album *Dark Side of the Moon* is one of the most renowned and best-selling of all time. I can only listen to their work with the volume set at 'ear-splitting' so headphones are mostly needed. It has got me through black days, and days of jubilation and celebration when there has been no one there to share my feelings with. When I have had enough on miserable days Pink Floyd will snap me back to a mood of defiance and when my simmering temper has climbed to boiling point, half an hour of their music will turn off the power and return me to 'normal'. There were a couple of occasions, while I was having a lengthy phone conversation with someone who always brought out the worst in me, when Ray would stand by the music centre with my favourite disc set up and ready, waiting for the conversation to end so that he could throw the switch.

Although in the circle I reproduced the mirror ball (which opens up into petals) that Pink Floyd used in many of their later concerts, I never actually saw the group live. The nearest I got to seeing them was at the Royal Albert Hall when I was taken by my son to see the tribute band Australian Pink Floyd. They were at their very best that night. We had seen them before, but that particular night they were faultless. They played all of my favourite tracks and at the end of one the standing ovation was overwhelming. To say merely that their music has an effect on me is an understatement. And in this instance even the word 'understatement' is completely inadequate. I listened to them continuously as my work on the tapestry progressed and their music will be played when I 'pop off' to meet my maker.

– CIRCLE 9 –

RATIONING AND SHORTAGES

For me rationing was a way of life and I had never known anything other than a life of shortages. The system of trying to ensure equal shares for all was up and running as far back as I could remember, and would stay there until we were into the fifties. The suspension of restrictions on various items was a long, slow process and ration books were not formally dispensed with until 1954.

Mother was an absolute whiz at spinning out the meagre rations and we never went hungry. She didn't bother experimenting with any of the fancy recipes thought up by the brains who worked with the government's Ministry of Food. These were supposed to fool you into thinking that you were having some rare delicacy when you were not. For example, she could not see the point of ruining a perfectly good parsnip which could, according to some recipe or other, become a banana. Plain and simple but filling was the rule in our house.

The rule also extended to fresh foods in preference to processed. Although we did get used to omelettes made with dried egg, nothing could replace the taste or versatility of a real egg. We had National dried egg, National dried milk for babies and National margarine which Dad called 'axle grease'. He also believed that sausages were one of life's mysteries, in that it was difficult to figure out what was actually in them. However, there was no mistaking one ingredient: bread. There was so much bread in a sausage that the minute it was put into a hot frying pan, it would burst open. To counteract this, the manufacturers began making sausages with a thicker skin which was extremely tough, so we got into the habit of removing the skin altogether before cooking.

Bread was a very good filler, at least when it was both available and edible. As the war dragged on we were confronted with 'the grey loaf', which had a high chalk content. It was 35 per cent cattle food. Mother said it was like chewing asbestos and it tasted ghastly. Toasting it only made it a little more palatable. Bread was never rationed during the war but it was from 21 July 1946. It would remain rationed for about a year. Now, all these years later, it is believed that this was unnecessary and was only done at the time in an attempt to convince America that the nation was starving and we needed more help.

While it is true that our family never went hungry, don't be alarmed by the fly in the circle. We did not eat them but they came in very handy at the end of a meal. If we were still peckish, then one reply to the question: 'Have you had enough?' was guaranteed to get you something more to eat. If you replied in a small, trembling voice with the words, 'I'm just beginning to feel as if I've snapped at a fly and missed it', you were quickly offered something else.

Like everything that had to come from abroad, oranges were a luxury. A woman in the lane asked me if I would do some heavy lifting for her. Afterwards she took me into her front room and told me to take an orange from her fruit bowl on the table. I remember thinking at the time that it was unusual for someone to have so many oranges when there were none in the shops. I also remember thinking that the one I chose felt a bit funny in that it was very hard. When I got home I cut through it with a knife – it was as dry as sawdust and completely inedible.

Everyone from that period seems to recall their first sighting of a banana. Mine was probably in 1947 and was both exciting and disappointing. I had been sent to a local shop on an errand. As I went in I could not help noticing a large plain wooden box on the floor, looking suspiciously like a coffin. The shopkeeper lifted the lid and, using a knife, cut off a bunch of five bananas from a stem that ran the length of the container. He handed them to me and said: 'Take these to your mother. Tell her I will put the cost on her bill.' As I waited to cross the road a passing cyclist, noticing the bananas I held proudly aloft, fell off his bike. Sadly, after years of hearing about them, I was not impressed with the taste and am still not keen on them, though I eat one every day because of their nutritional properties.

We never got used to 'Pom', 'Spam' and 'Snoek'. Pom was powdered potato similar to that which can be bought today but tasting nothing like it. 'Spam' was a kind of tinned luncheon meat which tasted ghastly and we would only eat it if it was fried. Snoek made an appearance in 1948 after the government ordered 10 million tins of it from South Africa. It was rumoured that snoek was a ferocious fish which hissed like a snake and barked like a dog when it was in a temper. A half-pound tin cost 1s 4d, and used up only one ration point as opposed to fourteen for red salmon and six for pink salmon. In August 1949 a further 8 million tins arrived from Australia which were labelled as barracuda, but the contents tasted like snoek.* In 1951 much of it was re-labelled and sold as cat food for ten pence a tin but the majority of it was probably used as fertiliser. In the summer of 1947 whale meat was introduced, although Mother wouldn't have anything to do with it. It had limited success but by early 1950 there were still 4,000 tons of it in storage lying unwanted, in cans.

During the early months of the fifties restrictions on milk were removed. This was followed by flour, eggs and soap. Sweets were among the last things to come off the ration, although some alternatives were available long before then. For instance, you could buy a soft toffee, but it was not as good as the rationed one which was commonly known as 'stick-jaw' and had to be broken up with a hammer. When chewing an excessively large piece one's jaws could become welded together and a finger would be needed to manoeuvre the offending chunk around the mouth. Anyone's finger would do in an emergency.

When ration books were finally scrapped I quietly put away my sweet coupons together with a threepenny (3d) bit. I had long ago learned that one was no good without the other and three old pennies were sufficient for two ounces of liquorice

* Michael Sissons and Philip French, eds., *The Age of Austerity 1945–51* (London: Penguin, 1964), p. 54.

comforts. In putting away both I was ensuring that, if hostilities suddenly flared up again, I would be ready. I still have them.

When thinking about rationing most people of today's generation would naturally think that it applied only to food. This was not the case. Along with a ration book for food we also had a book of clothing coupons. All clothing, household linen and furniture had restrictions of some sort, and all of these would carry a utility mark which established that the item in question met government guidelines in its manufacturing process. Blankets and many other items could only be bought if you applied for a docket. I still have a label from a wartime blanket which shows a utility mark and has the 'set in concrete' selling price of 37s 6d (£1.87) printed on it.

Both cigarettes and razor blades were hard to find and it was as well to keep in with a local shopkeeper. It was easy to tell when Dad needed a new blade. If, after shaving, there were no bits of paper stuck to his face, the blade was in good condition. If there were five or six we would know he was getting desperate. The better known brands of cigarettes – Woodbines, Park Drive, Craven A, Players or Senior Service – were kept under the counter. Dad's preferred brand was Woodbines, which were known as 'coffin nails'. These were often in such short supply that they were sold in packs of five so that more customers could have their fix. The brand that was readily available was Pasha, a 'gasper' in the proper sense and believed to be capable of rotting your socks. These were Egyptian and the smell of them burning was enough to put anyone off.

Dad usually had to work on Sunday mornings. One Sunday, when he came home just after noon he gave Ted some money and told us to go off on our scooters and get him some cigarettes. We were told not to come home until we had some. We eventually managed to get him five from a little shop in Aston.

When we got back, we found that he and Mom had been very worried about us. He had been joking when he said 'Don't come back till you find some.' I mention this only to show how little traffic there was on the roads then on Sundays. This was due to the chronic petrol shortage. To get to Aston, some five miles or more from home, we had used the main road through Birmingham and we were travelling on two home-made scooters.

If someone left a pile of builders' sand unattended it would be pounced on by young women who would rub their legs with it, leaving them a bright orange colour. This was supposed to give the impression that they had a tan or were wearing silk stockings. Some went to the trouble of getting a friend to draw a seam down the back of each leg with a pencil in an attempt to fool others into believing that they were wearing the finest stockings. I doubt that they fooled anyone, and Mother said at the time: 'I'd like to know what their bedclothes look like.'

In February 1946, the old wartime standby – dried egg – disappeared from the shops, but when national newspapers took up its cause the government grudgingly brought it back. After crop failures that year, the government urged farmers to plant again and offered them some of the 40,000 German prisoners of war who were being held in Britain to help. From January to July that year Europe was short of millions of tons of wheat. As 1946 drew to a close, something was approaching which would prove devastating to our beleaguered country. It would eventually test all of us to our limits.

The winter of 1947 began with a fall of snow on 16 December 1946. The winter would grip us quite mercilessly for months. By the end of January the country was paralysed. In March, 300 main roads were still impassable. A final storm on 16 March released floods which affected everything. These covered, at least in some part, 31 counties. About 600,000 acres of arable land disappeared underwater, destroying 80,000 tonnes of potatoes and 70,000 acres of other crops.[†] We lost nearly a third of the country's flocks of hill sheep and 30,000 head of cattle. London lost its fresh water supply and the Underground was closed. All of this was a devastating setback in our recovery programme and today, when historians discuss the winter of 1947, they talk mostly about the weather and not about its overwhelming consequences for a distressed and ravaged nation.

By 1948 rations had reached an all-time low and were even below the wartime offerings. Bacon and other meat, cheese, butter and margarine, cooking fat, sugar, tea and eggs would continue to be rationed for a long time to come, and queues still formed for things which were scarce. Today when I stand in a queue at a supermarket checkout I look at the overflowing trolleys and remember how hard people once worked on so little.

[†] Michael Sissons and Philip French, eds., *The Age of Austerity 1945–51* (London: Penguin, 1964), p. 51.

DECORATING

With restrictions and a shortage of money it was Hobson's choice when it came to decorating any of the rooms in the old house. There was no need to paint doors and skirting boards because ours, like most people's, were always dark brown and looked as if they had been that colour since the houses were built. If a bit of paint flaked off it would only reveal another layer of brown underneath. It would be some time before restrictions were lifted and money was available to allow the delights of choice when it came to decorating.

During the interim period all that seemed to be available was a 'ball' of whitewash for the ceilings, which was about the size of an ostrich egg and had to be grated into a bucket of water and stirred with a stick. For the walls we could buy tins of something called Walpamur. Ready prepared, it was thicker than whitewash, came in three colours – white, beige or pale green – and was known to everyone as 'wallop'. Women would proudly inform anyone who crossed their path that they would be giving the kitchen walls a 'walloping' over the weekend.

Dad hadn't done any decorating while the war was on, and he took us all by surprise one Saturday lunchtime when he came in from work and declared that he had decided to paint the front bedroom. He had settled on pale green for the walls.

I was despatched forthwith to the ironmongers. I asked the woman behind the counter for the paint. Before I could say what colour Walpamur we wanted, she asked: 'Do you want the white, beige or eau de nil?' I looked at her blankly and replied: 'I'll be back in a minute.' I scurried off home where I told Dad that they hadn't got pale green; only white, beige or eau de nil. He became very agitated for he had set his heart on the pale green. He said, 'Go back and ask her why she hasn't got pale green. Tell her it's the green we want.' When I returned from the shop and explained that eau de nil was French for pale green, Dad said that he couldn't understand how the paint company could expect the likes of us to know that.

Mom prepared the whitewash while Dad moved the furniture about. Dad, having covered his clothes with one of Mom's old nightgowns, tied an old scarf around his head and put on an old cap, was ready to start. He began very carefully, anxious not to make too much mess. The whitewash was very thin and watery. After a while, keen to get on, he threw all caution to the wind and slapped it on vigorously. At this point the cat ran for cover.

The Walpamur was a little thicker and not so messy. Even so, by the time the walls were done, everyone and everything that was not protected was liberally splashed with white and green splodges. We had a wonderful time. It was such fun. By Sunday teatime, with the room thoroughly clean, polished and tidy, it looked grand.

The following Easter Dad decided to spend the holiday week-end doing the same to his and Mother's room at the back of the house, only this time he wouldn't be using whitewash for the ceiling as it was too messy. This time it was wallop for the walls and the ceiling and hang the expense. The weather was typical English holiday weather and on the Saturday it didn't stop raining, but we were happy. Sunday was no different, and by 10.30 Dad was washing the brushes and buckets.

While lunch was cooking we all beavered away cleaning and polishing the furniture. Even the ornaments had a wash. After lunch Dad decided he had earned an afternoon nap. The rain was still coming down and he had been asleep for about an hour when a two-foot-square section of the ceiling came down on him. At first he thought that the weight of the Walpamur had been too much for the poor old ceiling, but we could clearly see through the gaping hole that there was a slate missing from the roof. The bedspread was removed with all the debris inside it. The landlord had the roof repaired quite quickly, but he would never do anything about the ceiling. When they left the house in 1962 the hole was still there, but daintily concealed by a piece of white American cloth.

Dad came home from work another day with a tin of gloss paint which he had picked up cheap, no questions asked. With the door to the stairs in the kitchen no longer being used as a chalking board (see Circle 34), he decided that the time had come to paint the doors to the stairs and coal place. I got quite excited until I realised that the tin contained brown paint. Within a couple of hours the job was done. As the time went by, we noticed that it didn't seem to be drying too quickly. Dad said we had to have a bit of patience and give it time. The weeks went by and it remained tacky. One of us would often get stuck to the stairs door in passing, especially if we had a woollen jumper on. Dad eased the situation by saying: 'For what I paid for it you can't expect miracles.'

The kitchens in these types of houses all had something which is no longer seen. This was known as a 'canting patch'. It was common practice for women to stand outside someone's kitchen door in twos or threes, having a cant (a chat). On cold or wet days they would stand just inside the door by the canting patch. This patch was a four-foot-square area of lower wall just inside the door, and it was usually timbered and painted brown. It was probably done this way to stop the wall being scuffed as people walked in or out. These can still be seen occasionally in very old pubs.

Fashions in decorating came and went as the wallpaper and paint industry came into its own again, but we were never too adventurous. For one thing, at least in the kitchen and front room, we were so overcrowded that you couldn't see much of the walls. For another, we had great difficulty in getting the paper to stick to the porous plaster. One family got around the expense by never decorating behind the furniture, and another made the job easier by cutting the paper into *Daily Mirror*-sized pieces. They took their time over the actual hanging but, unfortunately, didn't bother to match the patterns. You can imagine what it looked like.

When I married and left the house the paint on the two doors was still tacky. Dad would still not openly admit to buying a pig in a poke, and would comment with a twinkle in his eye that we should learn to have a bit of patience. Rome wasn't built in a day. However, he did eventually repaint both doors in a delicate shade of cream.

The kitchen never looked right after that.

– CIRCLE 11 –

THE FORTIES

A few days after the bombing of Coventry in 1940, Birmingham received similar treatment. About 350 aircraft released 400 tons of high explosives and 30,000 incendiary bombs which left 400 dead. In total 77 raids were inflicted on the city killing 2,227 and bringing destruction to around 300 factories and damage to 12,000 homes.* A blanket of secrecy was thrown over this information for two reasons: the first was obviously to keep it from the

---

*Sunday Mercury, 9 June 1996.

enemy and, second, it could have lowered morale among a work-force which was crucial to the war effort. For instance, in Castle Bromwich a workforce of mainly women had assembled 11,000 Spitfires, millions of guns and mountains of ammunition. This was only a microcosm of what it took to achieve the victory that would be signified by Churchill's famous V-sign.

One night an area close to where we lived was bombed and the next morning the emergency services were being coordin-ated from our street. Mom got us up early so that we could look around before we went to school. Ted was always on the lookout for shrapnel. In the street there was a great bustle of activity. The men in charge were busy discussing the pros and cons of various different approaches. We couldn't find any shrapnel so we went up the entry to the yard which was very quiet. We were the only ones there.

Behind a shed Ted found something which made him very excited, though we didn't know what it was. Ted said he was going to take it to one of the wardens in the street but I had doubts. We were constantly warned not to pick anything up that looked strange but Ted was having none of it and, with him carrying it flat across the palms of both hands, we gingerly walked across the yard to the entrance. As we emerged into the street one man glanced at us with an expression of horror. He raised his hand, palm outwards and said: 'Stop!'. He continued: 'Stay there and don't move an inch.' He left us for a moment but swiftly returned with a container of sand. He very carefully took the item from Ted and laid it on the sand. He barked 'Stay there!', and disappeared. When he came back he rebuked us for our stupidity and sent us home. As we walked back to the house Ted said that it might be a good idea not to tell Mother what we had been up to; he had been carrying an unexploded incendiary bomb.

On D-Day, 6 June 1944, Dad came home and said, with a lift in his voice: 'We've gone in then.'

'I know, but they say that we've lost ever so many of our chaps,' Mother responded.

'I know, I know,' Dad replied, 'but what we've got to remember is that they've given us a foothold, and that's all that matters today.'

From the tone of his voice I finally knew that the war would end. Paris was liberated on 25 August and Brussels on 2 September. Aachen was entered on 12 September and the following year, on 30 April, Hitler shot himself.

On Sunday 27 August 1944, my brother Jim was born, at home, downstairs in the front room. I was seven years old and did not understand the business of childbirth. I had been told that the nurse would bring the new baby in her black bag. Ted and I woke up at about eight o'clock and he was the first to notice that our clothes had been placed at the foot of our beds. On the dressing table was a bowl of water with soap, a towel and a comb. Ted commented that he did not know what was going on but it looked like we had been confined to the room until we had washed and dressed. While we were doing this I said that I could hear a baby crying. Ted thought that it was probably Auntie May with our infant cousin Barry. I replied that it was too early for Auntie May to visit and wondered why we were having to get washed and dressed in the bedroom if it was only Auntie May. Within seconds Ted's face lit up and he blurted out, 'I know what's going on. Mom's had the baby.' With that we increased our speed, finished washing and were dressed in record time.

Downstairs Dad was standing by the kitchen table looking very pleased. He looked down at me and said: 'Mom is in the front room and she has got something for you.' Mother's bed had been moved down to the front room a couple of weeks earlier in preparation for the birth. Ted and I had been directly above and had heard nothing.

At the end of hostilities many arrangements were made that attempted to sort out the mess and to ensure that wars would become a thing of the past. The Oxford Committee for Famine Relief had gathered for the first time in 1942 and we were told that with organisations such as this in place, the world would never again hear of people starving to death in times of trouble. In 1948 when the first Oxfam charity shop opened in Broad Street, Oxford it seemed such an excellent and simple idea. Sadly, in the twenty-first century starvation is still a problem in some parts of the world.

When Japan accepted defeat in August 1945 the country, at last, had much to look forward to. Well, at least that is what we were told. In 2001 a programme from the series *A Year to Remember* on Radio 4 told us that 1946 was

The year of GI brides, food rationing, the bill that created the National Health Service and the launch of the new Ford Anglia, costing £225. It sounds cheap until you consider that professional footballers were threatening to strike demanding a minimum wage of £7 a week.[*]

1946 was also the year that saw the establishment of the United Nations. This was seen as our real hope for preventing wars in the future. And with the restoration of a television service in this same year, a TV licence fee of £2 was introduced. While the world continued to cope with misery, it was a creative time with many new products coming onto the market.

The bikini swimsuit was named after the Bikini Atoll in the Pacific Ocean, which had been the site of an American atomic weapons test. The bikini was said to signify the new emancipa-

---

[*] *Radio Times*, July 2001.

tion of women at the war's end. At the end of the First World War most women had returned to their kitchens and once again had to find fulfilment in their domestic lives. While this was not the case at the end of the Second World War women would still struggle for years in an effort to find equality with men, none more so than the younger women who were expected to toe the line, without deviation, and be married and settled for life by the age of 21.

At the end of 1946 there began an unprecedented wave of industrial unrest which was dominated by a growing fear of communism. There was constant talk of the workers' unions being infiltrated on a grand scale by communists. With memories of war still very fresh in everyone's minds this was seen as a type of creeping terrorism, and the issues of communism and industrial relations would come to dominate the next 30 or 40 years.

On 16 December 1946 a cloud crept towards the British Isles which was to paralyse the nation from the moment it descended on us. It would continue for months. The winter of 1947 had arrived while the country was still on its knees and unprepared for a catastrophe. It began by paralysing the transport system, which prevented coal from being distributed to industry. This affected everyone. The only way many employers could cling on was by letting thousands of workers go. These redundancies covered the length of the country from cotton mills in Blackburn to Austin's in the Midlands.

Everyone was saying that the winter of 1947 could not have chosen a worse moment to hit our country, but now I cannot help wondering what course the war would have taken if it had gripped us five years earlier.

With the arrival of the National Health Service in 1948 the country was given a free medical service and never again would anyone have to worry about the cost of seeing a doctor, optician or dentist. However, it seemed that everyone suddenly needed glasses. Girls at school who had never had trouble with reading began wearing glasses. Any number of the elderly who hadn't had a tooth in their heads for donkey's years were now grinning like Cheshire cats. Of course it didn't last and a charge was quickly brought in for optical and dental care. As Minister of Health of the Labour government under Clement Attlee, Aneurin Bevan is credited with the introduction of this service. While this is true, the Health Service was not his brainchild. The man known as the father of the welfare state (which included the health service) was the Liberal Sir William Beveridge, although this is often forgotten. The Beveridge Report, which was published in December 1942, proposed a comprehensive scheme in which we would be taken care of 'from the cradle to the grave'. The report formed the basis of social legislation for the Labour government between 1945 and 1950.

With misery and rationing as bad as ever, facilities for the 1948 Olympic Games in London were basic. In the track and field events it was America's Olympics. They won twelve gold medals in this event while Sweden won five and Holland four. The 'Flying Dutchwoman', Mrs Fanny Blankers-Koen, won gold medals for the 100 metres, 200 metres, 80 metres hurdles and the 4 x 100 metres relay and became the star of the show. Britain managed four silver medals on the track.

However, in 1948 the main event for me was being a brides-maid to my cousin Alan in his marriage to Marie. It was a happy day. My dress was a dazzling shade of pink, which I loved, and I wore silver sandals and carried a flower arrangement of anemones. The reception was held at our house, with Mother and other helpers preparing the food which had been donated by relatives and friends of the couple, and I remember that

Marie's Aunt Gwen came from Yorkshire, bringing the wedding cake with her.

In 1949 the British frigate HMS *Amethyst* gave us cause to celebrate. During the last phase of the Chinese Communist Revolution under the leadership of Mao Tse Tung, HMS *Amethyst* was fired on by the communists while going up the Yangtze River to deliver supplies to the British in Nanking. Many officers and ratings were killed or wounded and several rescue attempts failed. The *Amethyst* remained pinned down for fourteen weeks, short on rations and equipment and in unbearable heat. It appeared in newsreels and was discussed at length on the radio and in newspapers throughout the period. Then, during the night of 30/31 July, under cover of darkness, it made a dash for it and covered the 140 miles to freedom at a speed of 22 knots, undetected by the five lines of Chinese forts which it had to pass in order to reach freedom. While it was unclear why the vessel was attacked, this was interpreted by many as an assertion of Chinese sovereignty over an international waterway.

In 1949 Piccadilly Circus was restored to its former splendour with coloured lights. George Orwell's book *Nineteen Eighty-Four* was published and we became aware that Russia now had an atomic bomb. The feelings of apprehension over the prospects of the Cold War developing into a nuclear war were exacerbated when Klaus Fuchs confessed that he had passed secrets to the Soviet Union. German-born physicist Fuchs, who was a communist, had come to England in 1934 to escape Nazi persecution. During the war he had worked in America on the Manhattan Project at Los Alamos and now held a senior post at Britain's Atomic Energy Research Establishment at Harwell. As the forties gave way to the fifties any hope that the Cold War between America and the Russians might fizzle out had gone.

The forties had much to be remembered for, good and bad.

The end of the war affected people in many ways. While every-one seemed to be beavering away to create a new and better world, it was impossible to forget what we had been through. In the first half of the forties, death and suffering were part of a war in which there had also been unbelievable examples of courage and bravery. During 1946 there was much talk of memorials, and films were made and books written about daring exploits and selfless determination to work hard and see things through. Even the children were not forgotten. To mark the first anniversary of the end of the war every schoolchild received a certificate from the King, but I have always thought that the wording of this was unfortunate:

To-day, as we celebrate victory, I send this personal message to you and all other boys and girls at school. For you have shared in the hardships and dangers of a total war.

And you have shared no less in the triumph of the Allied Nations.

I know that you will always feel proud to belong to a country which was capable of such supreme effort; proud, too, of parents and elder brothers and sisters who by their courage, endurance and enterprise brought victory. May these qualities be yours as you grow up and join in the common effort to establish among the nations of the world unity and peace.

Were we, too, not to be remembered for having these qualities of courage, endurance and enterprise in our childhood? Were we not to be remembered for displaying these qualities as we did for a further ten years, while the country sorted itself out? By that time we were young adults, and it seems that all of our work to help with the war effort – collecting scrap iron, salvaging paper, collecting halfpennies with ships on to help pay for military equipment and so many other things – had counted for nothing.

In the last 50 years I have seen memorials unveiled to every-one who did their bit during the war. In Park Lane in London there is one in memory of the work done by animals at such times, and rightly so. I have looked at this many times. Beautifully crafted, it does not leave out any animal that is capable of being useful and giving assistance in war. However, I have never seen one for children.

ADVERTISING

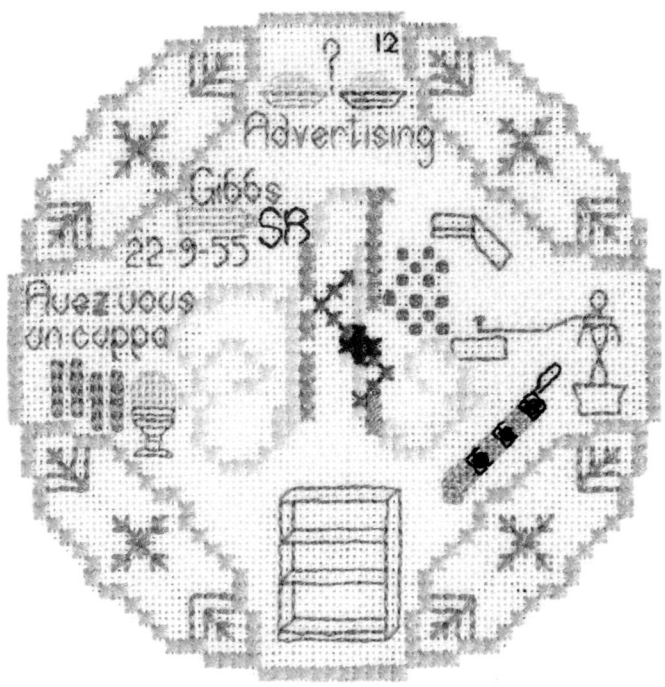

Advertising has always been part of our lives but in my early life we mainly saw adverts only in newspapers and magazines. In those days not only were there items advertised for sale, but there was also a form of advertising for things you could no longer buy. I suppose the logic behind these adverts was to keep the seller's name in the public mind and to show that these firms had a caring side but, perhaps more importantly, they were showing us that while some items for the home were not being made, designers and inventors were still planning for the future.

For example, in the following advertisement the GEC (General Electric Company) reminded us that:

The contrast between the elaborate silk-covered lamp standard of 1914 and its modern, elegant counterpart symbolises the rapid and continuous progress always being made in the electrical industry. Science did not stand still in 1914, and today the GEC is keeping abreast of developments and improvements that will result in better electrical equipment for the home when this war is over.

Another example gave us useful tips to help the war effort:

W.H. Smith & Son can still supply a fair choice of writing papers. But use it carefully – both sides of the paper please, little or no left hand margin, and smaller writing and closer-spaced lines. You get more on to a sheet if you use it length ways instead of upright. It is not simply a matter of making a little go a long way. Paper makes MUNITIONS so please don't forget to put out for salvage every scrap of old paper and cardboard in the house.

I believe that the slogans of the time, which were rules to live by and told you what you could do to help the war effort, were also a form of advertising. A few of these were:

Careless talk costs lives
Grow more food ... Dig for Victory
Paper for salvage helps to feed the guns
Rags for salvage will give the troops more blankets
Is your journey really necessary?

There were a great many of these and Dad's favourite, which he was always quoting, was 'Lend to defend'. But he would add his own threepenny-worth at the end: 'and borrow to live'.

I didn't care much for the nasty-looking Squander Bug which was covered in swastikas. He was seen as a sort of German agent who urged us to squander and waste our money with phrases like: 'Don't forget to take the squander bug with you when you go shopping.' He was used by National Savings who explained that as long as he thrived, so would Hitler and the Nazis. Only by being frugal could we buy National Savings Certificates and help to rid the world of them. The money raised from savings certificates helped to finance the war.

As the war became history very small advertisements appeared, attempting to sell objects which had been thought up by the enterprising but were not all they seemed. In those days it was quite legal to use all sorts of misleading statements to make money. Two of these are represented in the circle.

The first was for 'the sharpest pen knife you will ever own', which was sold at a very insignificant cost and also had an easily replaceable blade. Ted sent off for one and it turned out to be simply a razor blade in a tinplate holder.

The second advertisement spoke for itself. It featured a very simple sketch of a portable shower. This seemed to consist of a circle of tubing with holes in it which was placed round the neck and rested on the shoulders while you stood naked with your feet in a bowl. The circle had a length of rubber hose leading from it and you attached the end to a tap. The advert did not explain that you would have to stand very close to the tap or get someone else to turn it on for you. It did not tell you what to do if the water was too hot or, as in our case, stone cold. Neither did it tell you what to do when the bowl was full.

Advertising took a leap forward when great billboards were erected everywhere. They were used to disguise blots on the landscape by creating new ones of their own. The Pearl and Dean advertising slot became part of our 'viewing pleasure' at the cinema. The phrase 'for your viewing pleasure' was used frequently in a condescending manner. It was considered in those days that anything put on cinema screens would only add to our entertainment and would be warmly welcomed. It was my generation who developed the loud groan which can still be heard in cinemas when the advertisements appear.

With the advent of Independent Television, advertisements became part of our life at home. London was the first area in the country to get ITV in 1955, followed by the Midlands in February 1956. The first advert on ITV was for Gibbs SR toothpaste. Many television adverts were better than the programmes and used very memorable jingles or slogans. Esso Petroleum urged the modern driver to 'put a tiger in your tank'. A cheaply-made tiger's tail hung in cars everywhere in the country and was a very successful advertising symbol. The campaign which attempted to assure us that we really couldn't 'tell Stork from butter' wasn't convincing, but remains very clear in my memory because most people actually could 'tell Stork from butter'.

A good catchphrase became essential to an advertising campaign, and the series of adverts which had the most catchphrases was produced by the Egg Marketing Board in the fifties. They used Tony Hancock and Patricia Hayes to persuade us to buy eggs. The umbrella slogan which urged all of us to 'Go to work on an egg' encompassed all the others which were: 'Eggs is healthy', 'Eggs is easy', 'Eggs is cheap', 'Happiness is egg shaped', 'Where's me soldiers?' and 'How do you want your eggs, fried or boiled?'

We lived through the lives of two Oxo families and the developing love life of the dopey couple in the Nescafé Gold Blend series. If I had to choose one series above all the others it would be the one from Brooke Bond tea (PG Tips) which gave us the chimpanzees and featured so many characters. Mr Shifter, the piano mover, was one and another was the cyclist in the Tour de France who asked the immortal question, 'Avez-vous un cuppa?' Priceless.

As the century wore on TV advertising became an art form. By the end of the century some adverts carried enormous production costs and became a lucrative sideline for the famous. One of the most memorable of these more recent commercials was the one for Guinness with the horses surfing the waves. You could always tell Christmas was on its way when the Woolworths adverts began. These became more and more stunning every year and used the talents of many top celebrities. While we no longer have Woollies adverts to look forward to, we still know that Christmas is over for another year when commercials for wonderful holidays take over our screens on Boxing Day.

Probably as a salute to the new millennium the BBC astounded us all with an advert in which a whole host of their most important stars and presenters from radio and television appeared. It seemed to last a good minute or two and was eagerly enjoyed each time it was screened. It was obvious that no expense had been spared, but that was alright. The cost of this would have come out of the TV licence fee. As licence fee payers we were not only paying for the making of the advertisement, we were also paying for the programmes that the BBC was so benevolently telling us about. Unbelievable!

BATTLES AND WARS

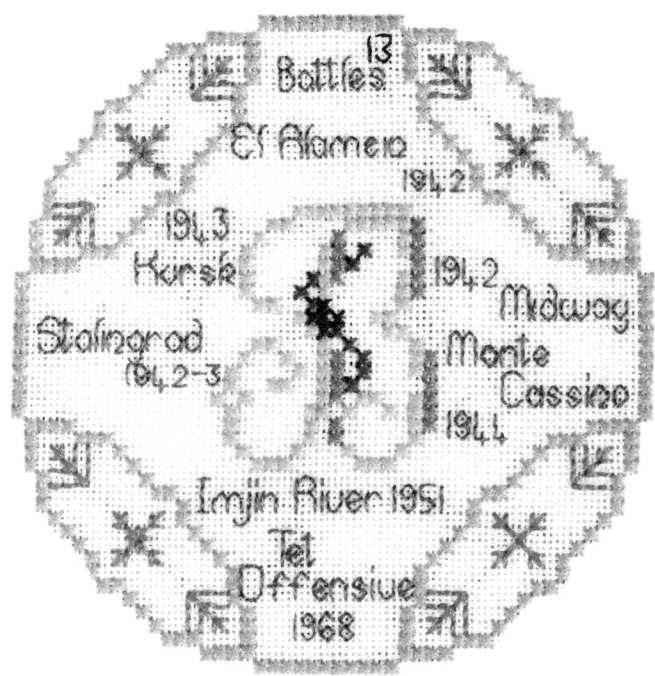

Like millions of children I was raised on battles. The first one to make an impression on me, in that I realised the importance to us of winning it, was the second Battle of El Alamein. The British 8th Army under the command of Auchinleck had prevented Rommel's troops from making a breakthrough, and in doing so had prepared the way for the decisive second battle at Alam Halfa. With Montgomery now in command, the 8th Army repulsed Rommel in October and November 1942. This battle was our first decisive victory. I remember distinctly the look of jubilation on Dad's face when he came home and spoke the words: 'We've got the buggers on the run at last.'

I remember the battle of Midway from the bombardment of the big guns of battleships in 1942 that we saw on cinema news-reels. Good intelligence by the Americans enabled them to anticipate the plans of Yamamoto and strike early at Japanese carriers. America lost one carrier and Japan four, and it brought to an end Japanese expansion in the central Pacific. This was a significant victory for the Americans. I also remember Mom's comforting reaction to the battle of Stalingrad which began in September 1942. She told us that Hitler had made his biggest mistake by invading Russia. When Ted asked her why, she replied: 'The Russians will show the Germans no mercy and the Germans are not prepared for a Russian winter.'

She was right on both counts. A large number of German divisions were deployed at Stalingrad and the Russians fought them street by street. In the maze of shattered buildings Russian snipers kept the Germans busy. In November the Russian counter-attack began on a scale never seen before. They continued to lure the German army into Stalingrad where the Russian army encircled them, and the Germans were forced to surrender. The battle was won at the end of January 1943 and had lasted roughly five months. It was the major turning point of the war.

I should add here that both our parents never missed an opportunity to remind us that the German troops were just ordinary people and, like our troops, were only following orders – and that any hatred that we might feel should be kept for Hitler and his henchmen. Ted explained that his henchmen included the likes of the Gestapo, the SS and the Storm Troopers. I remember having reservations about this with regard to the rest of the German servicemen. To me, at that age, all Germans were baddies and not to be trusted.

We relied very much on cinema newsreels to keep us in the picture, so to speak, with the progress of the war. Cinema news-reels showed us images of the greatest ever tank battle between the Russians and the Germans at Kursk in 1943, and of the desperate struggle at Monte Cassino in 1944. I remember the jubilation in the newsreader's voice at times of victory in skirmishes and battles, and the triumphant cheer from the children that went round the cinema as this type of news was relayed.

The world war ended but it did not bring world peace. The seeds were planted for the Vietnam War as soon as hostilities ceased. That country was then known as Indo-China and had been colonised by the French in the nineteenth century. A month after the Japanese surrendered, a Vietnamese Republic was proclaimed under the leadership of Ho Chi Minh and the French tried to regain control. French forces fought with the Viet Minh, and the fighting would last from December 1946 until the defeat of the French at Dien Bien Phu in 1954. The north-south division of the country at that time, implemented as a solution to the country's problems, would eventually lead to the disastrous Vietnam War.

The war in Korea had begun in 1950. I was growing up and, with the Imjin River battle in 1951, I began to realise that the wonderful world that should have been created after 1945 would not now come: all the promises that had been made were empty. I woke up to the fact that I, and millions like me, had been gullible to believe that mankind was capable of ever living in peace. By the time America began its interference in the Vietnam War I knew that war and strife were just another part of normal life; they would always be with us and there was not a lot I could do about it.

With the Tet Offensive in 1968 came the realisation that the mightiest military force on the planet could not defeat men who were armed very simply and hiding in bushes. The American troops could not see who they were fighting. The face of war was becoming even more sinister, and as I could do nothing to change these never-ending situations I decided I would concentrate more on the lives of my family.

However, during most of the second half of the twentieth century there was no escaping from the Cold War, though this was not really a war but a battle of wills. History tells us that the Cold War was already in the making during the Second World War. Stalin chose to extend 'hostilities' by his continued snubbing of attempts at interference by the Allied heads of state. This served two purposes. One was to conceal the numbers of Soviet war dead. The second was to discourage foreign infiltration should the country's plight become known. Victory for the Soviet Union had come at a price that no other country had had to pay.

An estimated 27 million Soviet dead had left a much reduced workforce which was mainly made up of women. We were unaware that they had suffered such loss of life. When pictures of Russian women doing heavy manual labour appeared in newspapers, Mother and other women muttered that the Russian authorities ought to be ashamed for using women in this way. Villages, towns and cities had been destroyed and most of the agricultural land had been rendered useless as a result of Hitler's 'scorched earth' policy.

Stalin avoided war by pretending that Russia was ready for it. This attitude would buy the time necessary to restore Soviet military power and rebuild the country. Stalin had to restore discipline. His position had become weakened. His every move was geared towards deceiving the West. There was no pity there for the starving because, despite their need, the export of grain continued in the Soviets' efforts to convince the West of their recovery. Stalin made use of the Cold War to conceal from the world the appalling consequences of his leadership. Within four years of the end of the Second World War Russia, too, had atomic bombs.

The secrecy, mistrust, threats, intimidation and fear would last, if we give 1945 as a starting point, for 44 years. But, by the time the Cold War was over, troubles in other countries meant that terrorism, mistrust and fear would remain. They are still with us today.

I was once asked by an older woman if I thought there was anything at all that could unite the people of this planet. I replied: 'Invasion from another one.' I went on to say that in making this statement I always kept in mind a play that I had seen on TV when I was a girl. In the play a peaceful planet was invaded by alien beings with a horrendously aggressive nature. After watching their activities with increasing alarm for over an hour I suddenly became aware of the obvious plot twist. The alien invaders were us.

CHRISTMAS

At the top of this circle is a hearthrug. These were hand-made by Mom. We knew that Christmas was on the way when, at the beginning of October every year, I would be sent off to all the people living in the area who were likely to have an old coat, skirt or pair of trousers to give away. Rug-making time was here again. These rugs were made by tearing waste fabric into pieces measuring roughly three inches by one inch. Having prepared a 'podger' by discarding one prong of a dolly peg and then sharp-ening the other to a point, you were ready to begin work on a rug-sized piece of hessian. Working from side to side a series of holes would be made by piercing through a fold in the hessian quite close to the crease line, thus creating two holes at a time. The fabric strips would then be fed through each pair of holes, again using the podger, and when the row was complete the fold would be stretched flat and the next fold created.

A lot of work went into those pegged rugs but they were worth the effort. They could never be called thin – when new, they were a good two inches thick and very, very cosy. You could work out how far away Christmas was by following the progress of the rug. It was usually finished with just a couple of weeks to go. This was a wonderful time. For the last two weeks before the big event we would have the excitement of the preparations and the knowledge that at the end of it all we would be spending a couple of days in the comfort of the front room.

With great enthusiasm we would get the festivities under way by spending an evening making paper chains and getting out the weary old Christmas tree, its baubles and other relics. We had a couple of Chinese paper lanterns, two large bells and a ball that opened up like a concertina. I seem to recall that even during the war scraps of holly and mistletoe would be available at the greengrocers for those who could afford them. Both the front room and the kitchen would be decorated so that we could enjoy the atmosphere in the kitchen during the build-up to the great day. During all this activity Mom entertained us with tales of Christmases when she was a girl. Sometimes we managed to get a few balloons, but they were of such poor quality that they would burst as they were being inflated.

Dad kept a few chickens in the yard so that we could have the luxury of extra eggs. I can remember his chickens so clearly. He liked Rhode Island Reds, White Leghorns and Light Sussex. As the big day approached the fattest one would be sacrificed. Dad wouldn't let anyone see him do this and it was then left to hang in the shed for 24 hours, after which Mom would strip it of its feathers. That evening, with due ceremony and great excitement, the kitchen table was cleared and prepared for action with a large packet of salt, plenty of newspaper and a sharp knife.

The first things to go would be the head, neck and feet. Ted would grab the feet as he knew exactly which bit of sinew to pull to make the talons work. It was horrible. While we were engrossed with this Mom would make a large hole at the neck end of the unfortunate creature, and as the smell invaded our nostrils the feet would be put to one side. Having thrown plenty of salt into the gaping cavity Mom would take a deep breath, plunge her hand inside and draw out the bird's innards. Ignoring the smell, we would be allowed a few minutes to probe the contents of the carcass. There were lots of 'yuks' and 'euughs' before Mom would say 'That's it', wrap it all up in plenty of newspaper and dispose of it. After more salting, picking and washing, the bird was ready.

On Christmas Eve the front room would be prepared. A bowl of fruit was put on the table and a bowl of nuts on the chest of drawers. A fire would be laid in the grate ready for lighting next morning and there would be a final flick with the duster before the finishing touch was added – the new rug. It would be placed ceremoniously across the hearth and the old one relegated to the kitchen, having hardly been used all year. In the kitchen mince pies were baked, vegetables were prepared and the best china was washed and put ready. Finally we children would be washed in front of the fire before we all settled down for an evening with the radio. The atmosphere was alive with excitement and expectation.

On Christmas morning we were always awake well before dawn. 'Santa' would have left our gifts at the foot of our beds and our socks, filled with an orange, an apple, some chocolate and nuts and a few bright new pennies, would be placed over our bedposts. With feverish excitement we would go through our respective piles of goodies. We quickly became frozen to the marrow and would have to leap back into one of the beds, curl up together and wait until our teeth stopped chattering.

Having thawed, we would leap out again. We would keep this up until about 30 minutes after Mom and Dad had got up. Then they would call us. This was the best part of all and for me nothing has ever equalled it. With Christmas music on the radio and the smell of breakfast being cooked we staggered downstairs carrying our presents straight into the front room, where there would be a blazing fire in the grate and the table would be laid. All of our meals were eaten at a table which was always spread with a nice tablecloth. What made Christmas special was that we were in the front room, and the table would be spread with the best tablecloth and laid with the best china. Dad would be hovering around the hearth waiting for us and from the satisfied look on his face it was easy to see that, despite all the troubles of life, all was well in this tiny corner of the world. After a few minutes on the new rug Mom would start bringing in the breakfasts.

In those early years I don't remember Mom and Dad ever having any presents but they seemed happy enough. One thing they had every year as a Christmas treat was a small bottle of whisky and, during the two days of festivities, they would lace their tea with it. One Christmas morning there had been a heavy snowfall during the night and just after breakfast there was a knock at the door. Ted answered. It was a tramp asking if we could spare him a mug of hot tea. Mom told the tramp to wait and she would make him a fresh pot. She ended up giving him an egg sandwich, two hot mince pies and a mug of tea with a splash of whisky. She left him eating it by the front door and went out later to collect the plate and mug. He came every Christmas for several years and Mom would prepare a hearty meal for him. Then one year he didn't come and we never saw him again.

All the stops were pulled out for that one day every year. And, for that one day, we had the world. On Christmas night it was Dad's privilege to have a drop too much to drink which simply meant that by ten o'clock he would be unsteady on his feet, deliriously happy and guaranteed to have a hangover the next morning. He would spend his 'happy hour' falling about to make us laugh while Mom sat in the comfort of an armchair, full of plumptiousness* and blissfully contented, cracking nuts with a pair of pliers.

When she was using the pliers she was in one of her more refined moods and eating only the smaller nuts. This mood rarely lasted very long. Being anxious to savour the delights of the walnuts and Brazils, she would turn to our favourite method for tackling the larger nuts. With one of her flat irons turned upside down and firmly wedged between her knees, and using one of Dad's smaller hammers, she would tap and chip away. Of course, walnuts were easy but Brazils were a different matter. She had neither the patience nor the delicacy of touch to extricate one of these from its shell intact. Just at the crucial moment she would come down a little too heavy with the hammer and the kernel would shatter, whereupon she could be heard to mutter: 'Bugger that.' Sometimes Dad would take over and pass around the shelled nuts to all of us, but the whole Brazils were always for Mom. Dad was the only one who could remove a Brazil kernel from its shell in one piece. That he always gave it to Mom when he was successful was one of the many

---

*'Plumptiousness', though not in the dictionary, was a well-used word in those days and could be applied to anyone who was sitting like a mother hen, all plumped up and feeling thoroughly contented.

small ways in which Dad showed his regard for her. Sometimes we would all be beavering away, cracking nuts using various methods, and it was great fun. We never did get around to buying proper nutcrackers. Years later it became the done thing to buy nuts ready shelled. It was hellishly boring and they didn't taste the same.

One Christmas, during his 'happy hour', Dad hit upon the idea of stumbling while holding a metal tray. He did not tell us of his plan and hoped that the tray would make a tremendous crashing sound, intensifying the slapstick effect. Unfortunately it all went wrong and ended with him getting a nasty cut on one of his eyebrows. Fortunately Mom remembered that one of our neighbours had in-laws visiting, and that one of them had something to do with a hospital in Birmingham. This man was summoned to administer first aid. Next morning Dad not only had his usual hangover but also sported a memorable black eye. Things became very heated later when Mom found out that Dad, in devilment, had told our next-door neighbour that she had hit him. She threatened to blacken his other eye and God knows what before Dad, wearily holding his head, told her to 'shut up and give it a rest. It's Christmas. Where's all this peace on earth and goodwill to all men?' Mom opened her mouth to retaliate but thought better of it. After an initial period of sulking we then got back to 'normal'.

Boxing Day was run on similar lines to Christmas Day but the atmosphere was different. We still had a fire in both rooms and plenty to eat but the magic had gone. Dad, knowing that he had to go to work the next day, couldn't get legless. In those days factory workers only had two days off for Christmas and nothing at all for New Year, and so on the 27th we would move back into the kitchen having enjoyed our break and feeling as if we had been away for a fortnight.

Years later, when Ray and I prepared Christmases for our children, times had changed. While I never sat laboriously making a rug, we did have *Blue Peter* and the efforts of its presenters who tried to get the nation to make things out of wire coat hangers, toilet roll tubes, washing-up liquid bottles and yoghurt containers. We bought oven-ready chickens, and I made mince pies. We still made paper chains but that was it. Ray didn't feel the need to drink much or fall about and we had proper nutcrackers; although there were still times when a small hammer and a flat iron were needed.

DIETING

During rationing many people kept their bellies full by eating stodgy food. It is surprising that more of them were not overweight. Nevertheless, it has been established that by the end of the war the people of this country had never been so healthy.

However, at the start of the fifties more and more people were putting on weight. By this time food restrictions were easing. It became fashionable to put yourself on a diet and the phrase "Er's gone on one of them diets' came into common usage. It began innocently enough with the banana diet and the bread-and-butter diet, or you could simply start the day with fresh lemon juice. Previously happy, jolly-looking women started to look drawn and haggard. Others, Mother included, would sniff meaningfully and comment that it was not natural to deny yourself food. I do remember that she did give the bread-and-butter diet a try. We knew she was doomed to fail when, sitting behind a veritable mountain of bread and margarine, she was heard to say: 'I can't see this working.'

There had always been a few dramatically obese women before dieting began, but they had always been looked upon with reverence as 'fine big women'. It always came as something of a shock when one of these 'fine big women' dropped dead, because anyone with some good solid rolls of fat was seen as the epitome of good health. It was the painfully thin, those obviously not getting enough to eat, who were pitied because it was assumed that they had one foot in the grave. A breakthrough came in the late fifties when someone worked out the calorie-counting system of controlling weight. Counting calories became a nationwide obsession. For those who were failing to shed the pounds doctors could prescribe Dexedrine or Duraphet which had marvellous results, but the minute you stopped taking them the pounds piled back on. Of course, the drawback to these drugs was their addictive qualities and they had to be withdrawn as slimming aids.

At some time in the sixties Weight Watchers became a thriving business worldwide. As the years went by a lucrative industry flourished that tried to give women, and men, the body shape that they craved. Every year at least one new slimming plan hits the bookshops and sails to the top of the best-selling lists. We have seen the F-plan, the Hip and Thigh, the Hay, the Mediterranean, the GI and the Atkins diets. Any one of these might be accompanied by a string of sessions at the gym. I wish someone would explain to me why so many people go to the gym in their car; one could ask why these gyms provide a car park in the first place.

Many people now make New Year's resolutions promising themselves that they will lose weight. In January they begin a regime designed to rid themselves of the blubber in preparation for the summer when it is essential to be stick-thin. By the end of the summer the weight is creeping back on and after Christmas the whole business begins again. Accompanied, of course, by a new diet regime riding high in the bestseller lists.

You might ask how I know so much about these methods of losing weight. The answer is that I've tried them all, although I've never been to a gym. For years I've been waiting for someone to come up with a 'how to keep it off forever' diet plan.

In this circle you will notice an industrial crane. This represents a very large piece of equipment belonging to a firm by the name of Danks. In my early life, while this crane could not be seen by all that many people, it could certainly be heard. It desperately needed some oil of some kind as it screeched and whined its way through its day's work. It was always a relief when it was shut down at the end of a shift. You may now be wondering what this has got to do with dieting. Let me enlighten you. As a woman's waistline expanded her husband might be heard saying to her: 'If yoh get any bigger we'll have to get Danks' crane to move yoh.'

In the meantime I continue to ponder why it is that in one half of the world many people are on a diet, and in the other half many are starving to death.

THE EVERGREENS

The Evergreens was a local concert party attached to a chapel in an area of West Bromwich called Greets Green. They had already been going for a number of years when I discovered them in the fifties and as far as I know they still are. It was all the brainchild of Ivy Round, one of the very nicest people I ever met. Her life was dedicated to the chapel and its activities. They would put on shows for the elderly and other deserving groups. The highlight of the year was their annual pantomime. Ivy would be in total charge. She would write scripts, select songs, play the piano, choose the cast and have a say in the costumes. These locally famous events began in 1933 and were still going strong in 2003. By 1983 Ivy was no longer just locally famous. That year she was honoured by the Queen in recognition of her outstanding work for charity. She visited Buckingham Palace where she also met Princess Diana.

I did not play an active part in the shows, but helped out where I could behind the scenes. Everyone, including the cast, mucked in and hoped for the best. The small hall, complete with stage, was behind the chapel and above a kitchen and dining hall. Although the group frequently played at homes for the elderly and in other church halls, the building behind their own chapel was also well used. The Evergreens would put on concerts in this hall for the general public, for which a small charge would be levied. There was always a full house and money raised in this way was used for repairs and improvements to the building, or donated to some local worthy cause. If they did arrange a show for the elderly in this hall a meal would be provided in the room below after the performance.

In around 1953 a chap from the group was doing his national service in the RAF but became quite ill. He was spending a lengthy period of time at Wroughton RAF Hospital in Wiltshire and had no immediate prospect of being allowed home. Ivy rallied us all into preparing a show for the benefit of as many of the hospital's patients as we could manage. Performances were quickly rehearsed, costumes and props organised and away we went in a hired coach. We probably managed to put on the show in four wards, pushing the piano around with us. The performers were well received and it was a splendid day.

The chapel was eventually bulldozed and the congregation merged with that of another chapel, in Great Bridge. I can still name most of the people involved and I remember them all with pleasure. The tower depicted in the circle represents Blackpool Tower and the famous illuminations, which we memorably visited as a group. They were lovely people back then and I'm sure that this remains true for all those who are still there spreading good cheer today. Although she was born in 1915, I hope that Ivy is still with us and will read this.

THE FIELDS

'The Fields' was an enormous piece of open land with no fences or trees, the sort of land which W.G. Hoskins[*] would have described as 'scrubby'. It consisted of a thin layer of soil on a rocky plateau, a type of outcrop which is common throughout many parts of the Midlands. While these pockets of land could support broom and other shrubs, they were no good for trees.

---

[*] W.G. Hoskins (1908–92) founded the first university department specialising in English landscape history, and his book *The Making of the English Landscape* (1955) remains the seminal text on the subject. He has greatly influenced environmental conservation.

Cows from nearby Bullock's Farm grazed the land but we never saw wild animals, such as rabbits. However, Ted, Jim and I spent much time irritating newts and frogs and never failed to turn over a dried cowpat to study the insect life beneath it. To get to the fields we would go to the bottom of the street and along the grassy track at the side of the foundry, pick our way over the brook and climb the clover bank on the other side. Having skirted the 'tocky banks', which had been formed years before from unwanted wet slurry from the mine workings below, we would come to the sunny bank and from this little vantage point we would see this enormous piece of land spread out before us.

There were houses at the right perimeter and running along the left was a canal. Two cottages stood at the side of the canal. One of these would have been the lock keeper's cottage in the past, but was now occupied by a woman who lived alone. In the other lived a couple who shared the property with one of their mothers. This woman had senile dementia and when the weather was fine she was allowed to wander the fields, talking to herself and shouting. Sometimes we could see and hear her in the distance ranting and raving and waving her arms about, and we always kept our distance.

If we crossed the lock to the other side we would come to an overflow. When a boat prepared to enter the lock the displacement of the water from the canal would create a waterfall with a drop of about four or five feet. The water would then flow into the canal basin. To stand under this waterfall on a hot summer day was hair-partingly exhilarating. We would sit on the grassy bank at the end of the paved and concreted passage, eating our bread and 'scrape', wearing what passed for swimming costumes and waiting for the cry to go up: 'Boat!' Then we would scramble to the overflow. Some days, when we were not at school, we would spend the whole day there. Further along the canal, on a piece of land at its side, was a natural spring which kept some people supplied with watercress. This was always a lovely, vibrant green. Mother didn't use it as she was doubtful about it, but we would sometimes pick some to give to one of the neighbours.

In wartime a barrage balloon was tethered near to the canal, a short distance from the cottages. Occasionally we would see someone in a khaki uniform putting some air into it. These balloons could, I think, be a bit temperamental if they hadn't got the right amount of air in them but generally it didn't seem to be used much.

The fields were dotted with pit holes. These were unbelievably dangerous but we didn't see them that way. I always thought they were ventilation shafts but I have since been told that men would have been lowered down them in baskets to mine the workings below. They were holes about three feet in diameter and had the skimpiest of brick walls around them with the merest suggestion of rusty barbed wire. These walls were less than two feet high and crumbled to the touch. We would lean over a wall and silently drop bricks into the dark, black hole, then wait for some sort of noise which would indicate how deep it was. It is unbelievable now that we got away with it but Ted could remember one catastrophe, when a boy fell to his death.

In the fields was a reportedly bottomless pool surrounded by bulrushes. This pool was called 'The Sinkings' and the name speaks for itself. It had been created when one of the mine workings had collapsed and the deep hole that this left behind had gradually filled with water. All around the edge of it bulrushes grew and I would have loved to pick some, but we were constantly told to keep away from it and, in this instance, we did as we were told. Not far to its right stood the engine house.

The engine house was empty, derelict and abandoned, with its doors and window frames long since gone. Inside, the enormous rusting machinery was still there. I was told it was used to pump water from the mine workings below. It was quite gothic in appearance and resembled a chapel with a chimney stack. There was something very creepy about it and only the very bravest of the boys would venture inside. It was rumoured to be a front for a German SS cell. Apparently the SS were secretly using it as a base as they conspired to take over our town and the surrounding area. 'Them Germans' used to get about a bit.

Behind the engine house was a memorably huge rusty iron girder. When I was small I would run along it, and it gave out a wonderful plinking sound. I always looked forward to this, and Dad would find something to sit on and have a rest while giving me time to enjoy my game. I have often wondered what happened to the girder. I like to think that it is still there, even if buried beneath a road or industrial building, and that on warm summer nights a plinking sound can be heard together with childish laughter.

There was an abundance of wild flowers in the fields, especially buttercups, clover, coltsfoot, daisies and dandelions. We also had garden flowers because one small area, quite close to the engine house, was a tip where local gardeners could get rid of their garden waste. Each spring and summer the tip would come alive with nasturtiums, lupins, tiger lilies and poppies. They added a lovely splash of colour. In time, with 'progress', the 'tocky banks' were levelled, the brook was encased in a concrete tunnel, the pit holes were filled in and the whole lot disappeared under bricks, tarmac and concrete.

It was as if my memories of many happy times in the fields with my brothers Jim and Ted were also buried beneath tarmac and concrete.

COMMUNICATION

The meaning of communication depends on how you see the word. If you can only interpret it in the sense of modern technology then you will probably be surprised at the way communication worked in my early life. The only people I knew who had a telephone at that time were the local doctor and Mr Black at the post office. We managed perfectly well without them. I suppose the main reason for this was that people tended to stay in the area where they were born and whole families would live within a few streets of one another.

Mother's two sisters and her brother all lived within walking distance, as did Dad's sister.

This also meant that we had close contact with ten cousins. Families could see each other regularly, and if one of them was ill the rest would quickly rally round. Cars can now also be seen as an aid to communication, but it would be years before they were taken for granted. Again, the only people I knew who owned a car were the doctor and the man at the post office. This does not include factory owners, for I could not say I knew them. Petrol rationing would have had something to do with the very limited use of cars, apart from the obvious reason of cost.

From Monday to Friday we could also have managed reasonably well without a clock during the day as there were bells, sirens and hooters going off at the local factories all day long. This daily cacophony began at ten minutes to eight every weekday morning. I would be roused from sleep by the sound of tramping feet as men started making their way to work, greeting each other as they passed by. At five to eight a klaxon would wail and the sound of feet would intensify. The eight o'clock bell from one factory and the hooter from another would then go off at the same time.

After the noise subsided, the street was silent for a couple of minutes before the lorries started rumbling past and the day's work began. At this point I would curl up into a tight ball and wish I could disappear, as I knew Mom would be coming up the stairs at any minute to get us up. There were hooters for the beginning and end of morning breaks, lunch breaks and afternoon breaks. The last one would go off at six o'clock when the weary workers began plodding their way home in silence, worn out by the day's labour.

Some mornings the footsteps would have a sort of hollow sound and from that I knew it was raining. If the footsteps had a muffled sound I would leap out of bed and look excitedly through the window because that meant it was snowing. If the sound of feet was drowned out by the window rattling for all it was worth then there was a gale force wind blowing.

The lack of telephones in no way impeded the spread of news and gossip, for there was no shortage of the greatest uninhibited communicators in the world – children. We called it 'passing on the gen' or 'getting genned up'. The slightest bit of news, boring or otherwise, was quickly spread from child to child and then from child to parent, and then the adults would take over. If an adult wanted to let the world know of any fortune or misfortune they had only to tell a child. It was as efficient and reliable as the bush telegraph.

One summer's day it came through on the network that a man had been spotted in a local field 'showing himself'. There had always been reported sightings of these unfortunate people but we had never had the experience of seeing one for ourselves. We were warned by parents to keep away from the field or there would be dire consequences. But the warnings fell on deaf ears. Some of us decided to meet in a nearby park after school and go off in search of this chap so that we could see for ourselves what it was that he had got to be so proud of. We ran all the way to the park but screeched to a halt as we went through the gates. Assembled there were about 40 children, all with the same purpose in mind. Not to be put off by the size of the crowd we set off on foot and converged on the field. If the flasher was lurking there he probably fled in terror, never to unfasten his buttons again.

We also knew of goings-on among the rich and famous. I don't know how we knew, but we did. Several times we heard that Hitler had been spotted strolling along the front at Blackpool with Eva Braun on his arm, but even we found that a bit hard to swallow. Twice, Mother knew that Princess Elizabeth was expecting a baby a couple of weeks before the official announcements. That is probably an example of women's intuition, something we don't hear much about today.

The first announcement of an impending royal birth came as something of a surprise to some of the kids. They had been reliably informed when the Princess married Prince Philip that they couldn't have any children because 'he hadn't got any naughty bits'. It was apparently well known that they had been blown off during the war. How did they know? Well, in our gang was a lad whose dad worked at the foundry, and he worked with a chap whose uncle had a cousin, on his mother's side, who knew a woman whose grandson served on the battleship HMS *Valiant* with Prince Philip, and he was there when it happened. Now, I ask you: could you have a more dependable source of information than that?

We depended on the grapevine, radio and newspapers, and we could not anticipate the means of communication that would come to be taken for granted in the later years of the twentieth century and into the twenty-first. Cinema newsreels and radio, always important in my early life, were overtaken by television although radio still has its place. Computers and the internet have become a terrific source of information and communication with people throughout the world, either in chat rooms or via e-mail, but I am not happy with modern technology and always approach my computer with caution and suspicion.

There is still much pleasure to be had from receiving letters or getting a phone call or a fax, but in the twenty-first century there is no doubt that the mobile phone must be regarded as the preferred method of communication, used by most people and particularly the young. It has a dual purpose: text messages and verbal communication. However, mobile phones are a continuing source of dissatisfaction in that they are bought one day and out of date the next. The mobile phone, for some, appears to be an extension of their arm. In the future this may actually be the case. I have read that some say mobile phones will eventually consist of just two rings, one on the thumb and the other on the little finger. Apparently, with the first three fingers bent into the palm, a call will be made by placing the thumb to the ear and the little finger to the mouth, and any connection between the two will travel through the bones of the hand. These rings will not necessarily have to be removed, even for washing. It is difficult to envisage what could possibly replace this type of equipment but undoubtedly someone somewhere has the matter in hand.

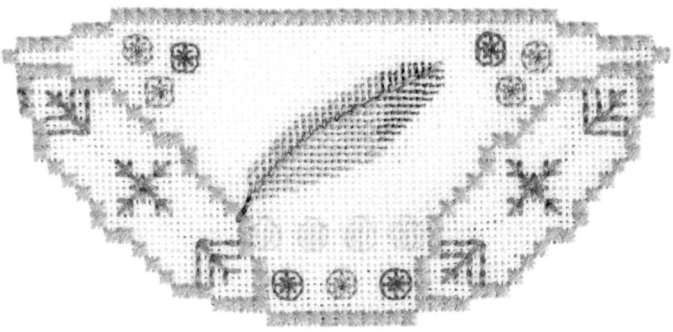

HANGINGS

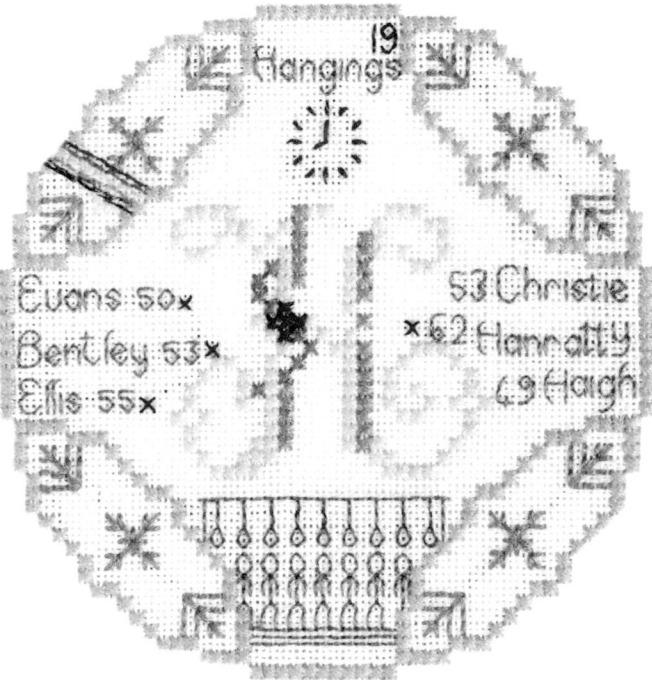

Hangings could not be ignored during my childhood, at least not in our house. During the war, newspapers often carried pictures of a line of men who had been marched to a makeshift gallows and hanged somewhere in the world. It seemed to me to be the way that opposing armies dealt with things and, on reflection, these photos were probably used as a method of propaganda. Our parents did not purposefully show us these pictures; the newspapers were simply not hidden away. In any case, we saw similar scenes on cinema newsreels. It seems that if our troops came across a line of people who had been hanged their first reaction was to take a photograph, or film it, to show us how barbaric the enemy could be.

Many of the hangings of murderers in this country seemed to be carried out at 8 am. Between 1932 and 1956 Albert Pierrepoint, the official executioner, hanged 600 people. This equates roughly to 25 per year, or one a fortnight. On the day of an execution Mother would get us up five minutes early so that we could listen to Big Ben chime eight on the radio. Then some newsreader would begin the bulletin with the announcement that the deed had been carried out. How many of them, I often wondered, had been innocent?

In the circle are the names of six people whose hangings I can remember. Four of them have a cross by their names. It is now generally agreed that, for various reasons, they should not have been executed. Whenever there was even a tiny shadow of doubt I found it difficult to believe that the death penalty could be justified. Even so, there have been those for whom I have had no sympathy and all of them were child-murderers.

– CIRCLE 20 –

ICONS

In this instance 'icons' are people who have lived during my lifetime and whom I have admired for various reasons. My very earliest icons would all have been film stars, of which there were many. Like most children I loved Laurel and Hardy. For me, their best film is *The Music Box*, in which they have to deliver a piano to a house at the top of a hill, which involves climbing hundreds of steps carrying it. A silent movie star who made an impact on me, and I hasten to add that this was many years later when his work featured regularly on television, was the genius Buster Keaton. One of his greatest films was *The General* which I have in my collection.

An exception to film stars as the icons of my early childhood was Douglas Bader who had lost both his legs in 1931 when he was 21 years old. Undaunted, he went on to have a distinguished flying career and played his part in the Second World War. He was well known to us during this time because, as a prisoner of the Germans, he became a headache to them with his escape bids. He was an inspiration to those who needed to be inspired, and their numbers increased daily in wartime.

We had been taught never to stare at anyone who was disfigured or who had a disability, but my resolve was greatly tested when I sat in a friend's house one winter's night. We were sharing the kitchen table with her father who was doing some woodwork. I sat transfixed watching him work. He had been a skilled craftsman before going to war but had been invalided out when he lost an arm. Now, with his empty shirt sleeve rolled up and pinned at the shoulder, he was a skilled craftsman still. While I like to think that Bader might have inspired my friend's father, it was probably Black Country determination which spurred him on. Bader was knighted by the Queen in 1976 for his work with the disabled.

In those first years after the war there had been many additions to my list of 'all-time greats', but there were just as many who I did not care for very much. As a girl I thought Mohandas Gandhi was a troublemaker; at that time I saw anyone who voiced opinions of discontent as a troublemaker. I did not understand the problems of India; I only saw the fighting and bloodshed. I thought that they would have had enough of this during the war. Gandhi believed that independence was the only solution to India's national grievances. We in Britain had been taught, more or less, that we were the charitable benefactors of all the countries in 'our Empire' and I couldn't understand why they wanted us out. As I grew older I came to understand the problems that faced India and many other countries in their changing times. Only then did I begin to appreciate Gandhi and his policy of non-violent non-cooperation. It was not surprising that he had enemies – most people in his position do. When he was shot dead in Delhi in 1948 many mourned and many did not.

In the fifties I began to take a general interest in sport and was carried along with the consensus that the American boxer Rocky Marciano was one of the best heavyweight champions we would ever see. He was champion from 1952 to 1956, and after winning all of his 49 professional fights he retired, the only heavyweight champion to retire undefeated. Of his 49 opponents he knocked out 43. He was a highly respected boxer in the often murky business that boxing was at that time. When radio commentators spoke of him you could detect from their tone that they thought highly of him. Marciano had the sense to retire undefeated but sadly, in 1969, at the age of 46, he was killed in a plane crash. I have always admired those, like him, who reach the top in their profession while still keeping the respect of others.

One sportsman was respected by everyone who either knew him or knew of him. Sir Stanley Matthews was born in 1915. He was an English footballer who only ever played for three teams: Stoke City, Blackpool and England, and began his career with Stoke in 1932, aged seventeen. He won 54 international caps for England between 1934 and 1957 and played in almost 700 league games. In all of those league games he was never once booked. In 1956 he became the first European Footballer of the Year, but was 38 before he gained an FA Cup winner's medal. He was the first Footballer of the Year in 1948 and won the title again in 1963. He later became the first footballer to be knighted while still playing, and continued to play first division football until he was in his fifties. Everyone who knew him says the same: that he was a gentleman.

Another gentleman, this time on the athletics track, was Roger Bannister. In 1954 he became the first man in the world to run a mile in less than four minutes at Iffley in Oxford. His actual time was 3 minutes 59.4 seconds. He broke four minutes again at the Commonwealth Games at Vancouver in Canada in the same year. I twice had the privilege of speaking to Mr Bannister when I lived in Oxford during the nineties. He wouldn't remember me, but I have never forgotten him.

Winston Churchill will be forever remembered for his role in the Second World War. Despite a speech impediment, he was an inspirational orator during the period when the world seemed at its bleakest. However, for me Churchill's greatest attributes had nothing to do with his political career, which had some tremendous highs and catastrophic lows. What impressed me most was his ability to be a master of so many other occupations, from bricklayer to author to renowned artist. His power with the pen was his main source of income throughout his life. Included in the formidable number of books written by him is a six-volume memoir of the Second World War and the four-volume *A History of the English Speaking Peoples* which covered the period from 55 BC to the First World War. He was knighted, made an honorary citizen of the US and awarded the Nobel Prize for Literature in 1953.

The book *The Lord of the Rings* has been voted the best book of the twentieth century in at least one survey. For years the only thing I knew about J.R.R. Tolkien was that he had written a very thick book called *The Lord of the Rings* which was a remarkable story about a fantasy world and a fellowship of rings that had become a cult classic during the sixties. It was published as a trilogy during the years 1954–55. My son read it when he was a student and remains a lifelong devotee. I did not take any real interest in it until 2001, when I went to see the first of Peter Jackson's film trilogy. While the films were spellbinding they also served to show that the ability and imagination used in creating the original story bordered on genius, and Tolkien deserves his place in literary history.

A couple who deserve their place in ice dance history are Jane Torvill and Christopher Dean, who conquered the world with their style of ice dancing. They won the world title four times and became Olympic champions in 1986 which gave us all an overwhelming feeling of national pride. Millions followed their progress avidly on TV, and in the end they received respect and admiration from all over the world with their distinctive interpretations of music that will always be associated with them.

A piece of music that will forever be linked to Luciano Pavarotti is, of course, Puccini's aria 'Nessun Dorma' from *Turandot* which brought him worldwide celebrity status when his rendition was used by the BBC as its theme music for the 1990 World Cup in Italy. He was an Italian operatic tenor whose voice had a clarity of tone that endeared him to millions in all walks of life. His career had begun in 1961 and by the mid-seventies he had appeared at all the major opera houses in the world. 'Nessun Dorma' is considered by many to be his greatest work, but I have always thought his recording of 'Ah! mes amis …' from Gaetano Donizetti's *La Fille du Régiment* takes some beating.

Having been brought up to listen to the radio and appreciate all types of music, the Last Night of the Proms was an annual highlight for us. Actually watching it on TV for the first time gave the proceedings a new dimension. Malcolm Sargent was every-thing we had thought he would be. He was a wonderful dresser. He had flair. He had style. While conducting he was the master of the grand gesture. He was the BBC Symphony Orchestra's chief guest conductor and also the leading conductor for the annual Henry Wood Promenade Concerts. To the promenaders he became known as 'flash Harry'. By the mid-sixties, when he was too ill to conduct any more, he did make one final appearance at the Proms but not to take up the baton. He was helped onto the stage, immaculately dressed as always, wearing a Melton cloth overcoat which concealed how frail he had become. He stood for just a minute before the adoring, cheering crowd and then he was gone. He had given us all what we had wanted; one last glimpse of a legend.

Another legend, this time on the tennis circuit, was the Swedish player Björn Borg who won the Wimbledon men's singles title five times between 1976 and 1980. In some of those years, while others verbally took on the umpire, Borg quietly smouldered his way to victory. This was very attractive to young women and he had an immense following among them. At the height of his success I was in my forties and old enough to know better but I still gave him the nickname 'old fiery nostrils', which is a term I used for any man who had the ability to smoulder quietly. These days we still get glimpses of him on TV as he occupies a seat as a spectator during Wimbledon fortnight; he still has 'it' and, seeing him, I feel 40 again. In 1972, at the age of fifteen, he became the youngest player ever to represent his country, Sweden.

In 1961, at the age of fifteen, George Best left his home in Ireland to train for Manchester United. By the time he was seventeen he had made his debut with them. He became a product of the sixties, swept along in a decade of overwhelming change, when young people found a freedom that had been denied to previous generations. Consequently, he had too much too soon. There were no advisers then for someone in his position. It was just expected that at eighteen this working-class lad could some-how cope with all the money, adoring fans and swooning females. Though never short of money, simply because his name alone was worth a fortune, drink ruined his career. He always knew that he had millions of fans willing him on each time he attempted to give up alcohol, but he failed every time. George Best gave pleasure to millions. That he had a natural ability with a ball has never been denied. He should be remembered for this, not for the fact that he had an addiction. There was more to George Best than alcoholism.

There was also more to Lord Nuffield, but I didn't discover this until I was carrying out research for this book. I never under-stood why he was disliked so much. Everyone is entitled to their own opinions, but one of those who detested him was Dad and I was unable at the time to find out why he felt this way.

Nuffield was a self-made man. He made an unbelievable for-tune out of the motor industry. He was happily married, had no children and appears to have given everything back to the coun-try that had made him so rich. There seems to be no hospital in the country that has not benefited from his generosity. He endowed Nuffield College in Oxford in 1937 and the Nuffield Foundation in 1943, and left his house to the college when he died. In his lifetime he gave away over £30 million. For this I admired him. This admiration has now become somewhat taint-ed with the discovery that he is thought to have donated £50,000 to Oswald Mosley's fascist organisation before the war. As Mother would have said: 'It takes all sorts.'

IN PASSING

In this circle are just a few of the fashions and fads that have come and gone in my lifetime, although some of them have not disappeared completely. They passed into legend and have never quite left us.

In 1940 the American Jeep was a new type of car made by Willys-Overland and used as a General Purpose Vehicle (GPV) or Jeep for short. It was open-sided and designed for duty on the battlefield. It had a high ground clearance and its four-wheel drive meant good handling on the roughest terrain. During the forties it became instantly identifiable and appeared to be both indestructible and totally reliable. The fact that it was American made it awesome, like everything else that came from the other side of the Atlantic – and this also included dance crazes.

Be-bop was a style of jazz music and dance which originated in the black clubs in Harlem, New York, in 1945. This was shortened to 'bop'. It is thought that this style initiated the development of modern jazz as opposed to traditional jazz. A leading exponent of bop was the exceptional trumpet player Dizzy Gillespie. Any type of American music was extremely popular in the UK at the time, but music which included a style of dance was particularly popular with the young. To young people at this time, Britain seemed like the land that time forgot. So when it was announced that Britain was to hold a festival which would put us back on top, the news was very welcome.

On 4 May 1951 the Festival of Britain opened. It was an example of Britain's capabilities and had its showground on the South Bank of the Thames in London. Bright colours and displays were intended to remove memories of the war and the bleak austerity which had followed it. Mother thought that this would have to be some sort of miracle when bomb damage and austerity were still with us. However, the Royal Festival Hall was the festival's centrepiece; the Skylon, an aluminium tower, was the festival's symbol; and the Dome of Discovery, not unlike the Millennium Dome but smaller, was the place to see all the bold new inventions and ideas that Britain had developed. With an eye to future markets we needed to show the world how clever we were. Mother said: 'With the country still in the mess that it is who do they think they're fooling? They must think we're all bonkers.'

When I said that I wanted to go and see it all, Mother said it was not for the likes of us but Ted went to see it with the chap from next door. I ruminated on Mother's stock answer, which covered everything in which she herself had no interest. We had always been 'the likes of us'. Who exactly were we? Would we ever be anything else? I always had to be satisfied with listening to other people's criticism of, or praise for, anything that I would not be seeing for myself and the Festival of Britain received plenty of both. It was built on a 28-acre site and cost £11 million. To many critics this was a complete waste of money. The Skylon was likened to the British economy – it had no visible means of support. Years later, when historians began debating the pros and cons of the Festival of Britain, some of them agreed with Mother by saying that it was purely a middle-class festival. She would have been cock-a-hoop.

The hula-hoop was already a craze in Australia before it became popular in America in 1958 and anything that was coast to coast in America, be it foul weather, colds and flu, music or toys and gimmicks, would eventually find its way over the Atlantic to us. Originally made from bamboo, the hoop was improved upon by a Californian company and manufactured from plastic. Because it was a cheap and simple idea it became a worldwide phenomenon, and in the process caused many a slipped disc among those old enough to have known better.

In 1959 the British Motor Corporation unveiled the new Morris Mini Minor and the Austin Mini Seven. They both became known simply as the Mini. Designed by Alec Issigonis, they had four seats in an austere interior which was very basic. In trying to think of a good descriptive word for the interior I came up with 'unlined', which my brother Jim assures me is perfect. It was capable of doing 70 mph and cost around £500. It was Britain's biggest-selling car and over 5 million of them were produced. It was the perfect sixties car.

Clackers – a children's toy made of strong acrylic plastic –

came to Britain in 1974. It consisted of two balls suspended from a handle by plastic strings. The two balls would knock together above and below the hand making a 'clacking' sound. They were also known as 'knockers', and one young lad told me how kind Angela had been by letting him play with her knockers. I managed to keep a straight face. Clackers eventually lost their popularity because children began suffering hand injuries when the balls didn't knock together, but knocked the hand or wrist instead. In some instances the balls would shatter on contact. Three years later another craze came along, involving glitter balls and a particular type of music and dance.

In 1977 the disco film *Saturday Night Fever* was a huge success and made a global star of John Travolta. His superb dancing, once described as loose-limbed, coupled with an exceptional soundtrack by the Bee Gees started a universal epidemic of disco fever whose symptoms would persist for some years.

The Rubik's Cube of 1979, a frustrating puzzle, was invented by the Hungarian Erno Rubik. It consisted of 54 small cubes of plastic in six different colours which had to be manipulated into the right pattern. You either could or could not solve the mystery of the Rubik's cube; it was as simple as that. If you could accept that you were unable to do it then you were home and dry and could chuck it in the dustbin with a clear conscience. If, however, you could not find it in yourself to admit defeat, you condemned yourself to a period of frustrating misery. You will have realised by now that I was one of those who could not do it. I tried for about ten minutes and then happily gave up. However, I didn't give up on the next craze to sweep the country until the invention of the iPod.

The arrival of the Sony Walkman in 1980 was a perfect example of a truly personal music player. It was a pocket-sized radio/cassette player which had superb stereophonic sound and, because it was listened to through earphones, it could go anywhere. My son was concerned that because I played it so loudly it might damage my hearing, but 26 years later I still listen to Pink Floyd or Sinatra at full volume. I once explained to Ray that it was remarkable to hear the music when it glided from one ear to the other, and he said that that was because there was nothing in between to stop it!

The internet phenomenon truly took off in 1991. Since then it has completely changed the way in which some of us live our lives. Where books used to be consulted in search of information, everyone's first port of call is now the internet. Those seeking someone to share the rest of their life with often start their search here. To many people, it has become as essential to everyday life as the mobile phone. But I suspect that it will be superseded eventually by something else which will be even more fantastic, because that is the way of things. In 1995 something truly fantastic and certainly out of this world arrived and stayed with us for weeks.

The Hale-Bopp comet was named after the American astronomers, Alan Hale and Thomas Bopp, who discovered it. It was a ball of rock, dust and ice and its tail was created by heat from the sun melting some of the ice. It became visible to the naked eye in April 1997 and remained so for several weeks. It was visible somewhere in the world for a total of eighteen months. It appeared to be at a standstill but was actually travelling at a terrific speed. If you looked at it early in the evening and again four hours later you would become aware of the distance it had travelled. My first sighting came straight after local television news had given tips on where to find it when weather conditions were right, which they were that night. I went to my bedroom window, opened the curtains, fixed my position, looked to the left and there it was. It will be back in the year 4530.

FIRES

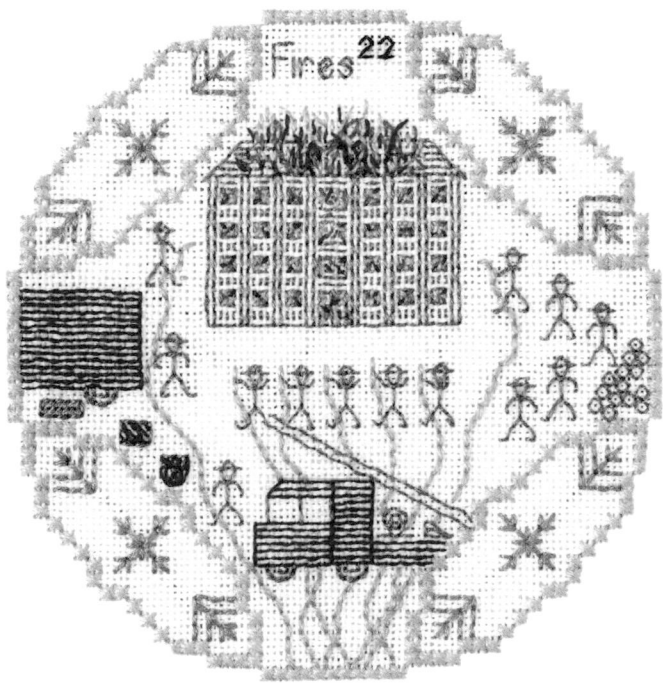

Building fires, and especially factory fires, were quite common during the Second World War and for some time afterwards. Most of the fires which occurred during the war were started by incendiary bombs or high explosives, and those after the war were started through neglect of the building in question or its electrical wiring. There has been no opportunity for me to stand and watch a building fire since those days, I am pleased to say, so for this reason the illustration I have placed in this circle comes from my childhood experiences.

I remember the first time we saw a turntable ladder being used; I believe this was after the war. It was very futuristic and exciting. Note the crowd of onlookers pictured at the right of the circle. I can clearly remember the names of the factories which caught fire. Some fires were quickly brought under control. Other times, buildings were reduced to a shell and one, which housed a paint factory, was reduced to a pile of ash. If we were playing in the fields and we saw a pall of smoke coming from buildings on the horizon, the boys would ascertain roughly where the fire was and off we would dash. We would call in to tell Mother where we were going as we passed the house. Her parting remark was always the same: 'Don't get in the firemen's way.' Sometimes we would travel miles only to find that the blaze had been dealt with by the time we arrived. We saw many blazes and many smouldering ruins.

Dad was in the Auxiliary Fire Service at the factory where he worked and spent many nights on duty. I remember Mom coming to get us up one morning. She was not her usual self and told us not to bother Dad, who had just come in from the night shift. He was sitting in his chair with a cup of tea, just staring into space, and did not speak a word. It would be several days before we found out what he had been through.

On the night in question a bomb had been dropped on one of the factory's huge machine shops and it had taken the auxiliary fire crew a long time to get the fire under control. By first light the fire was out, and when the fire brigade arrived to make sure everything was all right they said that the crew had done very well to achieve what they had, considering the size of the blaze. When they suggested that two men go up into the rafters to check that there were no remains still smouldering, Dad and another man volunteered to go. They were picking their way across the beams when the other man tripped and fell to his death. It was years before it occurred to me how Dad must have felt at that moment. Having witnessed this tragedy he then had to carry on making his way across the beams, carefully balancing himself as he went.

The fire depicted in the circle represents the one at a wharf on the side of a canal near our home. It was the fiercest blaze I ever saw. On the evening in question, as Dick Barton drew to a close on the radio, someone shouted through our half-open back door: 'The wharf's gone up.' Off we dashed and found the whole building ablaze. It quickly became obvious to the firefighters that they would not get this inferno under control. They remained on duty all night to make sure the fire didn't spread as it burned itself out. The building was a large old warehouse. It was crammed to the rafters with straw which a local firm used as packing material. I had never known there to be any glass in the window frames and the doors had long since gone. It was a four-storey building with a rope and pulley system for hauling goods to the upper floors.

We had often played in this building against our parents' wishes. It was a fearsome place. As each floor was identical in every way it was difficult to know which floor you were on. When a new supply of straw bales was stored it was sometimes hard to find the stairs. At these times I never ventured further than the first floor, and never moved far from the staircases. The place was a death trap. If a careless smoker had started a fire on the ground floor while there were children on the floors above, they would never have stood a chance. But this kind of building was a magnet for children, especially after the men had finished work for the day. They could play there unobserved until dusk. It was the sort of environment that was absolutely made for games such as hide and seek.

A week or so before the fire there was a great deal of furtive conversation among the adults. It had come to their attention that a much older boy had been fighting with some of the younger boys in this building, punching them with some force. The blows had been heavy enough to cause bad bruising. I remember my elder brother being stripped and checked for bruises by Mom and Dad and being asked questions, but he knew nothing and had no marks on him. Over the next few days the whispering between the mothers in the neighbourhood grew more intense. We were subsequently warned repeatedly by Mom and Dad that we must not go anywhere near the wharf. This was done with such seriousness and urgency that we did as we were told.

While none dared say as much, there never seemed any doubt

that the fire had been started deliberately. A day or two after the fire it was rumoured that a group of fathers whose sons had been attacked by the older boy had started the blaze. They had posted one man at the entrance and assigned others to check each floor. Having assured themselves that there were no children in the building, they had put a match to it. They had timed their arson carefully. Most children would have been indoors listening to Dick Barton.

Today I believe that the whispering before the fire was the fathers' way of letting the other parents know what was being planned. I do not remember the police being involved. What remained of the building was very quickly demolished and the whole thing was forgotten.

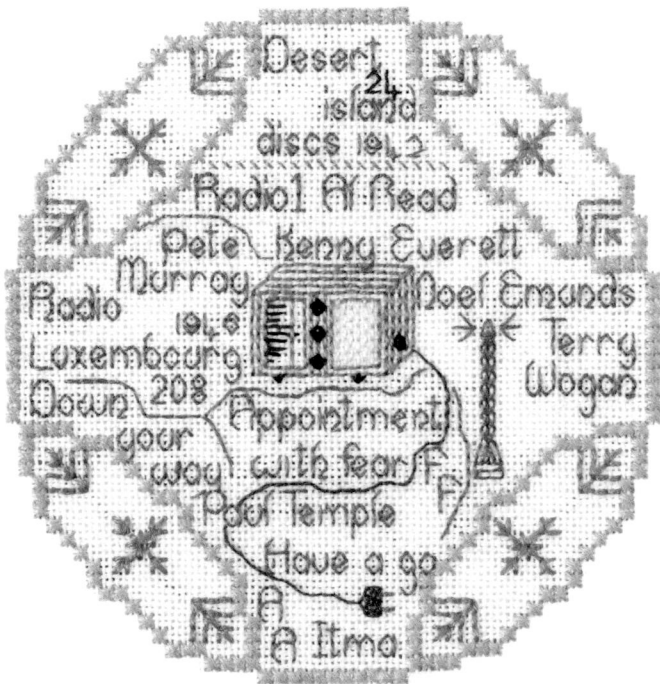

– CIRCLE 24 –

RADIO

Most of this chapter is about radio programmes of the forties and early fifties because, for a great many people, radio was the chief source of entertainment during that period. Our radio was a nice-looking piece of equipment, and Dad was very happy with it because it had a good receiver which gave excellent reception. It was made by GEC, which my brother Ted used to tell me stood for George Edward Challenger which made it very valuable. George Edward Challenger is a character in the book *The Lost World* by Sir Arthur Conan Doyle. At the time I believed him, which goes to show how gullible I was. It also shows that at some point before this we must have listened to *The Lost World* on the radio, either in story form or as a play.

While there was much entertainment on the radio there also seemed to be an overabundance of programmes that spread doom, gloom and misery. In my early days we did not need reminding that there was a war on or that times were hard, but there was always some killjoy who believed it was his mission in life to spell out our problems before sending us to bed feeling deeply despondent. Mother was known to comment sarcastically: 'I bet he's fun to live with.' There was often a police message at the end of a news bulletin, calling for information from anyone knowing the whereabouts of someone whose relative was seriously ill or worse. The number to call if we had any information on such matters was Whitehall 1212.

But radio was not all sorrow and woe and there were programmes that we simply would not miss. More than anything we enjoyed a good play, and to aid our concentration we would sit side by side in front of the radio staring at it intently while we followed the plot. There were also series and serials which, if you had listened to them, would secure you your place with the 'in crowd' of the playground the following day. Two examples of these were the Francis Durbridge serials in which Paul Temple and his wife Steve would solve a murder mystery, and the series about the light-hearted escapades of PC 49. Both of these would be on once a week for eight weeks. The serials of *Dick Barton – Special Agent* would also last eight weeks, but were on every night, Monday to Friday, at 6.45 pm for a quarter of an hour. The streets would empty as all the kids dashed indoors for another helping of the latest adventures of Dick and his pals Jock and Snowy which often dealt with espionage; he was, after all, a special agent. These episodes would be a full fifteen minutes of action, the cast list not being given until Saturday morning when an omnibus edition would be broadcast. The first series began in 1947 and the last one ended in 1951 when it was replaced by *The Archers: an Everyday Story of Country Folk* in March.

For women, in the afternoons at 2.45 there was *The Robinsons: an Everyday Story of Everyday People*, which I loved listening to when I wasn't at school. It ran for eighteen months and was sadly missed when it ended in December 1947. However, it was replaced, in a slightly later time slot, by *Mrs Dale's Diary*. This ran from January 1948 until April 1969 and is best remembered for Mary Dale's stock phrase 'I'm worried about Jim', to which Mom would add 'My heart bleeds'. Mom couldn't stand the imperious tones of Mrs Dale's mother Mrs Freeman, who she described as having 'more to say than she'd got to eat'. She was also irritated that Dr Dale always referred to her as 'Mother-in-law' when she would have preferred him to call her 'the old bat' instead. The programme was lampooned throughout the twenty years it was broadcast.

In the early fifties we were treated to 'Mrs Doom's Diary' which was just a small part of a comedy show called *Home at Eight*. This snippet always began with the snooty Drusilla Doom (Hermione Gingold) pouring Edmund, her doom-laden husband (Alfred Marks), a cup of tea and then asking him if he would like 'millock'. They had a servant named Trog who never spoke but made his presence known by heavy, vibrating footfalls which gave the impression that each foot weighed a ton. This was just one of the many variety and comedy programmes which went out in the evenings.

We used to listen to *Worker's Playtime* from Monday to Friday while eating lunch. This was a variety programme, the only one which would occasionally feature Dad's favourite singer of the time, Cavan O'Connor, who was known as the Irish troubadour. As he proceeded to murder his chosen songs we would groan and eventually renamed him 'Cavan O'Chronic'. Every Sunday, lunch would be cooked while *Family Favourites* was on. This was a request programme presented by Jean Metcalfe in Britain and Cliff Michelmore in Germany and was an exchange of requested, recorded music between the chaps in the forces stationed in Germany and those back home. For me, the programme and its signature tune 'With a Song in My Heart' will forever be synonymous with the cooking of Sunday lunch and with the Sunday atmosphere in general, which was completely different to that of the other days of the week.

When it comes to records programmes I have to mention the ground-breaking *Jack Jackson's Record Roundup*. Jack had a refreshingly friendly American style which was very much admired by the young. With his quick fire, very amusing patter and choice of recordings he definitely fitted the bill. He began with the BBC in 1948 and moved to Radio Luxembourg in 1954 joining other young men who had already made their names as disc jockeys such as Pete Murray, who began there in 1949. Radio in those days had so much to offer.

Oh, the delights of listening to tap dancers and trying to visualise what they looked like. The popularity of radio ventriloquists, though, was quite remarkable when you consider that their skill was judged on whether or not you could see their lips moving. The dummies became more famous than the men who manipulated them. My own favourite dummy was Daisy May (voiced by Saveen) because, though her voice came from a man, she came across as a sweet girl as opposed to the usual cheeky boys, the most popular of these being Archie Andrews (voiced by Peter Brough). I didn't particularly like Archie Andrews but his shows were terrific. Many great stars got their big break into show business on Archie Andrews' show including Max Bygraves, Beryl Reid, Tony Hancock and Benny Hill.

Harry Hemsley, considered by many to be a ventriloquist, wasn't. His programme, which was enjoyed by children and adults alike, was *Hemsley's Hotel*. Harry was the leading character in the show which featured his fictitious family; Elsie, Winnie, Johnnie and Horace the baby. All of their quite unique voices were supplied by Harry but there were no dummies. It was very funny and I loved it, but my all-time favourite radio entertainer was, like Hemsley, another 'one-man' show.

Al Read used his own voice to portray other characters such as his nagging wife or his know-all neighbour. His comedy was based on observations of everyday life among working-class people which he transformed into humorous situations. I have never stopped listening to this man, simply because I love his brand and style of wit. Now I have two hours of him doing what he did best on my iPod.

Any fan of radio programmes from the 1940s decade will remember *An Appointment With Fear*. Every week the programme would begin with a sinister male voice announcing: 'An Appointment with Fear, and here is your storyteller, The Man In Black.' Then we would hear the deep, dark voice of Valentine Dyall, who would proceed to give us a rough outline of the play we were about to hear and put the fear of God into us.

Two of these plays had such an effect on me that I clearly remember them still. The first was called 'The Nutcracker Suite', and was about a couple staying in a weird castle for the night. The story goes that while they were lying in bed they suddenly realised that the walls and ceiling were very quietly and slowly, but surely, closing in on them. They did, of course, all the way. Hence the title, I suppose. The second was about a man who was making a lot of alterations to his house. It was a huge house standing in its own grounds, well away from the road. While he was building a wall to block off an enormous old fireplace he discovered that his wife was having an affair with his best friend. To cut a long story short he drugged them, tied them up, and put them behind the wall he was building. As he was putting the last couple of bricks in place, they came round and started shouting and screaming. But he only laughed as he finished the job. Then he went off on safari for six months and left them to it, while you were left with your imagination.

Though this programme was on quite late we were allowed to stay up and listen to it. Dad was not happy about this, but we would have lost all respect at school the next day if we hadn't listened to it. After this ordeal Ted was always all right, or at least he gave the impression that he was, but I would not go upstairs until Dad had been up and put on the lights to check under the beds and make sure no one was lurking there; I always had a problem with the space beneath my bed. Then I would refuse to get into bed until he promised to leave the light on until I was asleep. As the years went by I discussed this programme with others of my age and found that I was not alone in my fear. Frightening or not, it seems that it was a 'must-listen' which was at the top of everyone's list.

Even Dad had programmes he would not miss. We always had to listen to football and boxing as he was very keen on both. We hardly dared draw breath during a boxing match for fear that he might miss one word of the commentary. He would sit in his chair, deeply engrossed, unaware that he was himself ducking and diving. The British boxers from my formative years were Bruce Woodcock, Freddie Mills, Don Cockell, Jackie Gardner and Randolph Turpin. Occasionally there would be a boxing match broadcast live from America. These were important contests and because of the time difference they usually came on the radio at about two o'clock in the morning. Dad would not miss these bouts and neither would the rest of us. We were not compelled to get up, but whatever Dad did he would have such a quiet air of enthusiasm that you simply felt the need to join him. Most people thought we were mad but we didn't care.

We eagerly awaited 15 May 1953 because the heavyweight title fight between the fantastic Rocky Marciano and Jersey Joe Walcott was to be broadcast. Our plans were drawn up and included our next-door neighbour, who had asked to join us as her accumulator was flat. An accumulator was a rechargeable battery measuring roughly six inches by six inches by twelve inches, and it would cost 1s 3d to have it recharged at the ironmongers. That night we went to bed early, with Dad's alarm clock set for 1.45 am. In no time he was waking us up and telling me to knock on the wall to wake up our neighbour. In the kitchen the air was electric. Mother told me to put the kettle on. Jim automatically passed the cups and saucers from the sideboard and Dad twiddled the knobs on the radio to get the best possible reception. I had just lit the gas under the kettle when we heard 'Seconds out. Round one.'

As was his habit, Dad gave an ear-splitting 'Shhhhh' as the fight began, just in case anyone was thinking of speaking. The kettle had not yet reached boiling point when we all stared at one another in disbelief as the referee counted out Jersey Joe in a first round knock-out. Marciano's win was not a surprise but we had hoped for a better show from Walcott, at least half an hour of class action. I turned off the gas, the cups were put away, our neighbour went home and we all went back to bed.

In 1967 the Light Programme, the Home Service and the Third Programme disappeared forever and were replaced by Radios One, Two, Three and Four. With them we had the joys of listening to Dave Lee Travis, Noel Edmonds, Terry Wogan and

Kenny Everett and others of that ilk, while hanging on to *Desert Island Discs* and *The Archers* from before the change. I was never all that keen on *The Archers*, but I still listen to *Desert Island Discs* and other things.

POWER OF MEMORY

Towards the end of the forties, from about the age of eleven or twelve, I had no idea why but I suddenly began asking questions about the events of one night during the war when the street had been subjected to a shower of incendiary bombs. That night the double-fronted cottage directly opposite our house and the steel works next to it had been hit by clusters of these bombs. And it was a narrow street. All I knew was that something about that night was somehow linked to the four basic rules for survival which were, at the time, constantly drummed into Ted and me in preparation for a catastrophe. These were:

1. If we fell into the canal or the park pool we should wriggle out of our coats and kick off our shoes, the theory being that the weight of these when wet would hold us down.

2. If our clothing was on fire we should roll back and forth on the floor, preferably in a rug or something similar, to stifle the flames.

3. If we were in a room full of smoke we should lie face down on the floor because the air there would be cleaner and easier to breathe.

4. In all cases we should try to remain calm and stay in control. This last one was most important.

In my quest for answers I asked Mother many times what happened that night and her sometimes snappy reply was always the same: 'You slept through it.' Ted was noncommittal. Dad had been on duty all that night, fire-watching at the factory where he worked, so he could only say that he thought the bombing had happened in November 1940.

While I had no recollection of that night, I did clearly remember the next morning. I woke on hearing heavy footsteps coming up the stairs. The door opened and in came Dad wearing his fireman's uniform. He scooped me up from my bed and as he hugged me he said: 'Come and see what the naughty Germans have done.' He carried me to the window to see the smouldering remains of the factory and the cottage. Undeterred, I asked an elderly neighbour what she remembered of that night. She remembered very little of the night but could recall events the following morning. She knew that as Dad had pushed his bike through the factory gate on his way home, the gatekeeper had told him that our street had been flattened during the night. He had sped off on his bike believing that he had lost his wife, family and home. The neighbour remembered seeing Dad in a very agitated state. As he swung into our street his relief at seeing the houses intact caused him to fall off his bike.

The street was full of people from the emergency services trying to clear up the debris and some of the neighbours were standing in a small group at the bottom of the entry. Dad stood up and, out of what must have been sheer relief that our row of houses was still intact, he raised his bike above his head and threw it with all his might against the wall of the pub. He then raced up the entrance, across the yard and into the house. By the time I had pieced together what Mother had told me, what the neighbour had told me and my own memories, I had a clear picture of the morning after but could still remember nothing about the night before. My unanswered questions about that night never left me and would continue to haunt me for a further 48 or 49 years.

However by the mid-1960s, when I had a family of my own, I had established two things. One was that my nose was now finely, and constantly, attuned to the smell of burning. The other was that I disliked sleeping in a room with the door shut. By then, of course, I had little doubt that something had happened that night which had been so alarming that I had buried it deeply in my subconscious. It would be 1996 before a few simple words triggered my mind into spilling out that which I had locked away for over half a century. But other events would bring up unresolved issues before then.

One afternoon in the summer of 1984 we had a thunderstorm. I was alone in the house. I had never been frightened during a storm, just a bit apprehensive, but there was no doubting that this storm was going to be bad. The sky was blacker than I had ever seen it and everywhere was quiet. I felt the urgent need to prepare the house as we had done for Mother at such times (see Circle 42). Then I sat and waited. What followed was the worst storm I have ever experienced. The building rattled, and fitted carpets throughout the house were raised a couple of inches and then fell back as the wind whistled through the house. Hailstones perforated leaves in the garden and left a layer of ice so thick that at bedtime much of it was still there. This was to be the catalyst for years of fear and from then on, at the first signs of a darkening sky, I would start shaking.

During a storm in 1986 Ray set me thinking when he said: 'I can't understand you. I never knew you to be so frightened of thunderstorms until a couple of years ago.' As we tried to work out what had triggered this fear, it was Ray who figured out that Dad's death two years earlier had something to do with it. We agreed that the night in 1940 was involved, but couldn't understand why Dad's death had opened a can of worms.

In the early 1990s I went to see Paul Salkovskis, a young psychiatrist who was achieving great things with a new method of helping people to conquer their fears. I went because by this time my fear of storms had become so bad that I was beginning to feel frightened just at the prospect of going out of the house, in case a storm developed. Having helped me overcome my threatening agoraphobia, Salkovskis set to work on my fear of storms. He worked out that it was associated with smoke and that I was more afraid of the lightning flash than the thunder. He then explained to me that when incendiary bombs hit their target they break open with an enormous, blinding flash which in turn starts a firestorm that cannot be extinguished with water. He agreed that the root of my fear was linked to my experiences in November 1940. If we could find the answer to that, the fear might be erased.

When Ray died in January 1996 we had been living in our house for just under two years. We had bought it for our retirement. Significantly, it had two lavatories, one upstairs and one in the back porch. The door of the one in the porch was in the old style and made of planks of wood. My despair after Ray's death was eased a little when my granddaughter Megan was allowed to stay with me for most weekends. We had left the winter behind and spring was bringing some decent weather.

One Sunday morning Megan was playing in the back garden and I was working in the kitchen. She dashed to the porch and gasped, 'Grandma, can you open the toilet door for me please?' This I did and in she trotted. As I turned away I stopped dead in my tracks. I hardly dared breathe. The door had a latch. I had completely forgotten that the doors to both bedrooms in our old house had had latches. When she came out I cautiously said:

'Can't you open that door by yourself?'

'No,' she replied, 'not even on tip-toe', and she demonstrated her point.

'And how old are you?' I asked.

As she went back into the garden she answered proudly: 'I'm four-and-three-quarters.'

I stood there, rooted to the spot and absolutely stunned, as my mind flooded with the memories of that night in November 1940. I clearly heard a young voice shout: 'She's here Mom and I can't open the door.'

This was followed by my mother's voice saying: 'Come out of my way. Don't hurt her. Let me get there.'

At that time we had only gaslight in the house so light didn't come on at the flick of a switch. There were no street lights and in any case the blackout rules were rigidly obeyed. When we were in the bedroom the door had to be kept shut, with good reason. The top of the staircase was very dangerous, especially for small feet in the dark. In that house the dark was very dark indeed. My depiction of the staircase in this circle shows a red line for our bedroom and a green line for Mother's bedroom. There was no landing and the top two steps were difficult to negotiate. The blue line at the bottom represents the door into the kitchen. On the night in question, when the air raid warnings had been sounded my mother and Ted would have been in the kitchen and probably hoping that the warning wouldn't amount to much, while I was safe and warm in bed. They would have been unaware of what was on the way.

Although I was a good sleeper, the flash from the clusters of incendiary bombs and the noise of the people desperately trying to put out the fires had woken me. The light from the fires showed me that the room was full of smoke. Even at such a tender age I remembered the four basic rules for survival. I kept a level head and I remember getting down on the floor and crawling towards the door which was, of course, shut. I did not get up and try to open it because, at three-and-three-quarters, I knew I could not reach the latch.

The latch on this type of door was always high up. I don't know why. However, these doors also left a good gap at the bottom, probably a couple of inches or so from the floor. I lay there pressed against the door breathing the cleaner air from the staircase. It is possible that while lying there I passed out, but I think it is more likely that I went back to sleep, safe in the knowledge that I had followed the emergency drill and stayed calm. The next thing I knew was the door being pushed against me and Ted shouting: 'She's here Mom and I can't open the door.'

Though I had been alone in the house I would have been alone for only minutes. As children we were not neglected in any way. I believe that Mother, for a few fleeting moments, desperately needed to know that other adults were close by and for this reason alone she and Ted would have joined others at the bottom of the entry.

The reason that I had buried the events of this night so deeply in my subconscious is quite simple: I was told to do it. I can clearly remember that, as Mom's hand came round the door and she scrabbled to drag me away so that she could open it fully, I started to cry. Having carried me downstairs and comforted me, it must have occurred to her that she could be in trouble with Dad over this episode and she came out with her stock solution for getting herself out of such difficulties: 'Now you hadn't better let your dad know that you've been a naughty girl by crying and being frightened. He will be very angry with you and shout.' So the easiest way for me to keep out of trouble was to completely dismiss the incident from my mind and store it away under lock and key. Sadly, Mother must have spent the next 44 years worrying that I would remember.

The thunderstorm in 1984 which had had such an effect on me was just a few weeks after Dad's death. His absence left me free to show my fear at last. That night in November 1940 had remained locked away in my mind until my father's death turned the key some 44 years later. It would be another twelve years before a small girl, aged four-and-three-quarters, would draw my attention to the fact that I also needed to lift the latch for these powerful memories to be released.

PATENT MEDICINES

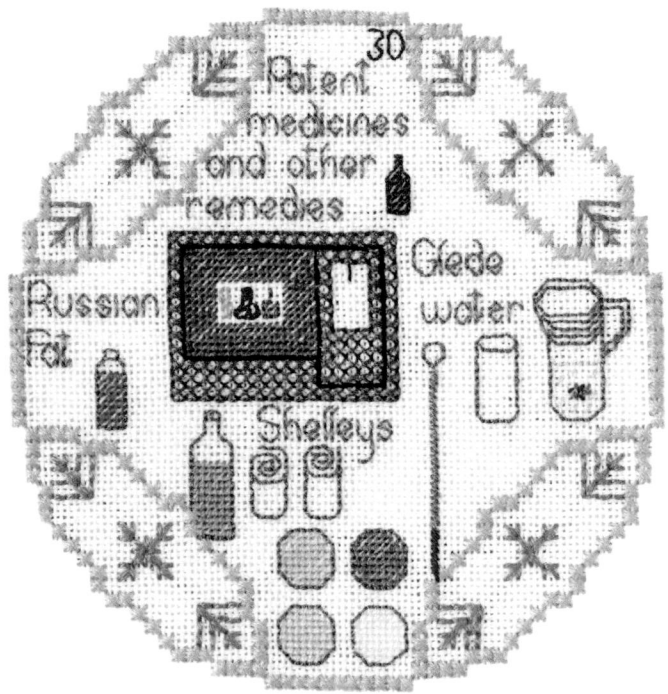

Patent medicines were many and varied because people would try everything possible before resorting to the doctor. Local chemists made up their own concoctions, and the best pharmacist in our area was Mr Shelley who had a shop at the far end of the High Street.

Many times I would toddle along there as a child when Mother was having trouble with our Jimmy. I would relate all the little horror's symptoms while Mr Shelley listened intently. He would disappear into his inner sanctum and emerge minutes later with a preparation in a bottle which Mother had provided. More often than not these remedies would do the trick. You could ask for some of them by name but you always had to supply your own bottle.

After a particularly long and stressful day with her little treasure Mother would heave a deep sigh, thoroughly wash out a bottle and, reaching for her purse, she would say: 'You'll have to go to Shelley's and fetch me three penn'orth of Mother's Comfort.' This mixture resembled cold, milky tea and was liberally spooned down the offending infant's throat. I could never understand why it wasn't called Baby's Comfort. I have no idea what was in it.

The three main ointments used in our house were Zambuk, Indian Cerete and Germolene. Dad didn't care at all for Germolene and it was only used when all else had failed. Zambuk was used for cuts and grazes and Indian Cerete was daubed onto anything that needed drawing, such as spots or cuts that had become infected. The Indian Cerete tin was white with a very fine black sketch of a railway engine printed on it. This was known to everyone as 'Injin Ointment'. Chemists and their assistants always knew what was meant when a breathless child asked for 'Injin Ointment'. We also kept Vaseline in the house to use on chafed skin but Dad didn't think much of it. He some-times used it as a hairdressing, and often remarked that that was about all it was good for.

We never had proper bandages, just torn strips from worn-out bed sheets which Mother kept rolled and ready in the sideboard in case of emergency. Dad was very much in charge of dressing all wounds. He was so much gentler than Mother and always seemed to know what to do. For headaches Ted and I were given Aspro tablets. For herself, Mother swore by Phensic. For the little misery in the corner, too young to let us know his problem,

Mother would assume that he might have a headache and would administer half a dose of powder from a small fold of white paper printed with the words 'Fenning's Fever Cure'. Dad's personal cure-all was a Beecham's Powder.

My favourite cold cure was Dad's armchair with a blanket and a hot water bottle. Sometimes it was worth having a cold just to get this treatment for a couple of days. As the evening drew to a close the patient's bed would be thoroughly warmed and then the transfer from warm kitchen to cold bedroom would be done as quickly as possible. During this period the whole house would reek of camphorated oil as the patient coughed and sneezed their way back to health.

Sometimes this bit of pampering wouldn't work and Mom and Dad, having talked the matter over, would decide to try the 'Russian fat'. At this point there would be a flurry of excitement. It wasn't often we saw the Russian fat. It was kept in Dad's top cupboard, wrapped in several sheets of very greasy brown paper. It would be placed on the table and ceremoniously unwrapped. It resembled a very large block of hard cheese but was pure white. Dad would slice a portion from it with a knife and then place it on a piece of woollen flannel, which was used only for this purpose. This was then put in front of the fire where the fat would melt and be absorbed into the fabric. When it was all nice and warm it would be slapped onto the patient's chest.

It invariably worked. I never knew, and still don't know, what it was. I don't remember there being any smell from it. It was, as far as I know, there when I was born and was still there when my parents left the house in 1962.

We used butter for bumps, salt bags or olive oil for earache and vinegar or Mother's blue bag for insect bites.* One advert in

---

* A salt bag was made by heating a tablespoon of salt in a saucepan before tying it up in a clean handkerchief. The patient would then hold it against the ear. A Reckitt's blue bag was normally used to whiten the washing.

the newspapers made a marked impression on me. It began with the headline 'Girls Who Cause Anxiety', and was supposed to be a warning to all mothers. It went on: 'The anxious mother sees her daughter gradually droop and grow fragile, bloodless and nervous', before revealing that the answer lay in Dr William's Pink Pills. For 1s 5d a box thousands of unhappy, feeble, anaemic girls had been transformed into robust women. At eight years old I couldn't wait.

As for little Jimmy, he had zinc and castor oil cream to keep his bum blemish-free, jars of borax and honey in which his dummy was dipped occasionally to keep his mouth blemish-free, and gripe water to settle his wind. When the gripe water didn't work Dad had a remedy of his own that was always worth trying. This was called 'glede water'. A glowing red cinder from the fire was dropped into a jug of water and after a few minutes all of the bits would settle to the bottom. Then he would pass the clean water from the top through a piece of fine muslin before giving the little whinger a few sips of it.

With luck the child would then stop crying. He probably did so on the assumption that if he didn't shut up he would be given some more. The government gave him cod liver oil and the most delicious orange juice. Ted and I would drink the orange juice. It was wonderful – I can taste it still. We couldn't actually give it to Jimmy as it gave him belly ache.

But, as Mother said at the time: 'It doesn't take much to give him the belly ache. I've never come across such a miserable little bugger in all my life!'

At school the universal panacea seemed to be iodine. Each application was preceded by the words 'This might sting a bit' as they maliciously dabbed away. A definite case of the cure being worse than the symptoms.

Californian Syrup of Figs was dispensed on a regular basis to keep our innards clean and in good working order. Cod liver oil and malt was given once a week to keep us healthy. Ted and I loved this but it wasn't to everybody's taste. My husband Ray once told me he hated it so much as a child that he had to be held down while it was forced down his throat.

Nurse King, the nit nurse, visited the schools about twice a year to check that we didn't have head lice. Dad trimmed our toenails when necessary. If we were feeling a bit under the weather with backache we would be given a 'Backache and Kidney Pill', which had the fascinating effect of turning our water a bright greeny-blue.

There seemed to be a remedy for everything but with the arrival of the National Health Service, which originally was completely free, many people asked themselves: 'Why should we pay at the chemist's when we can get it for nothing?' This brought a whole new way of dealing with health, eyesight and dental problems, with the result that in time charges had to be made for some NHS services. Even with the advent of free health care, Mom and Dad went on using the old remedies. The Russian fat continued to make an occasional appearance and the house still sometimes reeked of camphorated oil.

STREET GAMES

With only six houses in our street we were often joined by children who lived in the lane, where occasional traffic prevented them from playing outside their houses in the evening. Anyone who thinks that street games were simple affairs where everyone played nicely together couldn't be more wrong. The street was where you shaped your character and determined the kind of adult you would become. Nevertheless, street games could be tremendous fun. Some, such as whip and top, bowling, skipping and some ball games, could be played alone. Some needed simple equipment which we didn't always have. Most games would end up with everyone falling out or dividing into opposing factions, with each faction booing or mouthing off at the others, but the following day all ructions from the previous evening would be forgotten.

The games requiring equipment would last only as long as the one who owned the necessary equipment was kept happy. Great care was taken so as not to upset or offend this person, as it was not uncommon for them to go off in a huff and take their equipment with them. It was at these times that games such as Film Stars, Hide and Seek and Tick came into their own.

In the game of Film Stars one child would stand on one side of the street and everyone else would stand on the other. The one standing alone would shout out the initials of a film star and if one of the others could guess the name they would then become the person to call out the next set of initials. This was only a good game if the child calling out the initials could spell. Problems would arise if you were trying to guess Humphrey Bogart from the initials U.B. or Phyllis Calvert from F.C. One snotty-nosed little oik got into deep water when he gave us the initials A.U. These were supposedly for Anouk, the latest French actress to try her luck in the British film industry.

Hide and Seek was always a good game if there was a decent crowd. A couple of times, if I was tagging along with older kids, I would cover my face and start counting while they dashed off to hide. I wouldn't see them again for hours. Bit sneaky, that. However, they did it once too often and after that they could never get rid of me no matter how cunning they became.

If everyone stayed happy, Tick could be an everlasting game in which a 'tick' meant simply a touch. To start, one of the crowd would be chosen to be the first to try to tick someone. The others would run around and do everything they could do to avoid being ticked. The one who was eventually ticked would then be the one to do the ticking. Sometimes all you would get for ticking someone was a hefty thump. You, of course, would hit back and when the rest of the gang joined in the fracas the game would be over.

For games needing equipment we had to be very inventive, usually changing all the accepted rules. But this wasn't always successful. For example, while most boys had a home-made cricket bat, wickets created difficulties. However, we had no problems with football since this game only needed a ball. Because our game would usually only have five or six players and a ball the size of a tennis ball, this was not the conventional game. There would be no teams and the chaps would run about kicking the ball; any one of them could score if they could get it past the goalkeeper. The person with the most goals at the end of the match was the winner. The game was greatly improved when one of them had the idea of putting me in goal. The number of goals scored during a match quadrupled, and both the game and I became very popular. It was only when I realised that I was being taken for a mug that I flounced off, taking the goalpost (my orange jumper) with me.

We made several attempts at playing tennis but for one reason or another it was not one of our favourites. We had no racquets or net but this was not a problem – we could have a reasonable game with two small tin shovels and a piece of rope tied across the street. Even so, arguments would arise when one player claimed that the ball had not gone over the 'net' but through it, leaving the other player without a leg to stand on. Someone had the idea of having the rope stretched across the road while two others would judge whether the ball went through or over the 'net', but there were accusations of favouritism and to be honest it all seemed more trouble than it was worth. Often a solitary game was deemed a better alternative. Even so, there could be problems with these in that they might require a certain amount of skill.

Of two such games, one was the frustrating Whip and Top. The idea was that by winding the string of your 'whip' around your top and then, holding the top loosely but steadily on a firm surface, you could set it spinning by snatching the whip away from it. After this you would keep the top spinning by whipping it. I could get the top spinning alright but no matter how much I whipped it, it would quickly slow down, wobble a bit and then fall over. After a couple of attempts I would give it up as a bad job. Likewise, I never took to bowling, so called because you would bowl along, like a demented fool, hitting an old car tyre with a stick, and see how long you could keep it going for. This would not, I feel, be enjoyed very much by today's kids. How could they keep their street cred if they admitted that they had spent the whole of the previous evening running along the pavement hitting a car tyre with a stick?

For girls probably the most popular games were skipping and hopscotch. While all my friends enjoyed the game of hopscotch it was beyond me. I didn't understand it then and I still don't. I used to stand and watch all the others hopping from one square to another until they were declared out, and they looked as flummoxed as I felt.

Skipping had no rules and was much easier to understand. We disliked proper skipping ropes, which had brightly painted handles, because the manufacturers would never make the rope long enough. The length they provided was fine for people much shorter than us. In order to demonstrate the required skill, we had to replace the rope. To Mother's great annoyance, we would often use sections of her washing line, leading her to exclaim: ''Ave yoh been at my lines again?'

Many of my friends could skip at great speed, but I was hopeless at this and usually ended up with the rope knotted round my ankles leaving me lying in an ungainly heap. We had skipping rhymes which the girls chanted endlessly as they skipped individually with their own ropes. One rope could be shared very successfully by two girls, but often ended with the two of them arguing because the one who owned the rope was top dog. Sometimes, if we could get a piece of rope long enough (usually Mother's washing line when she wasn't looking), we could play a collective skipping game which was such fun that the chaps would also join in. It was an elimination game and two of us would stand holding the rope, one each side of the street, and swing it while all the others skipped inside it. The last to be caught by the rope was the winner. However, of all these games nothing could compare with the thrill of our efforts at Gang Warfare.

Anyone in the vicinity, as we drew up our plans, would be included in our gang. To begin with, we needed an old pram. One could usually be found on one of the many pieces of waste ground that were dotted about. More often than not, our find would have only three wheels, but that didn't matter. Having fixed ourselves up with this most vital piece of equipment, we would fill it with tufts of grass, pulled up by hand at the bottom of the street. Our scout, having been sent off to reconnoitre other streets, would dash back to let us know where he had spotted a likely-looking bunch of kids whom we could attempt to intimidate. Then off we would go, ready for action.

We approached the designated battle area with great caution. Whoever we had democratically appointed as leader of the expedition would furtively move to the very corner and peer round, while the rest of us stayed behind, close to the ammunition, awaiting orders. Raising his hand high above his head the leader would indicate that we should prepare ourselves, and as he shouted 'Go' we would dash into the war zone hurling clumps of grass, complete with soil, at the unsuspecting enemy for all we were worth. It would only take a minute for the clumps that we had flung at them to be flung back at us as they retaliated. Sometimes we would fly back around the corner to regroup, and then, with courage renewed and whooping and yelling for effect, we re-entered the fray.

With missiles flying in every direction and kids screeching, it wouldn't take long for two or three women to emerge from their houses. One would shout: 'You little buggers. Look at the bloody mess here. You wait till I see your mothers tomorrow.' They would then look as if they were going to give chase. With that we would grab the handle of our empty battle wagon and, dragging it behind us, we would run as fast as our little legs could carry us, shrieking with delight, mission accomplished and leaving the women to bring out their brooms and sweep up the mess. Several evenings later, as we were engrossed in our games, a great clod of earth would come sailing through the air and the whole process would be repeated in reverse. If the mothers did complain to each other, and I doubt that they ever did, we never heard about it.

– CIRCLE 32 –

TALES

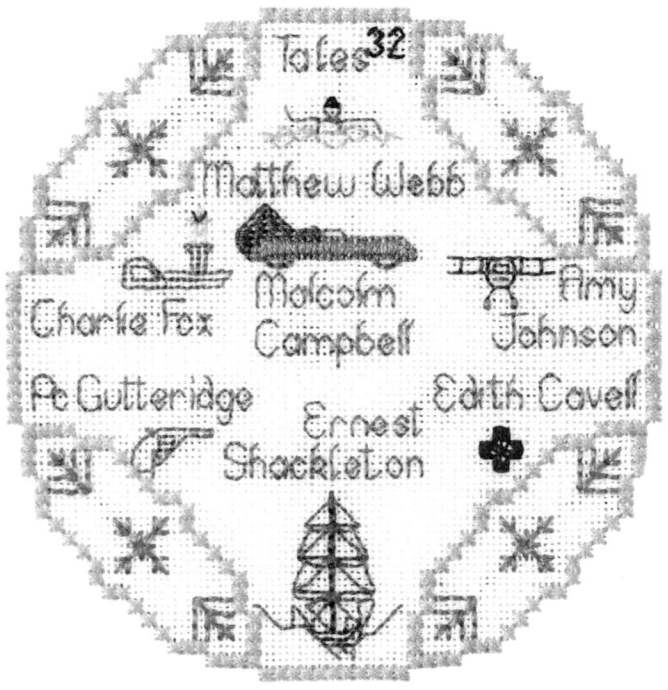

Mom, Dad and Ted were very good at telling tales. Mom's were always about when she was a girl and Dad's were about feats of courage, sportsmen and gruesome murders. Ted's were about anything that came to his mind. He could always spin a good yarn about footballers – Carter, Milburn, Finney and Matthews and so on – and he always seemed very knowledgeable about the Angles, the Saxons and the Picts. In Ted's case I think he saw me as very gullible so he could get away with saying anything. Gullible or not, when I look back to those days now, all I see is a girl listening to history which is something I am still doing. I will always be an eager audience for tales that are based on fact.

I have filled this circle with just a few names from Dad's long list of people whose stories I remember clearly. We had listened intently to all of his stories dozens of times but never missed an opportunity to listen again, while Dad never missed an opportunity to repeat them.

Captain Matthew Webb was the first man to swim the English Channel, from Dover to Calais, on 25 August 1875, without the use of artificial aids. He did the 22-mile swim in 21 hours 45 minutes, which at the time was a truly remarkable achievement.

PC George Gutteridge of the Essex constabulary was murdered in a country lane on 27 September 1927. Gutteridge was 38, a family man and a popular village bobby. He was based at Stapleford Abbots which lay between Romford and Ongar. He had spotted a stolen car being driven by two men, Frederick Browne and Pat Kennedy, and, having made the vehicle pull over, he was taking notes when one of the men killed him with two bullets. A further two bullets were fired into him after his death, one through each eye. The two men responsible for this murder believed that whoever or whatever was last seen by the victim before death would be imprinted on his eyes. They could not take the risk that this might be true. It was one of the earliest cases to be solved by using the study of ballistics. The two men were hanged. The way in which PC Gutteridge had been murdered caused outrage among the general public. This case was so gruesome that its satisfactory ending gave us a feeling of immense relief when we heard the story.

Malcolm Campbell was a British racing driver, who held both the land and water speed world records. He had broken the land speed record nine times by 1935 and broke the water speed record three times by 1939. His car and boat were both called

Bluebird. He was the father of Donald Campbell who famously emulated his feats in the sixties. Malcolm died from natural causes in 1948; his son would not be so fortunate.

Amy Johnson was the first woman to fly solo from Britain to Australia. She achieved this in a second-hand DeHavilland Moth with a Gipsy engine which had extra fuel tanks fitted, giving it a flying time of thirteen hours. She named the plane Jason. She began the 10,000 mile journey on 5 May 1930 and completed it in twenty days. Her plane disappeared in 1941 over the English Channel during the Second World War while she was serving with the Air Transport Auxiliary.

Charles Fox was a local murder victim. In August 1933 he was asleep in bed with his wife when she heard glass breaking. She woke him up and he went downstairs carrying a candle. In the sitting room the candle was extinguished by a draught from an open window. His wife heard a scuffle and a groan. Charlie staggered back upstairs with a knife in his back and collapsed dead at her feet. Later the murderer, Stanley Hobday, broke into the living quarters of a butcher's shop belonging to one Mr Newton, who did not wake from his slumber until the following morning. Before making off with a small amount of cash, Hobday took the time to wash and shave using the butcher's shaving tackle. He then sat down and made a few running repairs to his clothes using a work basket he had found in a cupboard. This told against Hobday at his trial, in that after committing murder he was sufficiently calm to thread a needle. He was hanged. Dad's theory was that if Charlie Fox had kept a torch by his bed he would not have been murdered, because a) a torch lights up a large area in front of the person carrying it whereas a candle only lights up the person carrying it, and b) the light from a torch cannot be extinguished by anything but its switch. Throughout my life I have always kept a torch by my bed.

Nurse Edith Cavell was the British matron of a Red Cross hospital in German-occupied Belgium during the First World War. She had been in Brussels when the war started and remained there during the German occupation, helping Allied soldiers to escape to the Dutch border. She was caught in August 1915 and later court-martialled. At her trial she admitted to helping 200 men to reach the border. During her final communion on 11 October she said that she must have no hatred or bitterness for anyone. The following day she was executed by firing squad. Her death was seen as an outrage and raised indignation everywhere, even in Germany where the Kaiser deplored her execution. I remember that after Dad's telling of this story there was always a long silence while we gathered our thoughts.

Ernest Shackleton's tale was, for me, the best tale of the lot. He was an Irish Antarctic explorer. He commanded the 1914–16 expedition which hoped to be the first to cross the Antarctic on foot. His ship, *Endurance*, left South Georgia on 5 December 1914. On board were Shackleton and his team of 27 men and enough dogs, equipment and stores to see them through a journey that would test all of them to a point beyond endurance. Just one month after their departure the *Endurance* became trapped in the ice on the Weddell Sea. Two hundred and eighty one days later – during which time, as the ship creaked and groaned while being crushed in the ice, everything that could be removed from the ship and saved was removed – the ship was finally abandoned to her fate.

During these 281 days, the ice in which the ship had been trapped had drifted 573 miles to the north-west and the men were now 374 miles from the nearest land. Dragging with them the boats they had salvaged from the ship, Shackleton and his men set off on a return journey to South Georgia which was to be completely stunning in its courage, heroism and fortitude.

When on 15 April 1916 they finally set foot on the bleak, uninhabited Elephant Island, it was the first time they had stood on land for eighteen months, but the worst of their ordeal still lay ahead. On 24 April, leaving 22 of the men on the island to sit it out, Shackleton and five others set sail for South Georgia in the *James Caird* to get help. After a nightmare of a journey they finally returned to Elephant Island to pick up the men on 30 August.

Sir Edmund Hillary, the New Zealand mountaineer and Antarctic explorer who conquered Everest in 1953 with Sherpa Tenzing, summed up for me the dogged determination and ability of Shackleton in his endeavour to bring all of the 27 men and himself back alive with the words:

For scientific discovery give me Scott; for speed and efficiency of travel give me Amundsen; but when disaster strikes and all hope is gone, get down on your knees and pray for Shackleton.

My love of stories of human triumph against the odds has never left me, whether in the realm of sport, personal sacrifice or survival.

Mother's stories are not mentioned in this circle simply because her stories were always about her childhood and I did not, at the time, see how I could represent these in needlework. However, there is one of her stories that I feel compelled to repeat simply because of its ending. Many of her stories made us laugh but even after all these years this one, while tinged with overwhelming sadness, still demands to be told. She repeated it to us whenever we asked her, which was often.

On the extreme right of Mother's circle (Circle 48), you will see a small basin tied up in a red handkerchief. When she was a child, many working-class men had a cooked meal taken to them at midday. The vegetables and gravy were put into a basin. On top of this was a small plate on which was placed a piece of meat which was then covered with an inverted saucer. The whole thing was held together in a large red handkerchief which was almost always decorated with white spots. When people talked about a 'spotted handkerchief' you always knew it would be red with white spots, and they were often known as 'dinner handkerchiefs'. The corners were knotted to form a carrying handle. Mom, aged I think about nine at the time, had the job of taking the meal for the man who lived next door to his place of work. One evening, on arriving home, the man asked his wife why there had been no meat with his dinner that day. She swore that the meat was there when she tied up the handkerchief. The woman may have been frightened to admit that she could not afford meat that day, but still she went to complain to Mother's stepmother. Though Mother protested that she had not eaten the meat no one believed her, and the stepmother chose to believe the neighbour. For letting the family down by stealing and for telling lies, Mom received a sound thrashing.

The next day she picked up the meal as usual, carried it halfway to the factory, then sat in the gutter and ate the lot. Then she tied up the empty basin and delivered it. She figured that as she had had a beating for nothing the previous day, today she would have a beating for something. However, that evening nothing was said. The woman must have confessed to her husband that there had been no meat the day before. They had probably sat in their house the previous evening and listened as a child was being beaten, the man feeling rather smug that justice was being done while the woman sat racked with guilt. This period in Mother's life, when it was common for children to be beaten, was known as the 'good old days'.

JEWELS OF WISDOM

Everyone seemed to have a few words tucked away which they could bring into a conversation when needed. Some of them were good advice; others were gibberish. My first example of these jewels of wisdom belongs in the latter category. It is just one of half a dozen that Dad would recite after a couple of pints of his favourite brew. While Mother would sit glaring at him he would, with the facial expression of a mischievous child, recite them one after another as if it were the first time he had spoken them. This one sounds more profound if spoken in the local dialect:

There was a bird upon a bough,
If 'e ay gone e's theer now.

However, Dad could give sound advice when it was called for. I still recall this one today when I have my eye on something expensive in a shop:

If you see something you want and you can see your way to paying for it, buy it. While you are hesitating the price will go up.

On a shopping trip to Stratford upon Avon, my granddaughter Emma experienced one of my moments of madness when Dad's words won the day. After much deliberation I spent a small fortune on a teddy bear named Charity. I have never regretted it.

This one is of my own making, which I drummed into both of my children:

You can do anything with your life. You just have to put your mind to it.

Never give up your dreams. While it is better to achieve sooner rather than later, it is never too late.

Many of these sayings have been handed down for generations and are known by everyone. I have heard the next one my whole life but my interpretation of it may be different to that of most people:

Never make a mountain out of a molehill.

I believe this is usually explained thus: never make an event or happening seem more important or serious than it is. It will only create repercussions. I see it differently, in that the molehill is an achievement for the mole. If he can see it as an achievement and be satisfied with his efforts he will have no reason to build a mountain.

I had been a smoker all my life; never a heavy smoker, but a smoker nonetheless. I had tried to give it up many times but always weakened in the end. At the age of 59, after a series of transient strokes, I was sent to the hospital for a scan of my carotid artery. In the room was the doctor in charge, a nurse and a young trainee doctor. On finding nothing wrong the doctor (quite rightly) snapped that I must give up smoking and left the room. Afterwards I was sitting on the couch, waiting for a note from the nurse, and the young trainee came and sat beside me. He took my hand and said very quietly:

You've been lucky up to yet. The next one could kill you. How many warnings do you want the good Lord to give you?

I never smoked again.

Older people are full of words of wisdom picked up during their lives. This piece came from an elderly friend:

Always look after your pocket. When you are elderly its contents might be the only friend you have.

This friend and I always had a lot in common and she also gave me a piece of advice, though it is not in the circle, which changed my life as it had changed hers:

You may never be rich, but if you can sew you need never be hard up.

On my way home I went straight to the local newspaper office and purchased a small advertisement inviting anyone who needed any sewing done to get in touch. It worked.

Our mother was full of jewels of wisdom. At the age of about twelve I rather dramatically informed her that when I grew up I would have six children, to which she replied:

If I was you I'd 'ave the fust one fust and then mek yer mind up.

Needless to say I kept it in mind.

This last example is a few words of advice she gave me just before I married. I leave her centre-stage:

Never let your husband know that you can move the wardrobe single-handed.

MOM'S KITCHEN

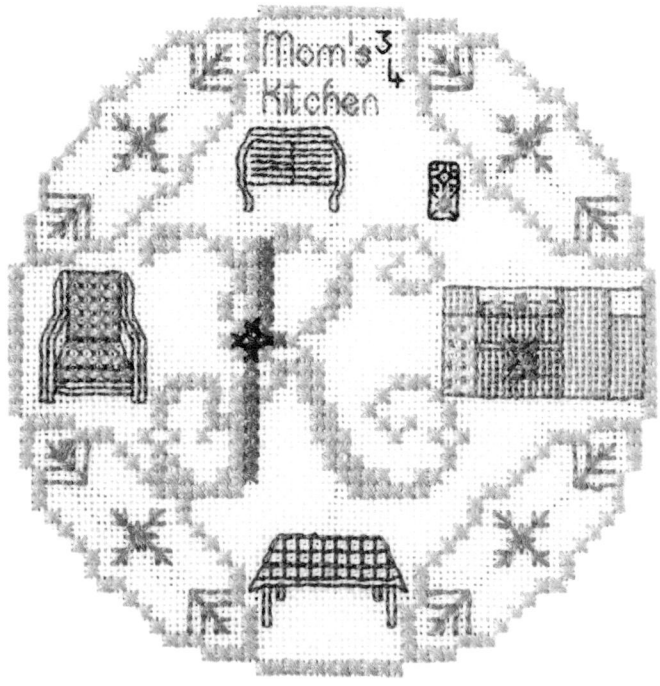

I see adverts on television and in magazines for labour-saving gadgets for use in labour-saving kitchens, and I smile. Labour-saving! They don't know what they are talking about. As you can see in the circle our kitchen had a black iron grate and to the left of this, concealed behind a curtain, was a very tiny sink with a cold water tap. To the right of the fireplace was the door to the stairs and next to this was the door to the cupboard under the stairs where we would take refuge during an air raid. The table in the centre of the room occupied more space than any other item. At the side of the table near to the fireplace sat Mother, always on a low stool so that her ample bosom was level with the table drawer in which she kept cutlery, carving knives and so on.

Opposite her, when the weather was too wet or cold to go out, would be Ted and me playing a table game or drawing. Behind us was the sideboard in which were kept food and crockery. No cooker, fridge or washing machine. The fireplace was the dominant feature of the room. It had a hob each side of the fire and a very small oven to the right. The whole thing shone like black satin because it suited Mother, with her aggressive nature, to attack it once a week with Zebo polish and show it who was gaffer. Because Mother needed a fire to cook our dinner, she lit a fire every day. On warm days the fire was left to burn itself out after she had finished cooking. When there was a fire in the hearth it gleamed and, when anyone mentioned the idea of a pot of tea, it was such a simple thing to move the already-filled kettle from its permanent position on the warm hob nearer to the fire. In no time at all the lid would start rattling, letting us know that the water was boiling. Of the two other doors in this room, one led into the back yard and the other into the front room.

Until I was almost eight we lived in the kitchen for all but eight days of the year. In these cramped conditions, the four doors in this room had to be put to good use. The door that led to the yard was where Dad hung his work clothes and his yard clothes. These included raincoats, jackets, caps, scarves, overalls and the dog's leads. The door to the stairs was wider than a normal door and reached from floor to ceiling. The kitchen side of this was strictly reserved for the use of us children as a chalking board. As it was painted dark brown, it was ideal for this purpose. The pleasure we felt when Dad furtively brought in two or three sticks of white chalk from work was wonderful. On the other side of this door were hung Mother's everyday coat, our coats and raincoats, and right at the very top, among other little-used coats, was an enormous old army overcoat which Dad kept for working in the yard on cold winter days. He could only reach it when the door was shut and by standing on the fourth or fifth step of the stairs.

On the outside of the stairs cupboard Mother hung her aprons, washing lines and peg bag. I also recall a hoopla game hanging on that door at one time. On the inside were hung shopping bags and school bags. Finally there was the door that led into the front room, known simply as 'the front'. This one had a dartboard hanging on it and, of course, it always looked as if it had a bad case of woodworm.

The doors were used in this way because we only had room upstairs for one wardrobe. This was kept for our very best clothes. I remember that Dad always had two best suits, two trilbies, best black boots and best brown boots. He had had them for years. Throughout the house not an inch of space was wasted.

We all went home for a cooked meal in the middle of the day at dinnertime, including Dad, so teatime was a simple affair. Tea and toast, that sort of thing. Mother would get comfortable on her stool with knives at the ready, and we would pass things to her from the cupboard behind us. If she decided to give us toast, she could easily reach the fire with the extra-long toasting fork that Dad had made for her. As Dad didn't get in from work until quarter to seven in the evening, it was always a divided meal.

Occasionally, at about eight o'clock in the evening, if she had the food to spare, she would make us a small supper. Dad, always a light eater, didn't partake. Our favourite was toasted onions. We would pass her everything she needed from the sideboard. Thinly-sliced onions were spread out on an enamel plate and sprinkled with scraps of cheese. It was a good way of using up the rind. She popped them in the oven from her key position at the table, and the kitchen was soon filled with the most wonderful, mouth-watering aroma. There would only be a small portion for each of us, spread on a slice of bread, but it made the evening special. All this activity, and yet no one had risen from their chair. Now that's what I call a labour-saving kitchen.

The kitchen table was the most important piece of furniture in the room. When we were children we played on it and Mother washed up, ironed, prepared vegetables, made cakes and rolled pastry on it. A bowl of water was placed on it so that we could wash. The baby was bathed on it. On winter evenings, if Dad was in a creative mood, he would commandeer the table and even Mother would have to move her stool. While she got on with her mending, Dad would keep Ted and me engrossed for ages making things. I thought he was so clever. He once built Jim a large train engine from pieces of wood, using a National dried milk tin for the boiler. He painted it with some of the ever-present brown paint and it was big enough for Jimmy to sit on when he was old enough.

He was always thinking up things to do but sometimes he bit off more than he could chew. The minute he was heard to mutter quietly 'Damn and blast it', we would surreptitiously look at Mother who, without speaking, would let us know that we must keep quiet until he had sorted out whatever it was that was giving him trouble.

Apart from the large pendulum clock which hung on the wall there were two other very important objects in this room. They were both in the corner, by the door to the front room. These were the wind-up gramophone and, on top of this, the radio. These two items of equipment completed our entertainment possibilities during winter evenings. The wind-up gramophone was a nice looking piece of furniture with Queen Anne legs and a lift-up lid. It was donkey's years old and wasn't used very much as it was a bit temperamental (see Circle 46).

When, on high days and holidays, we moved to the front room for a few days, these two items went with us. And why not? They were carried no more than four feet. By the time we moved into the front room for Jim's first Christmas in 1944, we had had electricity for some time and during this break Mother could see, for the first time, the advantages of using both rooms. So, when the break was over, we did not return to the kitchen. We were much more comfortable in the front room. We had a three-piece suite to sit on and we still had a table in the middle of the room on which we could work.

But the kitchen had many advantages over the front room. The atmosphere was not the same and the fireplace in the front room had no other use than to keep us warm. You could not boil a kettle on it or make toast. Mom could not pop something warming in the oven on a cold winter's night as a special treat. I never doubted for one minute that the family-sized kitchen, complete with large table, would return to favour again one day.

One winter's evening, years later when we lived permanently in the front room, Mother was doing a bit of mending when she remembered something upstairs that needed a stitch or two. She went off to fetch it but returned within seconds as white as a sheet, shaking from head to foot and unable to speak. Dad was the first to glance up from his paper and immediately bounced out of his chair. He gently led her to a chair by the table and started rubbing the back of her hand. Several times he quietly asked her what was wrong, but got no response. I asked if we should try giving her some water and Dad agreed. When I returned from the kitchen I had solved the puzzle and we all went to see what had caused Mom's trauma. She had gone into the kitchen and was too lazy to switch on the light. She groped her way to the stairs door and, as she opened it, Dad's enormous army overcoat had fallen on her from its lofty nail at the top of the door. In sheer terror she had thought for a second that she was about to be murdered. Ted saw the funny side of it. Back in the front room, Mother had started weeping. Spotting Ted's mirth, her tears turned to anger and things got very heated for a minute or two. However a nice cup of tea soon restored the peace and we settled down again. After that evening we never saw the overcoat again. Dad removed it from the house forever; we never knew what he did with it.

Ted was not being unkind. People in our part of the country often tried a smile or a joke first to calm a troubled situation. You would probably be surprised how often it worked. Mother herself got more pleasure from recounting her mishap than any of the rest of us.

– CIRCLE 35 –

THE LORD OF
THE RINGS

Although I briefly mention Tolkien in the circles on icons and cinema I felt that the film trilogy deserved a circle of its own. While I am not familiar with the books, most people agree that they will keep their place in literary history. Likewise, the films also deserve to be remembered in cinema history for the work of director Peter Jackson and his army of technicians. The three films all received Oscars; the first was awarded four, the second two and the third received eleven. Of these seventeen Oscars none was awarded to actors, highlighting the importance of the achievements of those behind the scenes. When I settle down to watch any part of the trilogy it is like being with friends and I continually ponder Tolkien's use of such a mixed bag of characters. He used them in an immense story. Did he use them for a purpose? Are there hidden meanings?

In his foreword to the books, Tolkien declared that his story was neither allegorical nor topical because he disliked both. While this magnificent tale was written by an intellectual I am assuming it was not written for intellectuals alone and I believe that, though it was never Tolkien's intention to be allegorical, there has always been the possibility that readers could interpret it for themselves or apply their own experiences. I am told that he wrote the books as a way of giving the English an ancient mythological history similar to those enjoyed by other countries, in particular those in Scandinavia where mythology goes very deep. For him, King Arthur and the Knights of the Round Table did not go deep enough. It is easy to see what he meant when we look at the pedigree of Aragorn, descended from kings who were nobler, wiser and longer-living than lesser mortals.

Portrayed in the films by Viggo Mortensen, he also – most definitely – had the 'fiery nostrils' factor. This was a major plus for me. At first sight, as he sat in the shadows of The Prancing Pony sucking on his pipe, I was hooked. Without a moment's hesitation, like Arwen, I too would have given up everything for him at that very minute.

This is more than I can say for Gollum. He has been described as a 'monstrous ghoul' and I detested him from the moment I clapped eyes on him. What Mother would have made of him I dare not think and she would probably have seen the sainted Gandalf as up to no good for most of the time. I have always thought of Gandalf as wise, trustworthy and completely believable, although I did spend a couple of weeks in 2004 hoping that the last of these qualities could sometimes be proved wrong. Having sat my exams in the summer of that year I then had a long wait to find out if I had passed or not. Feeling despondent one day I decided to occupy my mind by watching my video of *The Fellowship of the Ring*. As it neared the end I needed a cup of tea and, as I went into the kitchen, Gandalf shouted purposefully: 'You shall not pass.' I felt my knees go funny as I raised my hands to my face and I realised that what he had said was always a possibility. Two weeks later, with immense relief, I proved him wrong.

In *The Two Towers*, Aragorn, in search of the Hobbits, describes them to someone thus: 'They would be small, only children to your eyes.' I believe Tolkien saw children and hobbits as similar in many respects. The hobbits are always bare-footed, constantly eating, mischievously enjoying drink and tobacco and behaving in childlike ways, but always capable of great wisdom and maintaining clear distinctions between right and wrong. During grievous times children have always been old-headed and able to cope in alarming situations. They accept their lot without question.

I could go on about every character in this trilogy of films but I won't, because I do believe in allegory and could fill a great tome with what I see in them. To me allegory is nourishment for the brain. I shall continue to believe that there are many important lessons to be learned from *The Lord of the Rings* trilogy along with its main message, which is that good will always triumph over evil.

The books are a work of genius, and the films are a work of art.

MARBERRY

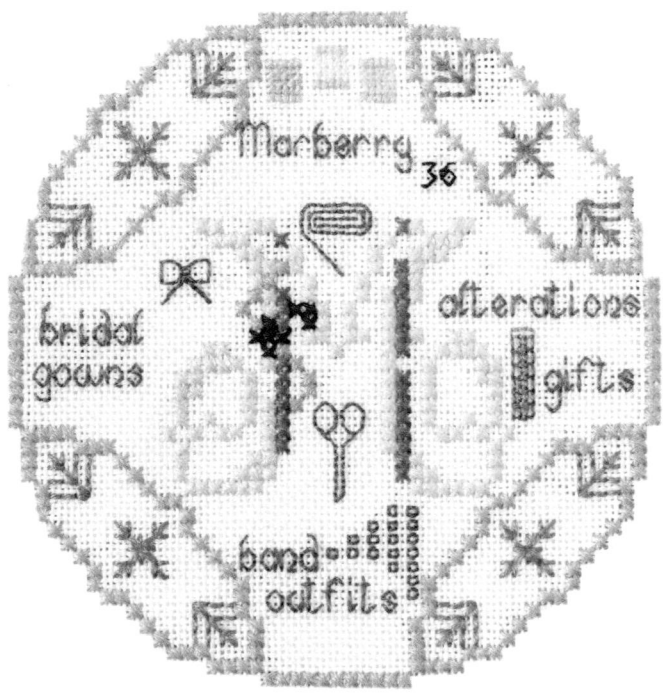

Marberry represents a period in my life when I became my own boss and happily dedicated myself to the business of sewing. Both my children were married by this time and I began by converting the dining room into a workroom. I called the business Marberry, a throwback to when my daughter Angela first started school. After a few days I noticed that she had begun imitating her teacher by talking with a posh accent. When I collected her from school one afternoon she told me that she had been taught a lovely song that day and she sang it to me. It began with the line: 'Here we go round the Marberry bosh, the Marberry bosh, the Marberry bosh.' So Marberry it was.

I consulted the Small Business Advisory Board at the town hall and sorted out my position with regard to income tax and book-keeping, and within a couple of weeks I was up and running. I ran my little sewing business for about eight years, and for two of these Angela worked with me. We would make bridal gowns and occasionally novelty items to sell as gifts. I suppose the defining moment of our time together was when we sold some of our nightdress cases to Harrods, in London. Apart from that there were no great highs or lows. We had good days when everything went right and bad days when we couldn't see the wood for the trees, but we were never without work. We were also never without bits of thread. They could be found anywhere in the house and they turned up in many unexpected places. It was quite common to find a bit in our lunchtime sandwiches.

While I never tired of the sewing I did eventually become disillusioned with the number of hours that I was working. It is amazing how many hours a week a dressmaker can spend on fittings and shopping around for the right buttons and colours of thread. I missed doing this type of work for years afterwards but continued to sew for myself. Eventually, after moving to Warwick, I gave it up altogether in favour of an education. Now I only ever thread the eye of a 'Crewel' needle and always with embroidery silk.

PARKS

As well as the fields (Circle 17) we also had two recreation grounds within easy walking distance of home and a number of parks where we could play. All of these parks were beautifully kept and had many facilities. They had a varying number of tennis courts, together with a sports field, a bowling green, a paddling pool of some sort and a drinking fountain. Two of the largest parks also boasted a boating pool, a fishing pool and lovely Victorian tea rooms. In all of them the glorious flower beds were a riot of colour in the summer, and there was friendly rivalry between the gardeners over which parks were the best. One park had a sand-pit, and two had a bandstand along with what were called 'Sons of Rest'. These were rooms where elderly, retired men could meet and have a game of cards, dominoes or billiards. 'Daughters of Rest' were tried but did not catch on. Mother said right from the start that they wouldn't because, she said, she had never come across a retired woman. Though they may have stopped working, they still had to look after the home while their husbands sat in the Sons of Rest playing with their friends.

The parks all had iron railings around them and park keepers to watch out for any hanky-panky. The bigger parks had resident keepers who would live in beautiful houses near to the park gates which they locked every night at dusk. My friend and I passed many a happy summer afternoon playing at being mothers in one particular park. We would make a beeline for our favourite bench which was at the side of the cricket pitch, under the trees, and make ourselves and 'our' children comfortable. I would have Jim in his pram, while she would have one of her sisters in hers and another one trailing along on foot. We would have the usual emergency rations of bread and 'scrape' and a bottle of drinking water, together with warm milk and spare nappies for the babies. We would talk like two old women, discussing the problems of wind, nappy rash and teething. The babies and the toddler were never any trouble.

Occasionally, as the babies became toddlers, we would all go off with a couple of fishing nets made out of the tops of a couple of Mother's old stockings which were threaded with wire to hold them open and fixed to a piece of cane, together with jam jars with a bit of string tied around their necks for carrying handles. We would spend the afternoon fishing and excitedly transfer to a jar any unfortunate tiddler that got trapped in our nets. I say 'unfortunate' because we were not like the dedicated anglers who would put their catch back in the water before they left. We took them home to show Mother. A couple of days later, when one or two of them began looking a bit sickly, she would chuck them all down the drain.

On one occasion, a warning was issued that an unexploded bomb had been found in an area near to Kenrick Park and Mother told us to keep away. Ted and I nevertheless ventured as close as we could, but there were guards on duty so this was not as close as we would have liked. When we arrived home from school at teatime the following day, Mother explained that the bomb had been 'dealt with', meaning that it had been disarmed. At the first opportunity, Ted and I were away. We approached the area cautiously to find only one guard on duty. Ted instructed me to just stand quietly next to him and say nothing. We stood there, with him holding my hand, looking at the guard for what seemed like an eternity. Eventually the guard put down his rifle and beckoned us forward. He told us to have a quick look and then go home. The bomb lay at the bottom of quite a deep hole which had straight, shored-up sides and a narrow ladder. We ran all the way home, exhilarated to have seen something that none of our friends had seen.

Every year, the summer floral fête took place in the town's main park over a weekend. We looked forward to it eagerly. On the Saturday morning the fruit, vegetables, plants and flowers would be judged in one of the huge marquees, and during the afternoon and evening we were allowed in to see who had won what. The vegetables and fruit always looked 'good enough to eat' and quite beautiful while the flowers, though equally beautiful, were a mystery to us. If we asked Dad what the names of the flowers were he would come out with words like 'calathumpians', and of course we believed him. I expect that there would have been a great deal of rivalry between the exhibitors but we didn't know anything about that. We only had a yard and it seemed to be incapable of growing weeds. In other words, it was pure poison to all flora and fauna. As dusk descended we would go to the area set aside for the fun fair and sideshows. The atmosphere was wonderful and when I was a small child I would have to be carried so that I could see it all. Dad would lift me up on his shoulders. While I held on to the top of his head he held on to my feet and Mother carried his trilby.

The parks were well used in those days. All the schools in the borough would square up to each other, again in the main park, during the town's annual sports day. Mothers would join their children in the afternoons as the competitors gave all they had in an attempt to beat the opposition at running, jumping and throwing things. I was never good enough to take part in any of the sporting events but I did belong to the country dancing display team, although one observer, who could only stand and watch sulkily, said I danced like a 'fairy on a gob of lard'.

The days have long gone when a family would join other families, if the weather was agreeable, to promenade in the park wearing their Sunday best, as music drifted across from the bandstand where a local orchestra would be playing. No doubt in 50 years' time the children of today will be reminiscing just as much about what they did when they were young. Times change, and nostalgia can be a potent thing.

NETLEY

Netley is a small village on the south coast of England, fairly close to Southampton. After our wedding in 1955 Ray and I lived there for about eighteen months, staying in rented rooms within properties named 'Rimpton' and 'Ronalda'. The village had a castle, which by then was used as a convalescent home, and a ruined abbey. It had a couple of pubs, a post office, a butcher's shop, an infants' school, two grocers and a really beautiful railway station. This station had been built there for a purpose, for this small village also had one tremendous jewel:

the Royal Victoria Military Hospital. Anyone who travelled by ferry from Southampton to the Isle of Wight before 1963, when the demolition crews got to work, could not have missed it. It was gloriously enormous.

If I had purposefully arranged my first sighting of this building I could not have planned it for a better time. Ray, his brother Ben and I all worked at the aircraft manufacturing company Folland Aircraft. We had to be clocked in by 7.30 am and this meant that we had to catch the 7.00 am bus. One morning, early in 1956, we missed it. Ben said that we might just get there on time if we took a shortcut through the hospital grounds. It was still dark as we set off. As we approached the hospital gate Ben said that we had to get past the guard, that it would be better if we didn't stop unless we were told to, and to leave the talking to him.

The soldier on guard took a step forward and demanded to know our business. Ben snapped back 'Staff', and we were in. As we walked through the grounds the dawn came up and to my left, in the early morning light, was the most magnificent building I have ever seen in my life. The two men were striding out, and I had to trot along to keep up with them while trying to take in as much of this building as I could.

The foundation stone had been laid by Queen Victoria in 1856 and she always took a keen interest in its progress. While the Queen carried a certain amount of clout, this did not guarantee the project freedom from its many critics, who viewed it with disdain as they felt that too much attention had been paid to the beauty and grandeur of the building at the expense of practicality. The design called for one large edifice consisting of a centre block and two wings. The length of the three together was 1,400 feet, eight feet longer than a quarter of a mile. The centre block would be used for administration and to accommodate sick officers and nurses, while the back of the centre block would house the chapel.* Behind the main building was a psychiatric block and stables. There was also a Welsh Hospital and an Irish Hospital, so called because they had been built from donations made by the people of these two countries. It was all on a huge site together with living accommodation for everyone, from nursing and maintenance staff to the guards on the gate.

Netley's grand village railway station was built in 1866 and used by the ambulance trains coming from the docks. Wounded servicemen would cover the last half mile from the station by road. Eventually the hospital was given its own railway system, continuing on from the village station to its own simple stop.

The first patient was admitted in March 1863. Two years later a cast-iron pier was erected which reached out some 560 feet into deep water. This allowed the worst-injured patients to be transferred directly from ship to hospital. At times of war, when the hospital's beds and wards were fully occupied, hospital ships would have remained on Southampton Water, treating the patients there.

Once up and running, the hospital was used extensively as the British Empire expanded. For example, by the end of the Boer War in 1902 Britain had employed 450,000 troops in an attempt to crush 50,000 Boers. The hospital was used extensively in both world wars and, for a period in the Second World War, it was given over to the Americans. A rumour circulated at the time that the Americans, finding that walking the long corridors was rather time-consuming (each wing was 554 feet long), used their jeeps indoors to increase efficiency.

By 1956, because of their proximity to the docks, the grounds were put to use during the Suez crisis. On 26 July 1956 President Nasser of Egypt had nationalised the Suez Canal Company,

---

* J.R. Fairman, *Netley Hospital and Its Railways* (Southampton: Kingfisher Railway Productions, 1984), p. 11.

whose shares were owned by the British government and French investors. On 31 October, after months of negotiations, British and French airplanes attacked Egyptian bases and on 5 November airborne troops landed at Port Said. I was quietly alarmed by these developments because Ray was still an RAF reservist, and we knew the seriousness of the situation from the amount of military activity in the village. Convoys were rolling through the village on a daily basis.

The grounds of the hospital had been crammed with every-thing that might be needed for all-out war. One local 15-year-old boy chose his moment carefully and managed to get through the perimeter fence of the hospital. He found the number of vehi-cles and amount of equipment, lined up and ready to go, diffi-cult to describe. He could only say that it was an unbelievable sight and he had never seen anything like it, not even in a film.

The Anglo-French invasion aroused criticism among people from both countries. It was denounced by the UN, America, Canada, members of the Commonwealth and many other coun-tries. This showed that both Britain and France could no longer act in such a gung-ho manner as they had in the days of Empire. America threatened to pull the plug on its financial aid. This was interpreted as a warning that the 'special relationship' had its limitations. The whole business had a damaging effect on this country's economy and the stability of the government. Prime Minister Anthony Eden had to resign through ill health, though he always claimed that his actions had been justified.

By this time the hospital itself was coming to the end of its usefulness and was being slowly wound down. The pier was demolished in 1955. Part of the main building was used for Hungarian refugees during the crisis of 1956. After that it lay unused for about five years and then, in 1963, there was a fire, thought to have been started by vandals, which badly damaged the building. In 1966 the bulldozers and cranes moved in. Ties with the army were finally severed in 1978.

The chapel is still there, as is the cemetery, where the remains of several hundred men from many nations lie at rest. There are other buildings which have been saved, along with the officers' mess, itself a most beautiful building, which has now been converted into luxury apartments.

The hospital had been built at the height of the British Empire and was already being dismantled when the Suez crisis removed all doubt that the days of Empire were over.

THE OLYMPICS

When it came to designing a circle for Olympians since 1948 I realised I had set myself a difficult task. I persevered, considering that while I had made some good choices for the circle it would be easy enough to make amends to those I had left out by mentioning them here. Simple, I thought, until I started writing. It had not occurred to me that, in over 50 years, the world has given us hundreds of memorable athletes, including many British ones. In this chapter, apart from the 1948 London Olympics which I must mention, I will refer only to the games involving the competitors whose initials appear in the circle, and I sincerely apologise to all the others.

In austerity-struck Britain the 1948 Olympic Games in London seemed to give the country the lift that it deserved after coming through the war and the winter of 1947. It seemed to signify new beginnings. At Wembley Stadium on a warm sunny day in July, in the presence of the King, the Queen and Queen Mary and a crowd of 85,000 spectators, the games were declared open. Throughout the world millions of people listened in via the radio. We kept up with events through cinema newsreels, newspaper articles and pictures and the radio. Names that I still recall are Emil Zatopek and Fanny Blankers-Koen who became known as the Flying Dutchwoman. The Czech runner Zatopek won gold for the 10,000 metres and silver for the 5,000 metres and we were very taken by the way his supporters in the crowd chanted in unison: 'Zatopek, Zatopek'. Blankers-Koen won gold for the 200 metres, 100 metres, 80 metres hurdles and 4 x 100 metres relay but, with a total of 38 gold medals, it was America's games. We in Britain didn't expect to do well but we did manage to get three gold medals, which could have been worse; and indeed things did get worse for us in the 1952 Olympics.

In the 1952 Helsinki games the chanting of 'Zatopek' became more intense, which was just as well because it kept our minds occupied. Emil Zatopek won three gold medals in the 5,000 metres, 10,000 metres and the marathon. Our only gold medal was won by a horse, Foxhunter, ridden by Harry Llewellyn in an equestrian event. Apart from this we also won two silver and eight bronze medals compared to twenty silver and bronze medals in 1948. It hardly seemed worthwhile switching the radio on for the closing ceremony.

By the 1960 Rome Olympic Games I was married and we had television so were able to see for ourselves the magnificent but unbelievable physiques of Tamara Press and her sister Irina. Tamara represented the USSR in the shot put and discus events and Irina was a track athlete. Between them they won everything except the distance running events. David Coleman, while commentating for BBC television on one of Tamara's events, exclaimed in disbelief: 'My word, she's a big girl!' He was not exaggerating. Tamara and Irina were both big girls but Tamara was the bigger. In the 1960 Rome games Tamara won a gold medal for the shot put and silver for the discus while Irina won gold for the 80 metres hurdles. The games belonged to the USSR with 43 gold medals in total.

In 1964 the Tokyo Olympics were dominated by America with their 36 gold medals. But by this time the determination of gender had become a problem. When Tamara Press won gold in both of her events and Irina won gold for the women's pentathlon, it was rumoured that both of them were being given male hormones to improve their performances. By 1966 gender verification became mandatory and that same year the Press sisters were both withdrawn from competition by the Soviet sports authorities. There were other athletes whose gender was in doubt and it seemed to me that it needed sorting out in order to be fair to the other athletes.

The 1968 Olympics in Mexico were America's games in more ways than one. While they won 45 gold medals, two of their men in particular caught the attention of the world. One of these was Dick Fosbury, who caused a sensation when he won the gold medal for the high jump by flipping over onto his back to clear the bar. This was immediately called the 'Fosbury Flop', and was watched repeatedly on television as experts discussed its pros and cons. The other notable American was the swimmer Mark Spitz who won four gold medals in the swimming events. But Spitz went on to even greater things when, at the Munich Olympics in 1972, he won a record seven gold medals, all in world record times. Unfortunately this Olympiad was marred by the murder of eleven Israeli athletes and coaches by terrorists. The victims were held hostage in their apartments but subsequently killed. Like the rest of the world I was deeply saddened that politics had once again encroached on sport. It was hardly noticed that the USSR had won 50 gold medals during the games.

The Olympic Games of 1980 and 1984 were witness to a wonderful period for British athletics. They were also witness to the continued turmoil of mixing politics with sport. Led by America's example, many countries boycotted the 1980 Moscow Olympics because of the Soviet Union's involvement in Afghanistan. Britain did attend the games, but it was no great surprise that the USSR won 80 gold medals. In those games, for Britain, Steve Ovett won a gold medal for the 800 metres and a bronze for the 1,500 metres, while Steve Cram, although hampered by injury, managed to win silver in the 1,500 metres. Sebastian Coe won gold in the 1,500 metres and silver in the 800 metres. Our champion all-round athlete Daley Thompson won gold for Britain in the decathlon and did so again in the 1984 Los Angeles games. Unsurprisingly, these were boycotted by the USSR and fourteen Eastern bloc countries as a protest against the boycott of their games four years previously. Again, it came as no shock that America won 83 gold medals. Along with Daley Thompson, Tessa Sanderson also won gold in the javelin, and so did Sebastian Coe for the 1,500 metres, as well as silver for the 800 metres. During this period Daley Thompson broke the world record for the decathlon four times. Though it was a splendid time, many of us would have been unaware that history was in the making because we had failed to realise the importance of Steve Redgrave winning his first Olympic gold medal in the coxed fours.

Redgrave won gold again in 1988 at the Seoul Olympics in the coxless pairs with Andy Holmes. He gained his third gold at the Barcelona games in 1992, again for the coxless pairs. It was the beginning of a 'dream team', because his partner in the boat was Matthew Pinsent. They would go on to achieve another gold victory at Atlanta in 1996. I could not watch this race for fear that I would put the mockers on it. It was the same again in the year 2000 at the Sydney Olympiad, when the coxless four race was eagerly anticipated because it would be Redgrave's attempt at an unheard-of fifth gold medal. The other members of the team were Pinsent, Cracknell and Foster, and the four of them pulled it off. Redgrave had got his five gold medals and was hailed as Britain's greatest Olympian. Pinsent had his third, which was no mean achievement, and he went on to win another at the 2004 Athens games in the coxless four event with Cracknell, Williams and Coode. Fantastic.

In 1948, 59 countries took part in the London Olympics. In 2004, 201 countries competed. The games have changed beyond all recognition during this period. Now the spectacular opening and closing ceremonies of the games are as eagerly anticipated as the events, and it seems that Britain does much better these days. We've come a long way since Foxhunter.

THE PARTY YARD

The party yard was a sort of communal area behind a row of houses. Our row consisted of six houses. The party yard was therefore shared by six families: six men, six women and ten children. Living in such close proximity to one another, rows and bothers in families could often be heard by neighbours. They were a regular occurrence, with each couple having their own style.

For example, the Lanes had real slanging matches that could last a full half-hour, flinging clocks and ornaments before they became exhausted and gave up. Mrs Walters would heatedly raise her voice while trying to have a set-to with her husband, but he would not raise his and responded with calm, well-chosen words which must have annoyed her no end. Their arguments were always such a let-down.

The Marshalls often rowed but we were never aware of it until the wife became tearful and started singing sad songs, which indicated that something was amiss. There is nothing much to say about the Hodgetts because I never heard the man utter a word, so there was simply never any chance of overhearing an argument between them.

Mom and Dad employed their own method. They would argue and bicker for ten minutes or so and then, when things started getting overheated and their voices became raised, they would shut up like clams and not speak again for two or three weeks. It was very uncomfortable during these silent periods. None of us could laugh or be jolly as Mother would snap: 'What have you three got to be happy about?' We would also get dragged in as go-betweens with demands such as: 'Ask your dad if he wants a cup of tea.' But the rejoinder would often come before we had time to open our mouths: 'Tell your mother no!'

If we had visitors, such as relatives, during one of these hostile periods they would behave in their normal fashion towards each other. They would laugh and chat away and the visitors would be unaware that anything was wrong. As soon as they had gone, though, we would be back to the wall of silence. Eventually, after an inordinate amount of time exchanging pleasantries, we would become a happy family again.

It was always such a relief when hostilities were brought to an end. One Sunday morning, when Ted was about sixteen and had been a working man for a couple of years, we were all seated around the table having breakfast. Mom and Dad hadn't been speaking for about ten days and the air could have been cut into blocks and stacked in the yard outside. Ted, shaking the sauce bottle vigorously and addressing them both very sharply, said: 'How much longer have we got to put up with this state of affairs? You're like a couple of kids!' I held my breath waiting for an angry response, but it never came. And we never again had to suffer these periods of silence.

It wasn't only married couples who quarrelled. The women could be relied on to have regular altercations, usually when the children were on school holidays. The children would start falling out, one would slap another and, mothers being mothers, they would fly to their offspring's defence. After a bit of a rumpus the mothers would grab their children and drag them home. As a final act of defiance both doors would be slammed. Minutes later the children would once more be playing happily together. Serenity would be restored and the women would have forgotten all about it. Most women, anyway. With our mother it was a different matter.

Mother was a seasoned campaigner. My favourite word for describing her has always been 'belligerent'. She loved an argument and would start a barney with anyone. Every couple of weeks she would have a go at one of the neighbours, one of the local shopkeepers, a bus conductor, a school teacher – anyone at all who crossed her path at the wrong moment. I remember one afternoon when I stood, cringing with embarrassment, as she took on all the staff, from the manager down, at a branch of Woolworths. She had bought a new roasting tin from them, but when she used it the following Sunday a small hole had appeared in it and she had lost some of her lard ration. She was going to sue them and issued all manner of threats, but it got her nowhere.

After a couple of rounds with a neighbour she would always give them the silent treatment. We would also be forbidden to speak to them. These episodes would always end in the same way.

After a respectable length of time, on passing these unfortunate people in the street she would, without warning, say something like: 'Good morning. It's such a lovely morning I'm just going to the butcher's and then I'm going to clean my windows.' The neighbour would be so taken aback by this sudden outburst of pleasantries that they would respond in kind. And that would be that. Often we would get back from school and be told: 'If you see Mrs S in the street you can speak to her as we are friends again, but if you see Mrs T don't you get speaking to her because we've fallen out.'

However life in a party yard wasn't all rows and bothers. There could be unbelievable kindness. If some of the women were at loggerheads it would only take bad news or an illness in one family for all the others to close around the woman who had troubles. If any of the women fell ill, one neighbour would take in her washing, another would care for and feed her children, while a third would do her shopping and run errands. When it was called for, there was also a bond between all of the children. It would only take one child confiding in another to bring the problems of a family into the open. Of the six families occupying houses in our yard, two had no children, two had one child each, ours had three and there were five in the last.

One summer's afternoon while we were at school the women were feeling low. The war had been over for a few years and things were getting back to normal, but very slowly. Food and some items of clothing were becoming more available but there was no possibility of getting new furniture. On this particular afternoon all six of the women were chatting in the yard. For some unknown and unfathomable reason, two of them decided to swap sofas. It would make a change and cost nothing. Then in next to no time all six of them had decided to make similar exchanges. I don't know how it happened but we ended up with

Mrs Lane's horrible, old, itchy horsehair sofa. When we got in from school Mother pretended to be thrilled, but you could see she wasn't.

In the evening, when Dad came in he took one look at it and said: 'Where's that thing come from?' Mother explained.

Dad replied: 'Well, you can just go and tell Mrs Lane that we want our old sofa back.'

'It's not that easy,' said Mother. 'Although we've got Mrs Lane's sofa, Mrs Marshall has ours and Mrs Coombes has got Mrs Walters'.'

'Well, I don't know how you are going to work it out, but work it out you will have to,' Dad declared, in a tone that indicated that that was his last word on the matter.

When it came to it, none of the men was pleased with the day's developments, especially Mr Lane. For, although he must have been pleased to see the back of their horsehair monstrosity, they had ended up with Mrs Hodgetts' squab,* and there was nothing on earth more uncomfortable than that. Later that evening the women could be seen working in pairs, quietly muttering instructions as they returned all the sofas to their rightful places. The men refused to have anything to do with it.

As we lived in the end house Dad, at some point, fenced off our section of the yard so that we could have some privacy. This gave Mother something of an advantage because she had found a convenient knothole in the fence that was at just the right height for spying on the neighbours. Dad gave her the name 'Keyhole Kate'. She only had to hear any of the neighbours chatting and she would be at the fence, her eye focused on them, blissfully happy, just wishing that she could read lips.

---

*A squab is, among other things, a sort of wooden sofa with a very straight back and no seat cushions.

QUEUES

These days, as I stand in the queue at the supermarket checkout, I think of the past and smile. Because Mother didn't like standing in queues, I spent many hours in my early days doing it for her. If I was at home she would always send me instead of going herself. She gave me the job of chief dogsbody and queue-stander when I was just seven years old. You can clearly see me at the top of this circle waiting my turn. From an early age I learned to accept it as part of life. I learned to stand quietly and listen. I learned that if I had a far-away look on my face, the women around me would think I was paying no attention and would continue with their gossiping. If they thought I was listening in they would change the subject. I could learn much from looking rather gormless.

There were queues for everything. We queued for meat at the butcher's on Saturdays simply because it was the only day of the week, for most households, when money was available. On Mondays we used up the leftovers from the weekend. Tuesdays, Wednesdays and Thursdays it was a bit of 'scrag end' or anything else that was going cheap. Fridays it was fish.

The Saturday queues at the grocers were caused by everyone getting in their week's rations. You had to be registered at a shop of your choice to get them. While standing in one of these queues some women would push in front of me but they didn't always get away with it, for in doing so they were also increasing the waiting time for those women behind me, who wouldn't stand for that. When it was my turn to be served I would put the shopping list on the counter and, without speaking a word, the assistant would gather the items in front of me; I would then pay up. In packing the bags I always had to be so careful with the eggs. Sometimes there would only be one egg per ration book while occasionally there would be none at all. On rare occasions there might be three which would be a total for me of fifteen, and egg boxes hadn't yet been invented. Trying to get fifteen eggs home intact, in a brown paper bag, was a physical impossibility.

However, the end of the war didn't mean the end of rationing or queuing. I stood in queues for Mother right up until I started work, although by this time rationing had come to an end for many items. At the start of my last year at school in September 1951 a new shop opened on the very edge of town They sold sausages, bacon and processed meats such as boiled ham and roast pork. All of these items were prepared on their own premises. It had become very popular before Mother heard of it. She had also heard that queues started forming at eight o'clock on a Saturday morning, and that it was really to your advantage if you could get there on the dot or earlier.

It was a long walk to the shop and, the following Saturday, I was dispatched with a shopping list and large bag; I managed to get served by nine-thirty. After the long walk back it was well after ten o'clock before I arrived home. The food lived up to our expectations and was delicious; as a result my Saturday mornings were, henceforth, taken care of. Just before I started work I asked Mother what she would do when I could no longer go to this shop for her, and she replied that she would have to go herself. She did, but only for one week. After that, she declared that she did not think their food was as good as it had been and had decided to go somewhere else. Somewhere that was nearer and didn't have such long queues.

– CIRCLE 42 –

COPING WITH
THE WEATHER

The houses in which so much of the population lived were like refrigerators in the winter and ovens in the summer. When the heat was overpowering many people would sit out on their front steps in the evening. Dad and the other men did not generally do this, because they considered it a women's thing. Nevertheless Dad would join us when all the other adults had gone indoors. On some nights as dusk descended, and if we did not have to go to school the next day, he would shut the door and we would go walking across the fields. These moonlit walks on hot summer nights were something special.

On hot days when we were not at school we spent much of our time in the fields or on the clover bank. We could safely play all day on this bank, with some bottles of drinking water and an old towel, splashing in and out of the water. On hearing one particular factory's hooter we would dash home, eat our dinner and then return to the brook.

In the scene depicted in the circle I have given all of us dark skin. This is just to emphasise that we did not worry about using sun cream. We could be out in the sun all day, and if one of us did get a little 'singed' we would either treat it with calamine lotion or dab it with Mother's blue bag. Small children had to wear some sort of hat or knotted handkerchief. We had wonderful long summers but then, as now, a hot spell would always be followed by a thunderstorm.

Mother had always been terrified of thunderstorms, and at the first sign that one was brewing we always had to go through the same ritual to keep her calm. First, we had to turn all the mirrors to the wall and hide all the cutlery, so that nothing could reflect the lightning. Then we had to remove any obstacles that were in front of the fireplaces and prop open all the doors, so that if a thunderbolt came down the chimney it would just roll out of the house. Apparently, if a thunderbolt came down the chimney into a closed room it was supposed to ricochet off the walls and furniture, doing untold damage. Finally, the electricity would be turned off at the mains and anything shiny on our clothes would have to be hidden.

When everything had been prepared Mother would sit on the bottom of the stairs with a heavy coat over her head, whimpering. With no radio and not enough light to read by, the rest of us would sit around and wait for the storm. Dad was very strict during this time and no one was allowed to make fun of Mother in her predicament. It was sad, because she got through the air raids without batting an eyelid.

We were having a terrible storm when I came out of school with a friend one afternoon and started the long walk home. It was very dark, and the heavens had opened. The raindrops hit us with some force and then bounced away. The lightning flashed and the thunder clapped. We thought it was great fun. We were halfway home when Mother appeared through the gloom carrying a couple of coats under her own coat. She was terrified and raving about it being the end of the world. We went the rest of the way huddled under her coat, as if she were a mother hen protecting her chicks. It must have taken great courage for her to leave the house. She always swore that the world would end during a thunderstorm. As far as she was concerned this was a well-known fact.

An approaching storm at least gives some advance warning, with a darkening sky and birds reduced to silence. But nothing could have prepared us for the winter of 1947. It had begun earlier in December 1946 but there was a gentle fall of snow at 9 pm on 23 January, and by the next morning we were left in no doubt that winter had arrived with a vengeance. Anyone who lived through it will never forget it. The Midlands was buried under 30-foot snowdrifts. Factories and schools were closed. Coal supplies ran out. Shops ran out of food.

When the temperature fell to 27°F (about −3°C) on 24 January it was colder in Britain than in Iceland, and the temperature stayed below freezing for five weeks. The country was in no condition to handle such a crisis. Just a few days later the temperature dropped to 19°F (−7°C) and Britain had another night of shivering. Seven hundred and fifty council workers, 105 casual workers and 126 prisoners of war kept Birmingham's roads clear as January came to an icy end and February blew in with a fierce blizzard.

On 2 February an estimated 2 million tonnes of snow fell on the Midlands and we found ourselves at the centre of a blizzard that stretched from Devon to Lincolnshire. Many children were absent from school because their parents had neither the money nor the coupons for suitable clothing or shoes. It was the same all over the country.

The RAF dropped food to isolated villages. The government announced that all domestic electricity supplies would be cut off for two hours every morning and again in the afternoon. They also announced that supplies to industry would be cut off altogether. Huge queues formed at coal yards. Ted and I used to push our home-made wheelbarrow to the coal supplier in the blacksmith's yard. It was lovely to watch the horses being shod as we waited in the queue, but even lovelier to feel the heat from the fire. We would be allowed a quarter of a hundredweight (28 pounds) of either coal or coke, which if used with great care would last a few days, and it was better than nothing.

Mom and Dad were as resourceful as ever at keeping the home fires burning; they had had enough practice during the war. Nothing was put on the fire until its potential for combustion had been investigated. An old shoe would be filled with a mixture of tea leaves and coal dust. Sugar bags would be tightly packed with dry vegetable peelings and other household waste. If it would burn, it was used.

We also went with many others to the old slag heaps in the fields and dug for coal, with some success – some had more than others. There was no point in going if you didn't have a sieve (which we called a 'riddle'). Many travelled quite a distance to try their luck, which caused some resentment among those who felt that they were not getting their share. One morning, while we were at school, a series of very unpleasant fist-fights broke out among the adults at the slag heaps. Mom told Dad this while he was having his tea that evening. We were then barred from going again, coal or no coal.

There was a glimmer of hope on 23 February when we saw the sun for the first time in 33 days, but the temperature refused to rise. It did not get above freezing for 36 days in a row. March brought the worst blizzards yet, and all this time food supplies were getting lower and lower. Farmers had been frozen off their land for six weeks and vegetables were becoming almost non-existent. Only 40 per cent of milk supplies were getting through. When the snow finally began to thaw, the country was stricken with the worst flooding for a century. We were lucky, as there were no great rivers in our part of the country. In a final flourish, winter departed with hurricane force winds on 17 March. The economic impact on the whole country was devastating.

The following are some of my memories from that winter:

- Dad wrapping his legs in brown paper and string, over his trousers, to keep warm, before putting on his oilskins and walking to work along the canal tow path because it was quicker and easier than cycling along the roads

- The teacher lending me her Wellingtons every lunchtime before I set off for home and dinner

- Wearing coats and hats in the classroom, and occasionally jumping up and down and waving our arms about to keep warm

- Mother weeping as she lifted the lid of a saucepan containing potatoes only to find that they had completely disappeared, leaving her with a watery mush. Many vegetables perished in the ground, which was frozen solid

- Going to bed at night dressed for a trip to the North Pole, and snuggling up with a hot house brick wrapped in a towel

- Dad keeping a spade in the house because, on several mornings, he had to dig us out of snow drifts before he could go to work

- Dad waking us up one morning and telling us to wrap ourselves up very warm from head to toe. We waited in the kitchen near the back door. When Dad opened it we were faced with a wall of snow. We were completely snowed in. Then we howled with laughter as Dad just threw himself at it

- Huddling round the fire in the evenings and watching the flames

- Jim being poorly and Mother setting a fire in the bedroom fireplace for him

- Long walks to school and back again which we had to do twice a day. No dinners at our school in those days

- The teacher trying to thaw out our frozen free school milk on the tepid pipes that went around the classroom.

On top of all this, food was still rationed and the country's transport links were unable to deliver the coal which was stuck at depots or in railway sidings. What had made this horrendous winter of 1947 worse was the poor state that the country was already in following the Second World War. Britain was close to bankruptcy and we were, though we did not know it at the time, close to starvation. Just how close was revealed by Andrew Marr in a BBC television programme a few years ago. In the government archives he found plans that had been drawn up during that winter of 1947 to deal with mass starvation.

That winter was followed by a very hot summer with a prolonged drought. Even with severe thunderstorms the rainfall was insignificant until late autumn and, spectacular to the end, Christmas night in the south of England saw a dramatic thunderstorm with larger than average hailstones. It was a year of great extremes but will be forever remembered for its winter. However, while it is true that the winter of 1947 had the most snow, the winter of 1962–63 was the coldest.

That winter began in November 1962 with the worst blizzards on record. Early in December a dense blanket of fog covered eighteen counties. This hung about long enough to develop into the worst and most lethal smog since the 'Great Smog' of 1952. By Christmas, however, the real winter had begun. Early on Boxing Day the temperature in many parts of the country was recorded as –9°C. That same day in Birmingham it dropped to –11°C. It was not until 6 March 1963 that the temperature finally rose, in London, to 17°C, its highest since 25 October 1962. For everyone involved in these severe winters, the difference between the two was fifteen years of progress. 1947 was harder because of the state Britain was in and the fact that the National Health Service was not yet in place. By 1963 the country and its people were better able to cope.

We no longer have such prolonged, severe winters, and we tend to blame global warming for this, as well as for the unpredictable weather patterns which have resulted in unprecedented flooding in some parts of the UK. Whatever the cause, most people of my generation prefer the old weather because it was predictable. We knew where we stood with March winds and April showers, and could be secure in the knowledge that a severe winter would have rid us of many of our germs and diseases.

WASHING DAY

I often think of Mom when I am preparing a load of washing, because if there is any one thing that has improved the lot of women it must be the automatic washing machine. When Mom was bringing us up, she did the washing on one particular day of the week. There was a reason for this. Most houses in working-class areas shared a wash house with a neighbour or two, so each woman would have to stick to the day she had chosen. And it was an all-day job.

Mom always did the washing on a Monday. The rest of us had nothing to do with this chore, but we all hated washing day because it disrupted the whole house. It would be stripped of anything that looked as if it needed a rinse. Anything that wasn't washed that day would have to wait for another week and, by then, would be even more difficult to get clean. By the time we went off to school our mother was already in the wash house at the top of the yard, up to her elbows in suds and surrounded by all that was necessary to achieve a perfect finish for the clothes and household linen.

There was a bucket of small pieces of coal in the wash house to keep the fire going under the boiler, an enormous mangle and a 'maiding tub' with 'maid'. In other parts of the country these last two were known as a 'dolly tub' and a 'dolly stick'. The clothes were put in soapy water in the tub, after which the maid was used to pummel the dirt out of them. As well as Fairy or Sunlight household soap, a scrubbing brush and a scrubbing board, Mom would also need Robin starch and a Reckitts' blue bag to give the whites a dazzling glow. Along with buckets, bowls and a ladle for transferring hot water from the boiler to the sink, I must not forget the boiler stick which was used to prod the clothes in the boiler occasionally, after which it would be used to lift them out of the boiling water and into cold water for rinsing. There was a choice of three washing powders at that time: Persil, Rinso and Oxydol. Mother was a loyal Persil user; although when I was sent to buy washing powder long after the end of the war, I was always instructed just to buy anything with thruppence (3d) off.

Sometimes, when I was on holiday from school, Mother would let me have a go at turning the handle of the mangle. Now and then I would be allowed to hang out the washing, but she was so particular about how it should be hung she wasn't always happy to let me do it. Monday was the only day when we didn't have a cooked meal, and on a wet Monday life was a misery as she had to dry all of the washing around the fire.

This all had to be done on Monday because Tuesday was ironing day. I remember winter Tuesdays of my childhood with pleasure because the kitchen was so warm and smelled nice. Ironing,
like washing, was a long job because the irons had to be heated
by the fire. Her washing and ironing was of such a high standard
that two of the shop owners in the lane would ask her to do
theirs. This consisted mainly of household linen and did not
include personal items.

Mother had always used her three 'sad irons' (flat irons),
which were heated at the fire in winter and on the gas ring in
summer. She was quite happy to continue using them, but eventually, when 'keeping up with the Joneses' became a way of life,
Dad bought her an electric iron. What disruption it caused!
First, although we had electric lights we did not have power
points. This was very common and we were not alone. So from
Woolworths, Dad bought a connection that went into the light
socket on the ceiling and allowed the light to continue working
while also enabling us to use two other appliances from a single
power source. Mother made it her business to find out the dangers of electric irons. She learned that for safety reasons, it was
advisable to wear rubber-soled shoes and stand on a wooden
floor while using them. Our kitchen had a stone floor, so Dad
had to make her a low wooden platform. She stood on this platform for the next ten years to do the ironing while wearing
Wellington boots.

It would have been in the fifties when Dad also bought her a
boiler with a hand-turned agitator, complete with a small mangle. This was kept in the kitchen which we were no longer using
as a living room. Washing day and ironing day, as we knew them,
disappeared forever. Freed from the Monday wash house
regime, Mother could do a bit of washing whenever she felt like
it – and she felt like it almost every day. There were times when

I thought she looked her happiest in the wash house with her sleeves rolled up, wearing two aprons and a long, heavy hessian one to keep her front dry. She always looked as if she meant business. Washing and ironing were her favourite chores.

There was a shop in the lane where people took anything which needed dry cleaning. Because of the cost, this service was not widely used. It was just a sideline for the shop owner, who was acting merely as an agent for a specialist dry cleaning firm. Most areas also had a pawn shop – these did a flourishing trade, accepting watches, jewellery and clothing as pledges. Ours was not the sort of area where people had much in the way of jewellery, so our nearest pawn shop dealt mainly in clothing, footwear and bed linen. Pawning things was quite a sneaky business, as no one liked to admit that they had to borrow money in this way. The reason why I have wandered away from the subject of dry cleaning will now become clear. Every Monday at teatime I went with a girl who was officially taking her dad's best suit to 'the cleaners'. Every Saturday morning it would be redeemed. We both knew what 'taking the suit to the cleaners' really meant, but neither she nor I ever mentioned it. One Monday after we had completed the transaction I went home to have my tea and Mom asked me how much my friend's mother had raised on the suit. I don't remember the exact figures involved, but let's say she was allowed something like 7s 6d on the suit and would have to pay 9s 3d to redeem it. Mother reacted with one of her favourite phrases: 'That's daylight robbery!'

However, the following Monday when I got back from school, she put a pair of Dad's best boots into a bag and said: 'Here, go and take these to the pawn shop and ask him if he will let me have 5s on them.' Off I toddled, calling for my friend on the way. We chatted away as we sauntered up the lane, she taking her dad's suit and me taking my dad's boots to 'the cleaners'.

After this first experience Mother used the pawnbroker's services again, though not very often. Just now and then, when she was in dire straits. But never again did I take anything that belonged to Dad, for that first week she died a thousand deaths worrying that he would find out what she had done. The following Saturday she heaved a big sigh of relief when she put the boots back in the bottom of the wardrobe.

Now Dad was no ogre, but he had a certain amount of working-class dignity. If you have never encountered working-class dignity for yourself you will have no idea how powerful it is. Mother understood this. He would have seen it as damaging to his credibility if it had become known that his wife was raising money at the pawn shop. Every time she planned to do something that she suspected Dad would not like, we were always sworn to secrecy. He did not mind her taking in other people's washing. He saw this as an example of enterprise, using her skills to earn honest money.

BONFIRES

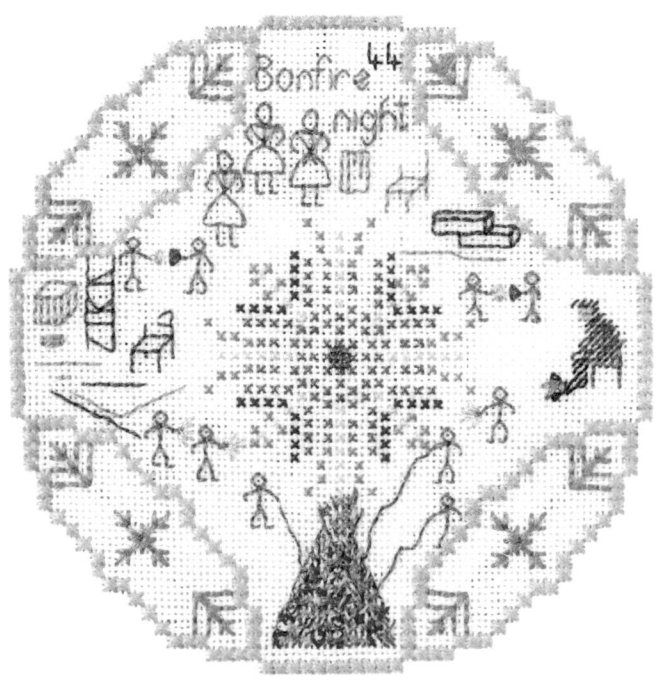

We had a bonfire to celebrate Victory in Europe (VE) Day and another to celebrate Victory over Japan (VJ) Day. After that we began having an annual bonfire on Guy Fawkes' Night. A couple of weeks before the event we began accumulating anything that would burn. There was never any shortage of rubbish for the bonfire but, in those early years, we could not afford to buy fireworks and only managed to get Bengal matches, sparklers or bangers. I never liked like bangers and later much preferred Catherine wheels or glitter showers, but these were very unreliable and were often referred to as 'damp squibs'.

We would start laying the fire on a piece of waste ground a few days before the event, and every evening before dark we would dash to our lovingly built mound of rubbish and pay homage by adding to it. We would make a guy well in advance, but never had much luck with begging. After accosting the same person for about the fourth time we would be politely told to 'goon bugger off'. The only child I knew to have any luck was our Jim. Still very young, he had been terribly ill with measles and peritonitis (see Circle 67) and all the workers who tramped past our door every day were aware of this. They had shown their concern by knocking on the door to enquire how he was. As Bonfire Night approached, Ted made a guy and Jim sat out on the step with a cap in his hand and the effigy sitting on a chair beside him. He did get a few coppers but mostly he was advised to try again on Friday. He did, and on that night hardly anyone passed him by.

Our bonfires were lit at around six o'clock after we had all had our tea. Once we had a good blaze going we would be joined by the mothers. We often had an old sofa, chair or mattress to burn and these would be among the first things to go on the fire, as we had a good use for the springs. While they were still hot we would uncoil them and stick a potato on one end. Holding the other end very firmly, we would fling the spud into the fire. Sometimes it would be lost, and there would be some cursing as the owner ferreted about in the blaze trying to retrieve it. On being asked what he or she was doing, the stock reply was: 'I've lost me tater!'

One after another of these supposed delicacies would be pulled from the fire and we would devour them as if we hadn't eaten for weeks. They would be burned black on the outside and raw inside and were awful to eat, but you wouldn't admit it to anyone. Adults would say: 'You can't eat that. It's raw.' But we would shake our heads and say: 'It's lovely.' We would then wait until the adults were engrossed in something else and furtively chuck them back in the fire.

The war had been over for some time when the local council, in its wisdom, decided at last to concrete and tarmac our street. What luxury. We even had pavements, but they drew the line at street lights. After this development it was decided that we no longer needed to have our bonfires on the waste ground. As soon as the last factory had shut for the night we dragged the collected bonfire material into the street and piled it up in the middle of the road outside the newly painted factory gates. After putting a match to the pile, the evening proceeded in much the same way as earlier Bonfire Nights had, but grander somehow. Very early the next morning the older boys came along to get rid of the ashes before the factories opened up, only to find that the fire had burned away the tarmac on the road and the recently-painted factory gates had blistered to the extent that the writing on them was now illegible. When the owner arrived to start the day's work he stood and surveyed the gates with a look of fury on his face while a couple of the lads stood waiting for the backlash. However, it didn't come and we heard no more about it.

When our own children were old enough for bonfires, Ray and I made quite a big thing of Bonfire Night in our back garden. Every year quite a number of friends and relatives would come along. Ray would organise the fire and be in charge of it all evening while I laid on suitable food. Any potatoes required were cooked in the oven. As time went by, these small family bonfires were increasingly discouraged, because each year would bring another series of tragedies involving children who had received horrible burns, some of which were life-threatening. Eventually family bonfires were replaced by large bonfires organised in parks which were, and still are, very successful and well-attended. The children still have the fun of the night and parents do not have the worry, but many people still enjoy garden bonfires. However – I ask myself – is it still possible to hear the heart-rending cry 'I've lost me tater'?

– CIRCLE 45 –

EDUCATION

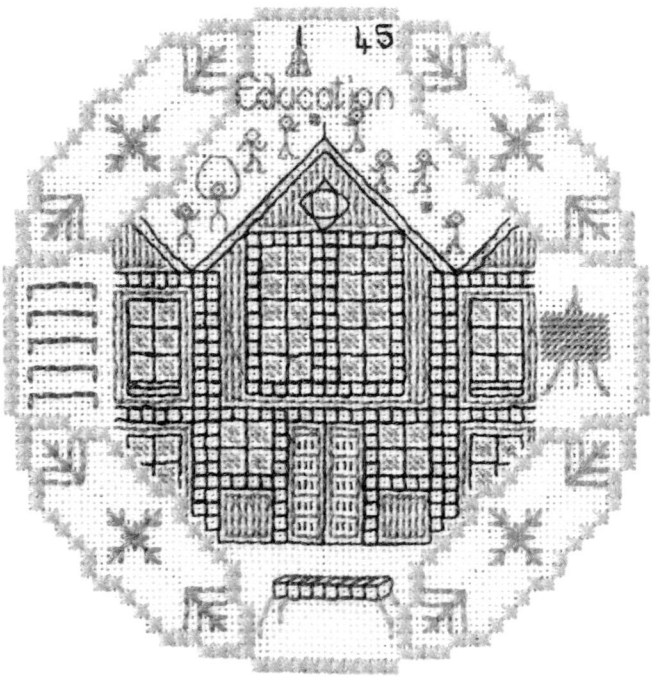

It was only when I had finished this tapestry that I became aware of how very important education is to me. It is the only subject out of 73 to take up both a circle and three corners of the tapestry.

I began my education at the age of four. I can clearly remember my first morning at school, which saw me standing by the teacher's desk, grizzling. I perked up when the teacher, handing out small bottles of milk, told me to sit next to the twins and drink mine. The twins were very nice and the rest of the morning was better. I was not amused when I found out that I would have to go back in the afternoon, but afternoons turned out to be better than mornings. On our return there were rows of small green beds laid out, and we all had to lie down and have a half-hour nap. Lovely.

At the age of seven I began a four-year stint at the junior school. Within a month I had had a life-changing experience. I had been in my first class for only a couple of weeks when it was decided that I was too advanced for that one, so I was moved up to the next class.

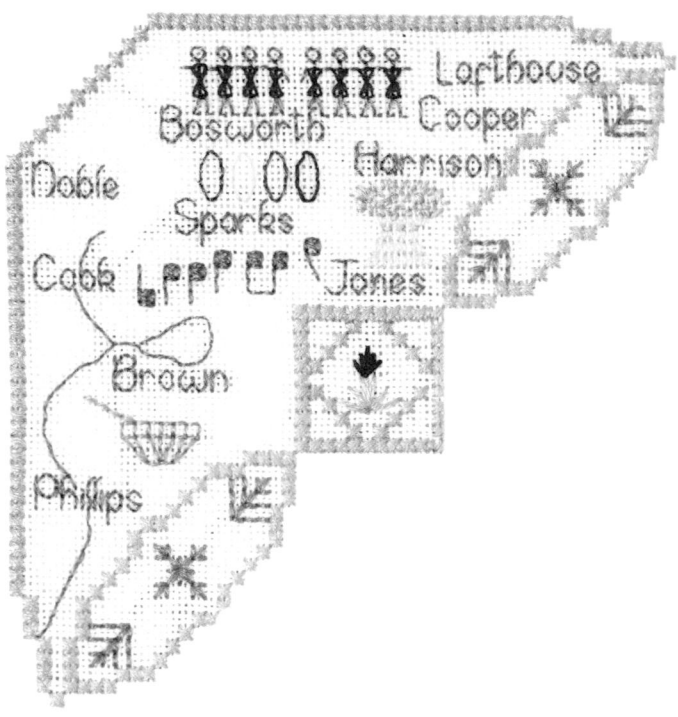

One afternoon, my teacher Miss Cook gave each girl a piece of calico measuring roughly five inches by three inches, together with a needle and a length of pink thread. Now, up to that point I had never seen pink thread, and it had a tremendous impact on me. And so my love of needlework began at the age of seven.

That afternoon I was taught how to do an embroidery stitch. In the top left-hand corner of the tapestry you will find embroidered a piece of pink thread, and I consider that this is probably the most important item in the whole work. If I had not been so besotted with that pink thread, this tapestry might never have been made. I did well at the junior school for one very good reason: every evening, Ted taught me everything he had been taught that day at the senior school.

After his merit exams Ted had been awarded a place at the secondary technical school (secondary tech), although it didn't do him much good. He had been there for only ten months when Mother, thinking that Ted would leave school at fourteen whichever school he went to, learned that if he stayed at the secondary tech and did well, God knew when he would leave. She invaded the local education offices and arranged to have him transferred to the secondary modern. Ted eventually started work in a foundry at the age of fourteen. It was a thousand pities. I know he would have made a very good teacher. But that's the way it was then.

The 1944 Education Act had been the brainchild of 'Rab' Butler, a respected politician, and was his most significant contribution to British politics. The evacuation of children from urban centres during the war had made it obvious that there was too much variation in the quality of teaching throughout the country. For many years excessive attention had been given to grammar schools which provided superior teaching facilities in manageable class sizes. The average number of pupils in a grammar school class was 25, whilst in elementary schools the average was greater than 40 and was sometimes as high as 50.

Ray went to a Church of England school which never had more than 30 to 32 in a class. I was not so fortunate. When we arrived in our classroom one Monday morning, we saw that the desks had been changed around. After calling the register the teacher became aware that she now had to teach 52 of us. She told us that she was not prepared to do this, not because of the workload but because it would be unfair to us. She asked us to support her for the next half-hour by quietly reading while she tried to sort things out. She left the room and returned ten minutes later with the headmistress who took stock of the situation. A short time later they were joined by a man who, after a short discussion, left with the headmistress. The teacher thanked us for our consideration and then we settled to our work. The following day our numbers had been reduced to 46.

The Butler Act of 1944 changed the structure of secondary education for all. It introduced a three-tier system: grammar school, secondary technical and secondary modern. The school leaving age would be increased to fifteen in 1947 and further increased to sixteen at some time in the future. With regard to Ted, it was this last policy that would have tipped Mother into taking action. However, as it turned out the school leaving age was not increased to sixteen until 1973.

At the age of eleven I sat the exams which would decide my future education. The results of these exams would determine what form of secondary education I would get, but we would not have the results until the middle of the long summer break. In the meantime we had the last class tests to sit before leaving the junior school for good. These were spread over a couple of weeks and consisted of a test on each of the subjects that we had been taught in the last year, probably eight in all. After each test we did not have to wait long for the results. After the outcome of the fifth test had been given we worked out, in the playground, that I was in the lead by one point. I was pleased but had never had a competitive streak, so it didn't matter that much to me.

In the evening I told Mom and Dad and their reaction was

along the lines of: 'Hmmm.' Ted thought differently, pointing out that whoever won this series of tests would be top of the school. He assured me that if I put my mind to it the coveted title could be mine. We sat at the table and worked out what was to be done. The girl one point below me was good and not to be sniffed at. The next test was on religion; I was quite good at that subject, and after a brief refresher course I got through that test with full marks. So did the other girl. The next, geography, was not one of my better subjects and two whole evenings were spent working on it. Again I scored full marks, but so did the other girl. The last subject was writing. My writing had always been quite decent and I knew the only way I would fail was if I dropped a blot on the page. I spent an evening practising dipping a pen into the ink bottle and soaking up the excess on a bit of rag. It worked. I didn't drop a blot on the day and I finished my junior school education at the top of the school. My best friend at school, Sylvia, was very pleased for me. She had come about fifth.

On the last day of school the parents were invited to view their children's work. Most fathers didn't come along to these open days as it would mean losing time from work. In my case Mother had never been to see my work, apparently for the simple reason that she couldn't be bothered. That year, because of my exalted position in the class, I begged her to come and she promised she would after she had taken Jim to school. I sat at my desk all afternoon waiting for her but she never appeared. My two aunts looked in and expressed opinions on what I'd been doing, but it was Mother that I had so badly wanted to see. When I got home she told me why she hadn't been able to come. It was nice to know where I stood (see Circle 61 for the full story).

During the summer the exam results came through and I had got a place at the secondary tech. I was very excited. Only one thing marred my joy, and that was the fact that my friend Sylvia hadn't made it. She was very disappointed. As the days went by Mother started thinking up all sorts of reasons why I would not be taking up my place. My uncle Dick came over one Saturday lunchtime to tell her that by doing this she was blighting my life, but she pointed out that she couldn't afford the uniform and that was the end of the matter; her mind was made up. When I pointed out that I was quite looking forward to going she reminded me that, if I went to the secondary modern, I would still be with Sylvia and I felt better after that.

Ironically my place at the secondary tech was given to Sylvia. After the new school year started, I never saw her again. To make matters worse, the secondary modern decided that the time had come when all girls would, henceforth, wear a uniform. So after all that, Mother still had to buy me a uniform while I became another brick in the wall.

I sailed through the next four years and the only time I felt challenged was in the gymnasium. How I hated anything energetic, especially the vaulting horse. One lesson ended with the small, trim teacher exasperatedly calling me a 'great useless lump of lard'. Well, she went right down in my estimation after that. When you are fifteen, tall and heavily built, you can really do without this sort of comment from people half your size.

Years later, it dawned on me that, having pulled Ted out of the secondary tech after ten months, Mother just couldn't let me go. It wouldn't have been fair. Needless to say, when it came to Jim's turn to sit the exams he saw no point in trying too hard. But the thing about Jim was that he didn't accept his situation as Ted and I had done.

When he left school at the end of July 1959 he had found a job but, as he would not be fifteen until 27 August, he could not start work until after that date. In the meantime he had discovered that there was the opportunity of a day release education at college if the company you worked for was prepared to pay your expenses and your wages for the day. Armed with this knowledge, after a few days at work he approached the management. They made him the offer of day release with wages and expenses for college, but on his part he would also have to go to night school. If at any time he missed an evening class without good reason, the day release would be withdrawn. It was as good as an apprenticeship. I have always admired him for this; Ted and I had accepted our lot too easily. We had assumed that education finished when you walked through the school gates for the last time.

One of the best things I got from my education was a love of English and of words. If only I could speak as well as I think. Words fascinate me. There were quite a few words that were never used in our house. One that springs immediately to mind is 'lunch'. We never ate lunch. We had three meals a day; breakfast, dinner and tea.

I also don't ever remember 'cancer' being referred to by its name. It was almost as if the word itself was a threat. The words used, and always whispered, were 'tumour' or 'growth'. The word 'cancer' struck fear into everyone's hearts and, even with the gigantic leaps in medical science of the last 50 years, that fear is still there. I well remember the first time I saw someone with cancer. I was still a child, and I shall never forget it.

Mother once received a letter from someone proudly announcing that her son's wife was pregnant. We wanted to read the letter but Mother hesitated because, to her, the word 'pregnant' was appalling. She finally allowed us to read it providing that we didn't ask any questions. Later I got out the old dictionary and looked it up, only to be completely confused a few days later when someone on the radio mentioned a 'pregnant pause'. The word we used was 'expecting'. Another time, I got a lecture from Mother for remarking that a woman who lived in the lane was pregnant again. Not only should I not have used this word, it was also a pity that I had nothing better to do than go around noticing such things. There was a time when the word 'sex' was only used as a means of defining whether you were male or female. Since then we have moved on to the word 'gender'. We seemed much slower in those days to become aware of what was going on around us. However our sex education blossomed in later years, thanks to my friend June's dad's *News of the World*.

Every Monday, at play time, we got into the habit of sitting and listening in awe as June informed us of anything she had managed to glean from the previous day's edition. We were all as thick as two short planks. She informed us of a court case where the word 'intimate' kept cropping up. She reckoned that this word had got something to do with some act of gross indecency.

Again from June's dad's *News of the World*, we learned of court cases where the word 'prostitution' kept appearing. Some women were imprisoned for doing it. We could never understand what it was all about. Even the dictionary didn't give a satisfactory explanation; in the end we came to the conclusion that these women were trying to sell something on the black market and, whatever it was, it wasn't very nice. Our actual sex education at school lasted 30 minutes and the talk was mainly about frogs. The most interesting thing about it, for me anyway, was that right at the start of the lesson the teacher put the stem of a white flower into a bottle of blue ink. By the end of the lesson the flower had started to turn blue. I thought that was fascinating, but I still don't know what it was supposed to have to do with sex. I may have to ask a youngster of today's generation to explain it to me. They seem to know more about sex than I ever did.

I didn't regret my lack of education until I got to my late twenties, and I seemed to spend the best part of the next 30 years trying to prove something. However, after that my time for an education did finally come.* After two years at Warwickshire College I was told about an access course that could get me to university. By this time the girl on the wall was an important part of my life and I made a promise that I would do it for her. I didn't find the access course easy but I stuck at it.

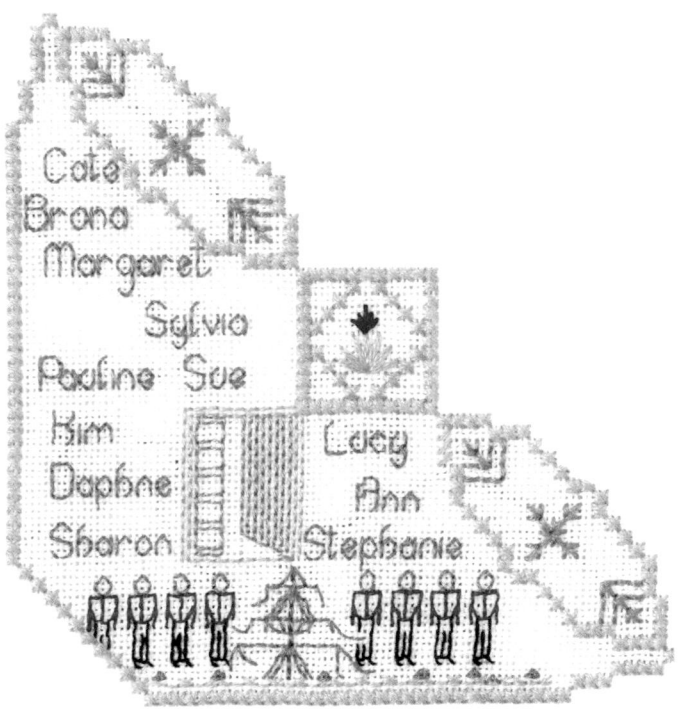

---

* At that time there was a further education advertising campaign featuring Floella Benjamin. She used the words: 'Education is your passport to life. Put your head down and go for it.'

Two years later, in my mid-sixties, I finally began work on her history degree at Warwick University.

These days, I do not regret the lack of opportunity to study when I was younger. If I had done it then I wouldn't be doing it now, although it might have made it easier to convince those who had always doubted that I had a brain. When you have a Midlands accent many people think you haven't got the sense you were born with.

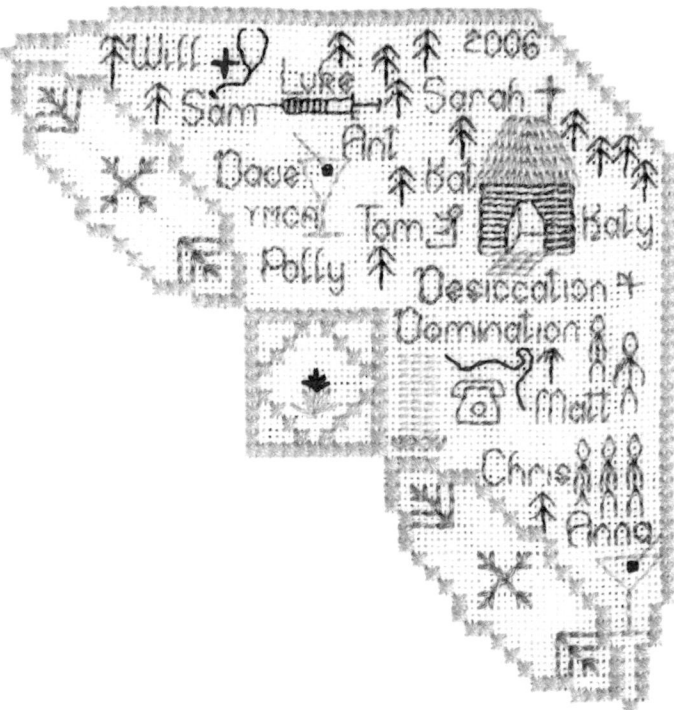

RECORDED MUSIC

I have always loved music, of all kinds. I am passionate about classical music, and I have seen popular stars come and go. I thought Vera Lynn was the best. I thought Johnny Ray was the best. I thought Nat King Cole was the best. There have been hundreds of them and all of them have, at some point in my life, been 'the best'. The list is endless.

It all began in Mother's kitchen. We had an old gramophone and a stock of probably 30 to 40 records, all of them ancient and rather worn. They were mainly sentimental ballads such as

'My Mother's Eyes' and 'I'll Take You Home Again Kathleen'. I will never forget 'The Mountains of Morne' and 'The Rose of Tralee'.

It was very exciting on those winter evenings during the war when Dad casually said 'I think I'll play a few records', but Dad was not a great music lover and after listening to half a dozen records he would give the job over to Ted and go back to his newspaper. However the gramophone had a temperamental spring and, having been warned not to over-wind it for fear that the spring would break, Ted would begin cautiously. On a wind-up gramophone the spring was long enough to play one side of an old ten-inch record, plus a little more in case you wanted to play a twelve-inch. If you over-wound it the spring would snap, with a vibrating 'boing', at the spot where it was attached to the machine and Dad would then have to fix it. Each time he fixed it the spring would be half an inch shorter.

The spring was a strip of very springy steel, half an inch deep, and wound into a coil. The time eventually came when the spring wasn't long enough to play one side of a ten-inch record and, as it got towards the end, the singer would begin to slow down and start moaning, at which point Ted would have to jump up and start winding again. The singer would stop wailing and, apparently regaining his or her composure, would triumphantly finish the song. By the end of the war playing a record was more trouble than it was worth and the gramophone was abandoned in its corner, although it did come back into its own years later when its function was upgraded to that of a TV stand.

During the war the big band sound and band singers were all the rage. I was always in thrall to the big bands and singers from America. I still enjoy listening to Woody Herman, Benny Goodman and Harry James, but my favourite two acts remain Artie Shaw and Glenn Miller. I'm not sure that recorded music's importance as a morale-booster and source of comfort during the war was ever realised at the time. Records were only occasionally played on the radio. Music programmes were almost always live, studio-bound, and featuring British bands. There were no weekly record programmes broadcast until after the war. The weekly request programme, *Family Favourites*, did not begin until October 1945 and the daily *Housewives' Choice* began in March 1946.

One Saturday, sometime after the end of the war, we were seated around the table eating our midday meal when Ted commented that one of the shops in the lane had started selling records. After due consideration, Dad decided to splash out and buy a new one. This was very exciting; I was dispatched with some money and specific instructions. I dashed into the shop and blurted out: 'Have you got a record of Cavan O'Connor singing "I'll Take You Home Again Kathleen", and Dad says can we have "The Mountains of Morne" on the other side?'

The chap behind the counter became quite flushed with irritation. Stroking back the hair from his forehead, he snapped: 'Does your dad think I've got Cavan O'Connor and an orchestra sitting out the back waiting to record any special requests that might come along? Go and tell him I have got Joseph Locke singing "I'll Take You Home Again Kathleen" with "Hear My Song Violetta" on the other side.'

I relayed the message and Dad was a bit put out. 'I've never heard of Joseph Locke or that song that's on the other side,' he said.

Ted was quick to say that Joseph Locke was all right and so was the song on the back, adding that he didn't think we would be able to do any better. After five minutes of head-scratching and chin-stroking Dad told me to go and fetch it.

After years of listening to nothing but 'The Miner's Dream of

Home' and 'My Mother's Eyes', all probably recorded in the twenties, Joseph Locke's record was wonderful. For a start it was a 'modern' recording, produced with modern technology so there were no scratches. But Dad was not destined to be a record collector. This fell to Ted who, by this time, was a working man and therefore in a position to buy any new recording that took his fancy. To get the best from these new records he bought one of the new-fangled electric radiograms. This was a table model with a radio at the top and a record player beneath which gave a choice of three speeds: 78, 45 or 33 1/3 rpm. The recording industry was progressing at a dramatic pace. Whether we were listening to the radio or the record player, the new radiogram had a beautiful tone compared to what we had grown used to. Our love of music was given full rein. Every Friday a man who worked with Ted would recommend a piece of classical music or an operatic aria, and on the Saturday morning I was dispatched to buy it.

Unlike all the fads in music that have come and gone in my lifetime, my love of classical music has never diminished. While Ted's purchasing power expanded my knowledge of good music, my love for it began much earlier and was due entirely to our mother. When we were children, sitting at the kitchen table writing or drawing with the radio playing in the background, Mother would sometimes say: 'Put your pencils down and listen to this piece of music.' We would put our pencils down, and we were never disappointed. For her anything by Tchaikovsky was a must, as were certain pieces by other composers. Operatic arias and choral pieces were also included, and one piece she really loved was called 'The Russian Creed' – it was stunning. These small interludes were simple lessons in musical appreciation.

Some would consider that I am now moving from the sublime to the ridiculous when I mention 'Rock Around the Clock' by

Bill Haley and the Comets, which came along in 1954 with the general rise of rock and roll. In cinemas this recording was used in the film *The Blackboard Jungle*; there was rocking in the aisles and, eventually, cinema seats were torn out to make more room for dancing. The music was responsible for the success of the film, which dealt with truculent American teenagers and indifferent teachers and gave out the message that if only teenagers were understood, everything would be all right. Nothing new there, then. While the sound was mesmerising, Bill Haley was not what young people were looking for. A new word, 'hip', had entered our vocabulary and with his kiss curl Bill was anything but.

But then, in 1956, came Elvis Presley, who held both the young and the not-so-young spellbound with his blend of black rhythm and blues, white country and western, and innuendo. While I appreciated Presley in some of his tracks, and still do, for me two singers remained far above any others and have stayed with me since the first time I heard them. They are Frank Sinatra and Ray Charles, and I have been fortunate enough to see both of them in concert. Ray Charles was simply the greatest rhythm and blues singer ever. He had a style that has never been success-fully imitated, though many have tried. After he recorded 'I Can't Stop Loving You', in which he showed what a black singer could do with the country and western genre, even Dad grew to like him – and that is saying something.

However, Frank Sinatra was always at the very top of my list of all-time greats. My admiration for him developed after Mother declared that she disliked him because he made the girls scream. The more she went on, the more I loved him. I never rated him too highly as an actor in films, but on the stage he was the con-summate performer. He never had to move about or perform any sort of ritual dance to improve his performance. He never had to wear bright colours or glitter. He only had to stand there and sing, and that is all his fans ever wanted. He had superb breath control which others tried to emulate but failed. It was not something he was born with; it was rather something he had worked to perfect, because he knew that breath control would give him the capacity to raise each performance to a higher level of excellence. From those early radio days to the present, Frank Sinatra has given my life some continuity.

Nevertheless, the first ever record I bought was not by Frank Sinatra but by Norman Brooks, singing 'A Sky Blue Shirt and a Rainbow Tie'. Ted tormented me at the time that I was wasting my money because Brooks was just imitating Al Jolson. His attitude was that it was not worth buying an imitation when you could buy the original. What he failed to see was that I was not buying an imitation, because Al Jolson had never actually recorded this song. As far as I was concerned I had indeed bought an original. But he must have changed his mind at some point because, many years later, he asked me if I would sell it to him. My answer was a very self-satisfied 'no'.

DAD

Dad was a master of trickery. He went about his endeavours so quietly that you never suspected he was up to anything. Having played simple tricks on us when we were children, to make us laugh or gasp in wonder, as we grew up and began work he became quite devious. He would seal the lining of a coat sleeve together using a dozen safety pins, then fasten all the buttons. He would tie a knot in your scarf and stuff the fingers of your gloves with tissue paper. It was also advisable, if you bought anything 'shop-soiled' or 'substandard', to destroy the labels straight away. Mother really lost her temper with him when she found she had sauntered through the town with one of these labels stuck to the back of her coat.

The bag I carried to work when I was sixteen was large enough to hold everything I needed to get me through the day. I could always tell when it was time to clear it out by the weight of it. As I trudged to work one morning it felt so heavy that I decided to sort it out after tea. That evening, after the table had been cleared, I took from the bag a scarf, gloves, a purse which never had enough in it, an umbrella, combs, a hairbrush, a makeup bag and a dozen other things that were essential for the peace of mind of a 'modern' girl. As the pile grew on the table I once more plunged my hand into its gloomy depths and among the numerous chocolate wrappers, bus tickets and shop receipts I felt a cold metal bar. I knew immediately what it was and looked at Dad, who was lurking behind his quivering newspaper. 'Oh, very funny,' I snapped as I pulled from the bag one of Mother's old flat irons, but he just grinned at me. I had lugged that blasted iron all the way to work and back.

I was in a pub one evening with friends. I was sipping my lemonade, sitting cross-legged and swinging my elevated foot backwards and forwards in a nonchalant manner when a couple of lads standing at the bar glanced my way and burst out laughing. Having been raised on Dad's devilment I knew immediately he had been busy again. 'I'll kill him,' I muttered under my breath as I made my way to the ladies. He had written on the bottom of each shoe in chalk '2s 6d', giving the impression that I had bought my shoes at a jumble sale. He, in turn, could take any amount of leg-pulling, and he always saw the funny side when we tormented him unmercifully as he worked on something which didn't work out as expected.

One Saturday afternoon, at some point in the fifties, he

decided to have a look around the shops. This didn't happen very often and it was obvious that he had something in mind. He returned some time later with a brand new cuckoo clock. Having hung it up on the wall he was disappointed that it appeared dull compared to how it had looked in the shop. We pointed out to him that the lighting in the shop would have had something to do with it. Jim was dispatched to a model shop for some tiny tins of paint in three specific bright colours. On Jim's return Dad put some newspaper on the table and, having removed the weights and the chains from the clock, began the delicate business of transforming it. When this was done he hung the clock on the wall and stood back to admire his handiwork. 'That's better,' he declared, and it was left there all night for the paint to dry. Next morning he rehung the chains and weights and set the clock in motion. All went well until it reached the hour. Instead of a happy little bird flying in and out of his hut letting us know the time, all we got was a series of dull thuds. As the paint had dried it had firmly sealed the door shut.

Winston Churchill played an important role in Dad's life. When Churchill spoke on the radio in the evenings he acted as Dad's safety valve. In Mother's kitchen Dad had someone who ranked highest in the land, someone he could blame or praise for his handling of the war. When things were going well it made Dad feel good that he could agree with Churchill's handling of the situation; however, what did him even more good was that, when the war was going badly for us, he could blame someone for the mess. It would be announced on the radio early in the morning and then intermittently during the day that Mr Churchill would be speaking to the nation that evening. The theme always seemed to be: never mind the hardship and the shortages, we could do it. Most of the time what he had to say went over my head, but I only had to take a look at Dad's expression to tell if the news was good or bad. Mother would sit mostly nodding or shaking her head, or tutting, leaving Dad to voice their opinions. Many times, as Churchill finished speaking, Dad could be heard to mutter: 'What does he know about it?'

On 4 June 1940 the prime minister droned on for several minutes before uttering the momentous words 'We shall defend our island,' and as he ended with 'We shall never surrender,' Dad leapt to his feet and declared: 'That's telling the buggers!' I remember feeling very secure in the knowledge that Dad was in agreement with the prime minister. This didn't happen very often. At another time both his and Mother's reaction to one phrase alarmed me. There was a gasp of disbelief and a shaking of heads from them after the words: 'If you think you are going to get it, don't forget you can take one with you.' I later asked Ted what Mr Churchill had meant and he explained that if we were invaded and thought we were going to die, we should try to kill one of the enemy before we did.

My reply was: 'I can't kill a German.'

To which he replied, 'Course you can. I'll kill one first and then I'll help you to kill one.'

So that was all right.

On 18 June 1940 France had just fallen to the Germans. Ted had drummed it into me that Hitler was only twenty miles away. This meant nothing to me. At that age I had no comprehension of distance but I knew things were bad. Again I found the speech boring but saw Dad pull himself into a more alert position in his chair when he heard the words: 'The Battle of France is over. I expect the Battle of Britain is about to begin.' Churchill finished that speech by saying: 'Let us therefore brace ourselves to our duties and so bear ourselves that if the British Empire and its Commonwealth lasts for a thousand years men will still say, this was their finest hour.'

The room went very quiet as the radio was turned off. Dad looked at Mom and shook his head. He said 'I don't know,' and buried his head in the newspaper. Ted and I went back to what we had been doing at the table.

There came a time in Dad's life when he realised that at last he could occasionally buy something without worrying about the cost. Sometime after that, the day arrived when he decided that he could start saving money. He began simply by saving his small change in a large glass jar which he kept in the kitchen cupboard. Sometimes in the evenings he would tip the contents of the jar on to the table and we would sit spellbound as he sorted the thruppenny bits from the sixpences and pennies. Then he gave up saving copper and hoarded only silver. Eventually he limited himself to saving only half-crowns. This went on for a long, long time and he never spent any of his savings. When the jar became full we never saw the money again, because he transferred it to an attaché case which he kept locked away under the bed. Sometimes, when he was nowhere to be found, on asking Mother 'Where's Dad?' her reply would be, 'If you mean Scrooge, he's upstairs counting his money'.

It would have been in the early fifties that the day finally came when the case was full and difficult to fasten. Only God knows how much there was in it by this time. Dad decided that now was the time to open a bank account. Mother held her hands up in horror. Well, everyone knew what robbing buggers these banks could be, but Dad had made up his mind. He opened his account with the 'Muni-cipple' (Oldbury's Municipal Bank). He never could quite get his teeth round 'Municipal'. The hoard was transferred a little at a time until it was all safely tucked away.

Why, you might ask, did he wait so long to put it away when it must have been risky to keep that amount of money in the house – especially when you remember that at that time no one locked their doors during the day? I think the answer is simple. I believe that he had had such a struggle during his early years of married life and the war that he could not believe that the hard times were over. For a long time he needed the constant reassurance of seeing his wealth.

Dad hated getting on buses. He much preferred walking. He loved nothing more than being out in the fields with Ted, Jim or me and the dogs, or pottering about in his yard. He always had a bike and continued riding one until he was in his late sixties, when he began having trouble with his left leg. At the hospital Dad was told that the leg needed to be removed. They sent him home and told him to return two days later when they would arrange for it to be done. The following day Dad was quieter than usual but still pleasant.

The following evening when I popped in to see him, Mom said he had shut himself in a darkened room. I opened the door and asked if there was anything he needed. He replied that he was all right but wanted to be left alone. I replied: 'Goodnight then, and God bless you.' Without any doubt he was dealing with his fear in his own way. The next day he stood tall and was ready. The quotation in the circle, 'Courage is fear that has been dealt with,' is a tribute to his courage and fortitude after having his leg amputated at the age of 70. Only when he realised that he was going to have to learn to 'hop' on and off the buses did he decide to part with everything he possessed that had anything to do with bikes.

He was a truly lovely man.

MOM

I had a happy childhood. We were well looked after and didn't go short of much. But Mother had been damaged in childhood. Although she could be great fun, she was incapable of showing affection. She was not unique. Many people of her age were products of the 'good old days'. Her mother had died when she was very young, leaving three little girls and an older son. Just five years old, she was the eldest of the girls. Her sisters were May, then aged three and a half, and eighteen-month-old Violet. There was some talk of them having to be placed in the local children's home, but their father found a widow to marry and then he went off to war.

She became accustomed to beatings, as did her sisters. It was the way it was then in many families. As a child her mouth got her into hot water on many occasions and for the rest of her life she was constantly on the defensive, suspicious that unlooked-for kindness from others masked darker ulterior motives. If only she had been shown some love instead of violence, she would probably have been a very different woman. I found the quotation 'Children need love, especially when they don't deserve it' many years after Mother had died, and always felt that it would have made an appropriate epitaph.

Mother never believed in saving money. As far as she was concerned, it was there to be spent. She would get very disgruntled with Dad when he refused to part with any of it; I don't know why, as he was always very generous towards her. She couldn't even leave her Co-op dividends to accrue. To her dying day, she never had a bank account or a Post Office savings book. When Dad died she took over his account at the Municipal and in less than a year she had got through its contents. She had had to take over the account because his company pension was paid into it, and she would be at the bank to draw it out every month. But when it came to making things last, she could be frugal to the point of being ridiculous. I have represented an example of this in her circle; you will see a pair of shoes with the heels worn down on the sides. To correct this she would wear the shoes on the wrong feet until the heels were level again.

She always had the highest regard for anyone who never married. She would say of one particular woman: 'I've always liked her. She's never bothered with chaps.' She expressed the same opinions about men who hadn't married. When she spoke of one of Dad's sisters who had sadly died in her forties having never married, she would say: 'She was the best of the lot.'

She was an excellent plain sewer and loved patching and darning. She had no patience with feminine fripperies. She was not very tall, but was well built and as strong as a horse. One incident illustrates just how strong she was. She would have been in her seventies when Dad, who by this time had lost a leg, decided he would like a tall stepladder so that he could climb up and look in the loft of the pensioner's bungalow they had recently moved into. He asked Mother if she would go and fetch him one. As it was made of aluminium it would not have been heavy, but it would have been bulky and cumbersome. At first she told him he would have to wait until my brother Jim made his usual visit to them on Friday. But Dad would not hear of it and in the end, to keep the peace, she set off for the shop on foot even though it was quite a breezy day. After making her purchase she asked the young chap behind the counter if he would help her to hoist it up on her shoulder. Apparently he looked at her as if she had gone mad and asked her how far she had to go. She replied that it was 'only' about a half-hour walk. She set off and soon realised that the breeze had stiffened somewhat. How did she know? Well, the stepladder was wrapped in strong plastic film and every time the wind caught it, she was blown around in a circle. This happened many, many times during her journey home. The weight of the ladder did not bother her. It was the fact that it was wrapped in plastic that was the problem.

Mother features throughout both the tapestry and this book. She was always there when we got home from school and could be tremendous fun.

MOON LANDING

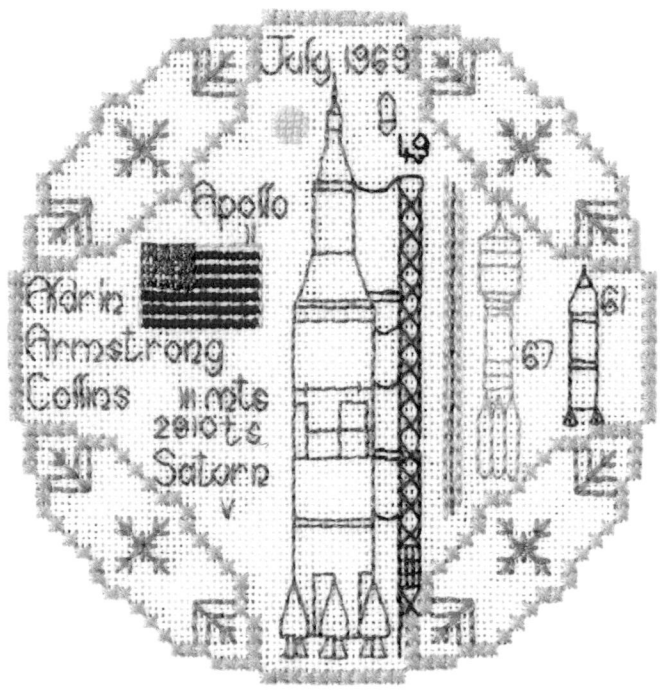

The build-up to the Apollo 11 moon landing in July 1969 lasted for years and, while the world seemed to be slowly going mad in the hurly-burly of the sixties, the space race was one thing that did seem to focus many minds. It was truly an 'out of this world' event for all of those who, all their lives, had thought of space travel as something that would only happen in the future. By the sixties the future was here and happening now.

In the circle is Apollo 11 which was put into orbit by the awesome Saturn V rocket. To the right of this is a representation of the 'iron curtain' and further right are Soyuz and Vostok, two of Russia's spacecraft.

As the Second World War ended, competition between the Russians and the Americans began. During the Cold War there was always a fear that confrontation between the superpowers would lead eventually to the destruction of the world. As the years went by the tit-for-tat mentality continued, and we were all too aware that great 'progress' was being made by these two countries in the development and stockpiling of nuclear weapons. Fear would strike me every time 'intercontinental ballistic missiles' were mentioned. These had the capacity to carry a nuclear bomb over 5,000 kilometres. America always professed to be open and honest about what it was doing and what its intentions were, but Russia remained secretive and uncommunicative. While both continued with their weapons development, they were also developing space probes and satellites. It became a matter of public conjecture which country would achieve what first.

Russia was the first to put a satellite – Sputnik 1 – into orbit in October 1957. Following tests to see how animals would cope with space travel, it was Russia's Yuri Gagarin who became the world's first cosmonaut on 12 April 1961. He completed an orbit of the earth in a Vostok craft. All talk of intercontinental ballistic missiles was abandoned for a time, although the British public converted the word 'ballistic' to mean an explosion of temper. The phrase 'He went ballistic' is of course still in common use today.

Just over a month after Gagarin's great achievement, on 25 May 1961, the American president John F. Kennedy gave a speech informing the world of the Apollo space programme. This would enable the USA to explore space with the intention of putting one of their astronauts on the moon before the end of the decade. The space race had begun in earnest.

Although this was a race in which the British couldn't compete because of cost, we nevertheless had some space-age technology we could be proud of. In 1945 Bernard Lovell had established the need for a radio telescope of gigantic proportions to support research on astronomy and develop a greater understanding of the universe. Jodrell Bank in Cheshire was opened on 2 August 1957. By October it had been used to track the progress of Sputnik 1, and would continue to play an important role throughout the space race.

There followed a long period of activity involving both Russia and America. There were space walks and exchanges from one spaceship to another, and a real buzz of anticipation as pictures appeared in newspapers and film footage appeared on television. We experienced the full range of emotions. We felt shock and sadness when things went wrong, such as the devastating fire on 27 January 1967 which killed three accomplished astronauts: Grissom, White and Chaffee. We felt immense pride when Apollo 10 sent back pictures of the earth rising as seen from the moon, just as we could see the moon rise from the earth. What a strikingly beautiful world we lived in. We perceived our own insignificance compared to the grandeur of the planet on which we were privileged to live.

Apollo 11 left the earth on 16 July 1969 with Neil Armstrong, Buzz Aldrin and Michael Collins on board. They travelled in the command module which, during flight, was docked to the service module. This contained the lunar landing module. When they reached the moon, Michael Collins continued in orbit with the command module and the service module while Armstrong and Aldrin landed on the moon in the lunar module. Then came the announcement: 'The eagle has landed.' After a period of rest Armstrong was the first to set foot on the moon's surface with his famous line: 'That's one small step for a man, one giant leap for mankind.'

At home, we had gone to bed the night before knowing that the astronauts were on the moon and we were anticipating with excitement what we would see the following day. Early next morning we watched the grainy images of the astronauts on our black-and-white television screen, moving around in what seemed like slow motion because of the moon's lower gravity. I called up to my son Jim, who at twelve years old had all the exuberance of his age, and he came dashing down the stairs. Angela, being Angela, followed more slowly, took a quick look and went back to bed. Armstrong and Aldrin set up various pieces of test equipment on the moon and collected rock samples before successfully lifting off and rendezvousing with the command module in lunar orbit. They returned to earth, mission accomplished and history made.

For three years in the mid-to-late seventies, Ray, Angela and I would regularly visit Jim in Manchester where he was a student. We travelled by train, and I would look forward to passing through Kidsgrove, especially if it was a clear day, because I knew that as the train made its way to Macclesfield I would have a tremendous view of Jodrell Bank and its radio telescopes. Gleaming white against a clear blue sky, they begged for admiration. By then the main dish, now known as the Lovell telescope, had slipped down in the world rankings to third largest but it was, and still is, an inspirational sight.

– CIRCLE 50 –

SCHOOL TRIPS

There were no school trips for us until well after the end of the war. My first one, to Lichfield cathedral and Dovedale, was on 9 July 1947. It was a typical English summer's day: dull, overcast and raining. The tour of the cathedral was very good and, of course, it didn't matter about the weather. Dad had told me the night before that I would love the cathedral with its three spires, which were known as the 'three sisters', and he was right. I have always had a special bond with that particular cathedral. There are some things about this building that still linger in my mem-

ory after all these years. One of these is the white marble memorial to two small children who appear to be asleep but actually
met an untimely end.

After Lichfield we then re-boarded the coach and went on to
Dovedale. We were all dressed up in our Sunday best, which in
my case was a pale green coat and nothing on my head except a
ribbon bow. It rained. Oh, how it rained! After crossing the river
on stepping stones we were supposed to go rambling along the
river as far as Lion Rock. The teachers didn't see why a drop of
rain should change anything and we set off. The riverside path
became a quagmire and we were slipping and falling all over the
place. My coat became soaking wet and caked in mud. Everyone
was in the same mess and we took turns complaining: 'Mother
will kill me.' We got to Lion Rock, said a few 'oohs' and 'aahs' and,
being unable to sit down anywhere, returned to the river crossing. When we reached it a few mouths fell open, including mine.

The river was fast-flowing because of the rain and quite wide,
with many of the stepping stones looking decidedly wet and slip-
pery. Of the first few brave souls that crossed, one or two fell in.
The water was not deep, and they got up and carried on regardless. I got halfway and almost lost my bottle but, despite the
wind, the weather and a raging thirst, I made it. We clambered
back onto the coach and compared coats and shoes. What a state
we were all in.

After a short journey we pulled up at a tea room and, leaving
our wet coats on the coach, we pushed and shoved our way in. It
was a large wooden building with lots of windows, so it was light
and airy. A couple of women bustled round with large enamel
teapots – we enjoyed our simple tea of bread and butter, and
things didn't seem so bad after that.

When we got off the coach after arriving back at school the
strangest thing had happened. There was no mud to be seen on

our clothes or shoes. It had dried and dropped off. It was obviously a much cleaner brand of mud than we were used to. On reflection, though, we never did call our local stuff 'mud'; we called it 'sludge', and there, I suppose, lay the difference.

The next outing was to Worcester on 25 June 1948. I remember this trip for two reasons. One was lunch and the other was tea. We arrived in Worcester and the weather was set fair. The plan was that, after a tour of the cathedral, we would have a picnic lunch in the public gardens by the river. We sat quietly on the coach while the two teachers and the driver decided that we would be handed our lunches in paper bags as we disembarked. These we would carry with us while on our tour. We carried them around for at least an hour and a half, and this included our jaunt up the cathedral tower. Those paper bags got a bit mauled, to say the least. The tower had a seemingly never-ending, tightly winding staircase and, as we were struggling to get up and then down, there were other people coming and going in the opposite direction. This had a peculiar effect on the lunch we were carrying. When we had all settled ourselves by the river and opened our bags we found that the contents of every one, with no exceptions, had been wound into a spiral. The sandwiches and two pieces of cake resembled a Swiss roll.

Tea that day was also a bit of a fiasco. At 2 pm we were scheduled to go on a river trip to Holt Fleet, where we would visit a local establishment for a tea of strawberries and cream. This was to be the highlight of the day. Many of us had never seen a strawberry, never mind tasted one, and the same went for the cream. But it was all a pipe-dream; there had been a mix-up with the bookings. The teacher was allowed to use the telephone and, after a couple of calls, we were told that we had to wait for the next boat and go back into Worcester. We ended up in a very ordinary, scrubbed-tables establishment, and on each table was a plate of bread and margarine, a jar of jam and pots of tea.

Unfortunately, the disappointment showed itself in the behaviour of some of the girls, and the next day we were given a very serious talking-to by the headmistress on the subject of table manners. The teachers in charge had been shocked to see one girl dipping into the jam pot with her knife, which they considered 'a disgusting exhibition'.

As the headmistress prepared to leave the room, one girl raised her hand. When asked what she wanted, she bravely stood up. In clear and practised tones she repeated a message from her father: 'As we had paid for Sheila to have strawberries and cream and she ended up with bread and jam, when can we expect a refund?', she said.

A tremendous hush fell. The headmistress and the teacher exchanged glances.

'The financial side of this matter will be sorted out in due course,' said the headmistress brusquely, and left the room. I do not remember if it ever was.

After I moved to the secondary modern at the age of eleven, my school trips took a new turn. Three times we went to the cinema with our dedicated drama teacher, Mrs Jones. The first time was to see June Allyson in *Little Women*, the second time to see Laurence Olivier's *Hamlet* and the third David Niven in *The Elusive Pimpernel.*

I also went to school camp for two weeks. It was out in the country, probably just over an hour's drive from the school. The camp was made up of three large dormitory huts, each holding about twenty girls, together with a recreation hut, an ablutions hut and a combined kitchen and dining hut. It was set in many acres of woodland and I hated every minute I was there. The only highlight for me was the forced route-march on both

Sunday mornings to a little country church. I can still see it in my mind's eye and would love to know exactly where it was.

Half a dozen of us had to leave the camp on the final Thursday as we had another school trip the following day that we didn't want to miss. This was the big one. At last I was going to see the sea. It was 1949, I was twelve years old and the long-awaited day was here at last. It was the first time for many of us and we were going to New Brighton via the Mersey tunnel. The tunnel was a wondrous thing for me. I never expected it to be so long, and from New Brighton there is a good view of the Liver and Cunard Buildings in Liverpool. We enjoyed the day and were left very much to our own devices, but it became a bit of a blur when I developed a headache.

The last school outing that I can remember was a theatre trip to Stratford-upon-Avon. It was 1951, I was fourteen years old and we were going to see Julius Caesar. We had spent several months preparing for it, reading the play in drama class and having it explained to us by Mrs Jones. Many of the girls were going just for a day out, but others were actually looking forward to the play.

However, once again there was a discussion at the booking office while we waited patiently outside, and eventually a deflated Mrs Jones announced that there had been a mix-up and we would not be seeing *Julius Caesar* after all. There was a bit of groaning, but we cheered up when she told us that we would be seeing *Henry V* instead.

The play had been running for about fifteen minutes when we realised that none of us knew what was going on. We had not had the preparation for this that we had had for Julius Caesar and so we found it rather boring. During the battle, and scenes with a lot of political dialogue, there was much tittering going on around us. Mrs Jones, sitting behind me, sighed with exasperation and tutted a lot. One of the girls two rows in front of me whispered something really funny and I succumbed to a fit of sniggering, whereupon Mrs Jones tapped me on the shoulder and snapped: 'Jean, I'm surprised at you!' I failed to see why she should be surprised at me and not the others, but there it is. Things changed dramatically later in the play when Henry, stripped of his armour, and having left the dire and dismal battle scenes behind him, came on stage looking absolutely gorgeous and proceeded to woo Catherine. Who was this gift to women who had transformed the St Trinian's-like mob? Even Mrs Jones went quiet. We watched the rest of the performance transfixed. What power a good-looking man can have over impressionable young women!

As the years went by I often wondered who that actor was. Had he become famous? Had he ever made any films? I had to wait until I was 63 to find the answer. It was Richard Burton, and also in the cast that day was another attractive male actor who went on to become famous, Anthony Quayle.

MAKE DO AND MEND

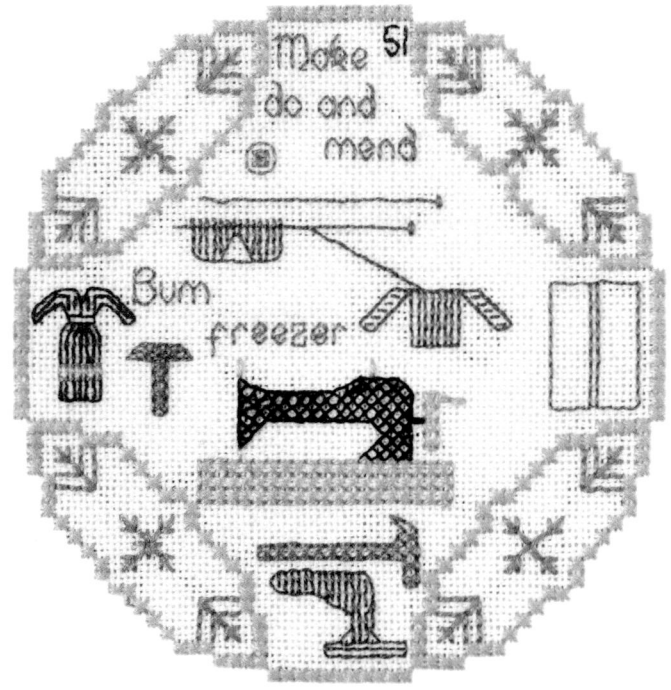

Today we live in a throwaway society. Of course, this does not necessarily mean that all of us adopt the ways of the majority. There must be many, like me, who cannot forget what we were taught when we were younger. I still look at everything I am about to throw out to check if there are other useful possibilities lurking behind their original purpose. The methods of 'make do and mend' adopted during the war years and for some time afterwards have stood me in good stead ever since; I have always made full use of my sewing and knitting skills.

As a small child I paid a lot of attention to the subject. Everyone was encouraged to 'make do and mend'. It became a national pastime. Newspapers and magazines gave useful ideas and printed government-issued suggestions, and there seems little doubt that 'making do' by sewing was top of the agenda in many houses. But we did not adopt a 'make do' attitude with clothing alone. Everything during the period in question was covered by this umbrella philosophy, including household linen and furniture, food, toys, games and entertainment. Anyone who could sing or play the piano, the accordion or even the spoons was in great demand when it came to entertainment.

From one article written by the Board of Trade on making clothing coupons go further came the words:

Every sailor knows his 'rig' may have to last him a long time. So definite times are set aside each week for the sailors to 'make do and mend', and clean and repair their clothes. Follow their example. Every time you avoid buying new clothes by mending, altering or 'freshening up' something you already have, you are definitely helping to beat Hitler and his gang.[*]

This always gave me visions of a sailor, halfway through some decisive sea battle, saying to his shipmates: 'It's no good, I'll have to leave you to it, I've got some mending to do and I always do it at this time every week.'

We were encouraged to consider the potential of every out-grown or worn-out garment before it was passed on. We were also given instructions on how to make full use of what we had to hand in the home, on a self-sufficiency basis; for example, it was possible to buy kettle or saucepan mending kits. Dad was very good at repairing our old shoes with one of his three lasts

---

[*] Brian Braithwaite, Noelle Walsh and Glyn Davies (eds), *The Home Front: The Best of Good Housekeeping 1939–1945* (London: Leopard Books, 1995), p. 76.

and a hammer, but he failed abysmally when it came to creating a sole out of a piece of old tyre.

Mom was a whiz at plain sewing with her old treadle machine and earned a little money doing jobs for other people. We were given tips on how to save coal, how to make firelighters, how to deal with draughts (thus saving fuel) and the best way of storing food scraps for use as pig food. There was advice on how to feed a family of six on eighteen penn'orth of scrag-end, how to make a cake without sugar, how to make a cake using no dried fruit, how to make a cake without an egg, how to make your sugar ration go further and what to do with bits of stale crust. I can vaguely remember a recipe for a cocoa paste covering for a wedding cake.

There were endless ideas on how to unravel an old jumper and knit a new one, how to make a good sheet or towel out of old ones, how to make a new coat out of an old blanket and how to make a new blanket out of an old coat. Mom was very good at using the tails from Dad's shirts to make new collars when the old ones had become too frayed. This did not please him at all and he constantly referred to these shirts as 'bum freezers'. Any woman without the talent to make a new hat *and* a dishcloth out of an old vest must have been consumed with guilt. But I have often wondered just how many women had the time, skill, patience or inclination to put a new foot on an old stocking? Instructions were given in many magazines on how to do this, including patterns to assist the cutting of a new foot and toe from waste fabric. I look at these instructions today and still don't know how this could be done, but I think it serves as a good reminder of just how scarce stockings were at the time.

It seems reasonable to say that 'making do' must have included birthdays, for it is also true that birthdays were non-events in our house. This was fairly common. Birthday cards were not sent to all and sundry as they are today. They were probably seen as an unnecessary luxury, as were birthday presents. Up to the end of the war, if I asked for anything on my birthday I was reminded that there was a war on, and that was the end of the matter. When the war was over, Mother could always think up another reason for ignoring the day. The usual reply was: 'I think you had all yoh'm likely to get, for Christmas.' (My birthday is in January.)

In time I became aware that some of the girls at school were getting birthday cards, so when my birthday came round one year I decided to try my luck. I came down the stairs and Mother wished me a happy birthday. Later, while I was getting washed and dressed, I asked if I could have a birthday card. After a bit of persuasion Mother grudgingly agreed: 'Go round to the shop and fetch one. Tell them to put it on the paper bill.' I ran around to the shop, chose one that I liked and dashed back home. I offered it to Mother. She said, flatly: 'You'll have to write on it yourself, I haven't got the time.' So I sat at the table and in my very best writing wished myself a happy birthday. I propped the card up on the sideboard and dashed off to school as proud as a peacock. I had got a birthday card!

When I had a family of my own, I always tried to make birthdays in our house a special occasion. Mother was always included in these little celebrations and she joined in with great enthusiasm.

– CIRCLE 52 –

THE FIFTIES

For working-class girls the fifties were no different from the forties. Life was still suffocating. You went to school. Then you left school and found a job, which was not difficult as they were plentiful. I left school on 4 April 1952, aged fifteen, and started work three days later. By the age of 21 a young woman was expected to be married; the life she could live for herself was over before it had really begun. Meanwhile, as the two superpowers dug in their heels and faced off against each other, we learned to live with the ever-present threat of nuclear weapons. The world seemed to be slipping closer to inevitable destruction, but we were all expected to be blissfully happy because the war had been over since 1945 and we were at peace.

The King died in February 1952. At the time we were informed that he had suffered a coronary thrombosis, when in fact he had died from cancer. As head girl it was my duty to go around the school and quietly tell all the teachers, who would then pass the news to their pupils. On the day of the funeral we had a service in the school hall and observed a two-minute silence. At the timber yard close by the circular saws were switched off, and for the first time we realised how intrusive the noise was. Since then I have always connected the two: the death of the King and the saw mill.

By 1953 I was working in a shop which had several departments. I worked in drapery. In this department the owners had stocked up with the best selection of bunting and flags in the town, and as the build-up to the coronation began we were very busy. In May the country went red, white and blue mad and by the time the big day, 2 June, came around there was nothing left. The Queen's coronation was a day off for everyone.

That year also saw a string of achievements. Just four days before the coronation Edmund Hillary and Sherpa Tenzing Norgay became the first to reach the summit of Mount Everest. After a successful 33-year career Sir Gordon Richards, the country's best known and most popular jockey, finally won the Derby on Pinza, coming in at 5 to 1. There was tremendous excitement when England's cricketers won the Ashes for the first time in nineteen years and Stanley Matthews won his first FA Cup winners' medal at the age of 38.

Much was made of these achievements. To perk us all up we were told that we were now living in the new Elizabethan age. It was said in a way that suggested that we should see it as a privilege to be citizens of such a forward-looking country, and that our continued hard work would reap its own rewards. Mother couldn't accept this at all. She was convinced that all these achievements were a set-up and had been arranged just to make us feel better so that we would all keep working hard. It was all a put-up job – the managerial classes were pulling the wool over our eyes to make more money out of us, and she was the only one who could see it!

In 1954, as mentioned in Circle 46, Bill Haley and his Comets set us alight with 'Rock Around the Clock'. It was a worldwide hit. One lunchtime I was in Littlewoods with a girl I worked with, buying a tin of soup, when the track was played over the public address system. We put our bags on the floor and showed the older shoppers how it was done. I loved dancing, especially jive and rock. Mother wasn't impressed at all. She said it wasn't ladylike and thought it was reminiscent of tribal dances in the jungle. I asked her what she thought the Charleston and the Black Bottom were reminiscent of, and she flounced off. These were two of the dances she had done as a young girl.

That same year 'Rock Around the Clock' formed part of the backdrop to the violence among the Teddy Boys. Young people had begun to break away from the tradition of dressing and acting like their parents. Social change was in progress. Often looked upon with trepidation because of their association with flick knives, Teddy Boys revelled in their new-found freedom. They paraded in their frock coats, drainpipe trousers and suede, crepe-soled shoes. Dad always referred to these shoes as 'muck spreaders', while Mother interpreted their gait as 'walking as if they've done something nasty in their trousers'. I found Teddy boys intimidating. They always went about in gangs and, at seventeen, I avoided them as much as possible.

Mother didn't like anyone who didn't conform in the way they dressed. In 1957 she branded a chap who had an alternative style of dress together with long hair as 'one of them beatniks', but I don't think she had any idea what a beatnik actually was. I believe she just liked using the word because it made her feel 'with it'. So-called beatniks used their style of dress to support the social philosophy of a movement in America called the Beat Generation, which came to prominence in 1957 as a group of writers who rejected the values of middle-class American society. They offered an alternative lifestyle assisted by quantities of mind-altering drugs. Written works from some members of the Beat Generation such as Allen Ginsberg and William H. Burroughs achieved notoriety, but it was Jack Kerouac's book *On the Road* that would be hailed as the group's seminal work. Jack Kerouac gave the blossoming new youth culture, eager to break free from the shackles of what it perceived as a repressive society, a new idol in the form of Neal Cassady.

In the fifties ration books finally disappeared. For the first time since 1939 people could buy any amount of food they liked, provided they had the money. Elvis Presley lightened the gloom with 'Heartbreak Hotel' and 'Hound Dog' as he began his rise to super-stardom.

It was in the fifties that Britain realised that the car would soon be king. As our own roads became clogged with traffic there was much talk of the superior German road system. It was probably 1956 when the talking stopped and the work began. The Preston bypass was the first 'motorway' to open in December 1958. It was eight miles long. The M1 motorway was opened in November 1959 and in January 1958 the first radar speed traps were used. In March of that same year, Mayfair in London was the first place in the country to get parking meters and parking tickets.

In this decade Jonas Salk, an American microbiologist, developed the vaccine that it was hoped would rid the world of the greatly feared disease poliomyelitis. In America, Rosa Parks refused to give up her seat on a bus to a white man, an incident that gave the civil rights movement a boost as the news spread round the world via television. At Wembley stadium in 1954, West Bromwich Albion won the FA Cup by three goals to two against Preston North End.

It was a decade of change for some, but a decade of standing still for many. In 1950 I was a schoolgirl and in 1959 I was a wife and mother, so the decade had brought me great change even though I still felt that I was at a standstill. I was without prospects simply because any chance of achievement was completely beyond my reach as a wife and mother. You could only do one or the other, not both. It sounds as if I am complaining but really I'm not. At that time, for many of us, it was just the way it was and we just had to get on with it.

THE SIXTIES

The sixties passed me by somehow. In 1960 I had a husband and a son aged three. By 1969 I had a husband, a son aged twelve and a daughter aged seven. The years continued to be shaped by Cold War rhetoric, the fear of nuclear weapons and major social upheaval. The baby boom after the Second World War meant that by the sixties there were many more teenagers in the population. These soon-to-be adults had no memory of the war and had grown up through the hypocrisy of the fifties. By 1960 the desire for social and cultural change among the young had quickened its pace, while I quietly dreamed of a life that didn't only consist of housework, cooking and playing games.

Class divisions were as strong as ever. Sociologists spoke of 'sub-cultures' among the working classes and 'counter-cultures' among the middle classes. National Service ended in 1960, leaving young men to make their own way from their teenage years to manhood. They were experiencing considerably more freedom than their parents – or I, for that matter – had ever known.

Youth became a restless driving force, and incidents of racism of various kinds were on the increase. While the sixties are remembered as a wild and carefree time when people broke free from the conformity of the recent past, things were not always as they seemed. Amid great achievements and hedonism there was just as much misery and dissatisfaction. Everyone seemed to be demanding more while I just got on with the housework, the shopping and the cooking.

OPEC, the Organization of Petroleum Exporting Countries, was established in 1960 and power shifted from big oil companies to the nations of the Middle East. The 28-mile-long Berlin Wall was built by the Soviet Union in just one week in August 1961. It was to remain as a symbol of the Cold War for 28 years. And in 1962, US military intelligence gained evidence of the installation of Soviet medium-range ballistic missiles in Cuba. In October John F. Kennedy moved US forces to a state of high alert and blockaded Cuba. The Soviet leader Nikita Khrushchev was asked to remove the missiles. The world held its breath. After much negotiation the missiles were removed along with the blockade seven days later. The world let out a collective sigh of relief; I was just so grateful that I could continue with my life for a few more years and watch my children grow.

To many who lived in the early sixties John Fitzgerald Kennedy had become a symbol of hope, but on 22 November

1963 he was assassinated by Lee Harvey Oswald. Oswald's reasons were never properly established. While glossing over Kennedy's weaknesses, the grief at his premature death extended beyond America to many other countries. It was difficult to accept that he had been cut down in his prime, so openly and before the eyes of the world. It tends to be only when such things happen that we become aware of our own mortality. The death of Kennedy, though it was felt very deeply, also coincided with the first of the James Bond films, and throughout the sixties the entertainment industry became adept at taking our minds away from the troubles of the world.

The first of the hugely successful James Bond films was released in 1962. *Dr No* starred Sean Connery and it served to define the attitudes of the sixties. Its combination of sex, violence and occasional camp humour was repeated in subsequent films in the series. Connery became a world star and *Dr No* was followed by *From Russia With Love* in 1963, *Goldfinger* in 1964, *Thunderball* in 1965 and *You Only Live Twice* in 1967. I didn't manage to see any of them. I was too busy washing, ironing, baking cakes and doing housework while trying to look thrilled with it all. The problem with household tasks is that there is never any end to it. What you do one day you have to do again the next.

While I do go on about household chores, I will always be eternally grateful that I never had the worry that so many other parents suffered in this period. Thalidomide was prescribed to expectant mothers in the early stages of pregnancy for minor ailments such as morning sickness, general depression and backache. It had been hailed as a new 'miracle' drug that was completely non-toxic and had been found to have no harmful side effects. What was not known at the time was that thalidomide contains two molecular structures that are mirror-images of each other. One structure provides the medical benefits that were claimed. But, given to women in the early stages of pregnancy, the other structure could cause deformities in the foetus.

As the medical authorities were unaware of the difference, the thalidomide that had been freely prescribed since it was first marketed in 1959 consisted of both structures. It was immediately withdrawn in 1962 when the link with a huge increase in birth defects was established. More than 400 British 'thalidomide children' survived and the numbers affected in other countries were catastrophic. Along with every mother this affected me deeply, and it was covered very thoroughly on TV. Today doctors are reluctant to accept that any new drug is completely harmless.

On the subject of transport, we viewed Dr Baron Richard Beeching as being 'capable of doing more harm than good' to our railway system. He was a British scientist and administrator and, during his time as chairman of the British Railways Board, he produced the controversial Beeching Report of 1963. This was a plan to concentrate passenger and freight traffic on railway lines running between cities at the expense of lesser-used lines. Something like 5,000 miles of branch and rural lines disappeared. Those most affected by the closures in rural areas could continue to live normal lives only if they had the use of a car. No one seemed to care about the others.

Because we lived in a busy town with good bus services we had no call for a train service on a daily basis, but thousands of others did. Even so, we did use trains regularly. It was only with the swift removal of the railway stations that it hit us. Always just a bit grimy and definitely draughty, they were there one minute and gone the next. We didn't know how much we cared about them and everything that they stood for until they were gone.

But because it was 1963 there was always something to distract us. That year the Beatles became established, and no other pop group has ever come close to the worldwide success that they achieved.

Most young people of today cannot understand their popularity, but you really had to be there to understand. I couldn't say that they were inspirational, they were just there at the right time – slightly irreverent, perfect for the sixties, appealing to all age groups – and they had global adulation. Peak time television news programmes would begin with: 'Good evening. The Beatles have gone straight to number one in the charts with their new single.' Just occasionally the rest of the news didn't matter. It was the same when the English football team won the World Cup.

England was the host nation for the FIFA World Cup in 1966, and we became the first host nation to win that trophy since Italy in 1934. In the final we were playing against West Germany and 98,000 people packed Wembley stadium to watch the match, while Ray and I, along with Jim and Angela, who were then aged nine and four respectively, were packed together with Mom and Dad in a small holiday caravan in the Welsh seaside resort of Rhyl.

There really wasn't room to swing the proverbial cat and we settled down to listen to the match on the radio. With the match under way Mother decided to cook everyone a late fry-up lunch and Ray was the first to be offered double egg, bacon and mushrooms. This he rested on a seat while he searched for the brown sauce. At this point England scored a goal and Dad and the children leapt to their feet and cheered. Unfortunately Dad had moved position slightly and, when he sat down again, he sat on Ray's late lunch. Dad blamed Ray, Mother blamed Dad, I blamed Mother and Ray wasn't bothered. To keep the peace he ate his meal while Dad changed his trousers. We beat the West German side 4–2 in extra time and nothing else mattered.

There were some good times during the sixties but just as many bad ones. People in high places couldn't let things settle;

they had to keep stirring them up. In 1968 the Conservative politician Enoch Powell delivered his 'rivers of blood' speech to a group of businessmen in Birmingham. It was blatantly racist and the speech revealed the depth of feeling of a section of the white population. Though Powell had achieved his fifteen minutes of fame, he lost all the credibility he had built up over many years in politics. He was marginalised. Before this speech he had been highly respected, and was probably one of the best educated members of the Houses of Parliament. He was immediately dismissed from the shadow cabinet and resigned from the Conservative party in 1974. There was so much that he could have done. Now this speech is all that he is remembered for.

So much happened in the sixties that it was difficult to decide what to put in the circle and what to leave out. The decade was all about sex, drugs and rock and roll but I wouldn't know about that. While it was supposed to be a time of worldwide euphoria with Britain at the centre of it all, it was also a period of calamities and tragedy when, occasionally, the Cold War would bring us to the edge of our seats. While it is fondly remembered by many people who say they had a wonderful time, I seem to have worked my way through it. But then, when it comes down to it, I wouldn't have had it any other way.

RELIGION

We were brought up to believe in God, but we didn't have to go to church to prove it. Neither Mom, Dad, Ted or Jim ever went to church except for christenings, weddings and funerals. Dad always looked a bit uncomfortable when the subject was mentioned. I think he was one of those men who thought that if he entered the house of God the roof would fall in on him. Mom, on the other hand, could become quite belligerent. Her attitude was that most of those who did go only went so that they could feel a cut above the rest of us and show off their Sunday best.

Going to church, she said, didn't necessarily make a good Christian. I went along occasionally to fulfil those sudden urges that would wash over me to show the world how pious I was. I considered myself good convent material. Mother didn't call me 'dramatic Alice' for nothing.

I think most youngsters found church services quite boring, and quite unlike the atmosphere we found at the religious meetings held in the large upstairs flour storage room at the back of Mr Hale's bakery. I would have been no more than nine at the time. We would congregate on Tuesday evenings at seven o'clock having been escorted through the bakery itself. We dawdled a bit to make the most of the warmth and the tantalising smell of fresh bread. Both were irresistible, especially on a frosty night.

In the room were rows of benches lined up in front of the sacks of flour, and at the far end of it was an upright piano on a small platform. This was played with great vigour by Mrs Hale, while Mr Hale claimed his spot at centre stage. They were a nice homely couple with pleasant, smiling faces. Their gentle way of leading us into religion was a huge success. The room was always packed. We would have about an hour or so of singing exhilarating songs such as 'When You're Down in the Dumps and Feeling All Alone' and 'Jesus Wants Me for a Sunbeam'. We would put actions to some of the songs. I remember that one of them was about rabbits, and we would make rabbit ears by waggling a couple of fingers behind our heads. The best song of all was about David slaying Goliath; its chorus ended with the words:

Oh round and round and round and round and round and round and round,
David put a stone into the sling and the sling went round and round.

For this one we would hold a scarf in one hand, high above our heads, and swirl it for all we were worth. We would never be satisfied with one rendition of this song, and we would stamp our feet and cheer until Mrs Hale started playing it all over again. It was a lovely atmosphere. We would end the evening with about ten minutes of serious prayer and then went straight home, feeling uplifted and satisfied.

One week I had a bad cold and Mother wouldn't let me go out in the damp night air. I was very upset. Jim wouldn't go without me so Ted went on his own. When he came home later he was very excited and said that Mr Hale, on being told that I wasn't very well, had called the crowd to order and prayers had been said for me. Well, you could virtually see the halo glowing around my head that night. The following day at school I was treated with awe and reverence when word went around the playground that I had been prayed for. There was no doubt: it would be the convent life for me when I was old enough.

These happy evenings went on for about eighteen months. Attendances never flagged and the room was always packed to capacity. Then one evening a radiant Mr Hale told us that there would be no more meetings at the bakery. We all gasped, but he quickly allayed our disappointment by telling us that the meetings would henceforth be held on Sunday afternoons in a room above a shop on the corner of Bull Street.

The following Sunday only a few children turned up, together with about eight miserable-looking adults. The first thing that struck us as we entered the room was that Mr and Mrs Hale were dressed in black. He looked rather pompous while she looked worried and doubtful. There was hardly any singing that day, only shouting, table-thumping and fire and brimstone. We didn't go again. It was very sad. I have often wondered if, because those evenings were such a success, Mr Hale thought he was destined for bigger things.

The vicar from our local church would spend some evenings visiting his flock on his bike. I don't know why, but he seemed to call at our house more than any of the others. If I was playing in the street when he came around the corner I would dash indoors and issue the warning: 'The vicar's about.' There would be an immediate flurry of activity as cushions were straightened and cups and saucers were removed. As Dad combed his hair and opened the newspaper Mother would whip off her apron. As sure as God made little apples the knock would come, and at this point Ted and Jim would scarper. I would open the door with great dramatic innocence (I was good at that), then turn and say 'It's the vicar, Mother,' to which she would reply: 'Don't leave him out there. Ask him to come in.'

Removing his bicycle clips he would enter the room as Dad raised himself casually from his chair and with great aplomb held out his hand in greeting, saying: 'Good evening, vicar.'

The two men would talk about the state of the nation and anything else of significance while Mother made a fresh pot of tea. This ritual would last for about 45 minutes and then the vicar would replace his cycle clips and be on his way, whereupon Dad would slide gratefully back into his armchair and heave a sigh of relief; relief that once again the vicar had not asked him why he hadn't been to church lately.

In fact, I don't think God, the church or religion were ever mentioned at these tea ceremonies. I don't know why the vicar called on us so often. Perhaps he thought that with a bit of extra effort we could easily be converted, or perhaps he just liked us. I think it is more likely that he just enjoyed a good challenge. Most people did not go to church and so it is therefore difficult to explain why both the christening of children and church weddings were nevertheless considered an absolute must.

I have always found great pleasure in going into a church and sitting peacefully while I survey the surrounding beauty. My religion has always been a quiet one. I particularly enjoy the majesty of our great cathedrals and have visited many of them. In the circle you will see Lichfield, which was the first cathedral I ever saw as a young girl in 1947. I have loved it ever since. I go back occasionally, just to see it again and renew my acquaintance with the memorial to the sleeping sisters (see Circle 50). I have also put the two Liverpool cathedrals in the circle. Each is splendid in its own way and I find the Anglican cathedral awesome. The Lady Chapel in particular contains much that is inspiring, but outside this majestic building the draw for me is Tracey Emin's sculpture of a small bronze bird atop a four-metre pole. I love it. The smallness and simplicity of this bird against the imposing backdrop of the cathedral is brilliant.

Also in the circle are representations of the old and new Coventry cathedrals. The old cathedral was destroyed during the Second World War. It was bombed on 14 November 1940 during a raid by the Germans which lasted for eleven hours. Five hundred and fifty-four people were killed and 865 were seriously injured. Almost everyone knew someone who was dead, missing or homeless. Coventry had been chosen because of its size. The Nazis needed an important city that was nevertheless small enough to be obliterated. When the new cathedral was consecrated in 1962 it was not well received by some who found it too modern, especially in such close proximity to the old. The 'spire' of the new was considered insignificant when compared to the old, but there had never been much point in giving the new cathedral a grand spire because that of the old one was still there. Only the walls remain of the body of the old building, but its spire is still open to visitors. The whole point of the new cathedral was that it was never intended to replace the old one. You cannot replace something that is still there and always will be. The old cathedral will remain as a reminder of what terrible things man is capable of doing, while the new will be a reminder of what man is capable of achieving.

For me, the beauty of the new cathedral lies in the fact that everything, both externally and internally, was designed at the same time. This includes the building, its windows and all its tapestries and accoutrements. All the gifts for the cathedral from other nations had to have their designs approved before work began. It is completely of its time. Throughout the world it symbolises co-operation and peace. What a pity that the new world, after the war, could not have been designed and rebuilt in the same way.

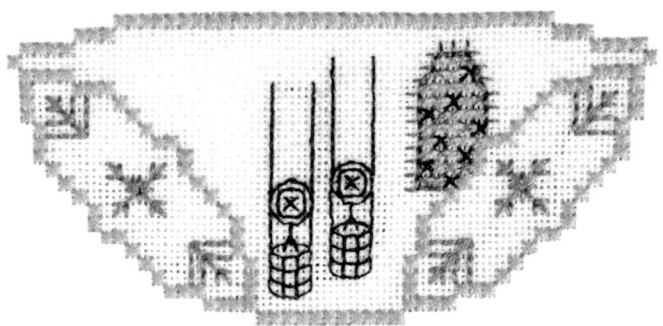

– CIRCLE 55 –

SUNDAYS

The Sundays of my childhood were something we all looked forward to. Although during my childhood Dad often had to work on Sundays, when he was at home the day was his. He was the one who made the decisions because, whatever we did, he would have to bear the cost if money was involved.

These days always began in the same way. We could not get up until we were called. After quickly washing our hands we would sit down at the kitchen table, where a cooked breakfast was laid out for us. We always had a cooked breakfast of some sort on

Sunday but, because of rationing, some Sundays were better than others.

As youngsters we had to wear our Sunday best. These clothes were only worn on Sundays and immediately made the day special. Some Sundays Dad would decide to simply clean out the sheds or tidy up the yard. If this was the case, we were free to do our own thing. But we still had to remember we were wearing our Sunday best. Whatever we did in the afternoon, we would have to be quiet as this was very much a rest period for the adults who were at home. Mother would lie on the sofa and Dad would go to bed. The silence in the streets was unbelievable. Throughout my childhood Sunday activities varied greatly, but the afternoons at home were always the same; you had to be quiet.

Dad was always happiest when he was doing something in the fresh air. He liked nothing better than tidying and reorganising the yard, but heaven help us all when Sunday was wet and cold. Before we moved to living in the front room, only one room in the house was heated and we all stayed in it. As we kids got on with some activity or other at the kitchen table, Dad would stand on the small hearth with his back to the fire and his hands in his trouser pockets. In this position he would mournfully sing one sad song after another as he gazed wistfully at the window with the rain lashing against it.

Mother would patiently keep squeezing past him as she prepared to cook dinner, but she would soon begin to get tetchy and we young ones would exchange knowing looks. Mother would start the ball rolling with the remark: 'Why don't yer sit down and let somebody else smell the fire', to which Dad would reply: 'Oh, 'er's off again.'

At this point he would start singing 'I'll Take You Home Again Kathleen'. This was guaranteed to make matters worse and

Mother would shout: 'Get out of me way while I put the meat in the oven.' He would sit down and grab a newspaper, but the minute Mother shut the oven door he would jump to his feet and reclaim his spot on the hearth.

This state of affairs would go on for a little while longer, with Mother getting more and more agitated as Dad dredged up one depressing song after another. She would finally explode with: 'Jim, will yer shut up and sit down, yoh'm getting on me nerves.'

Dad would look at her with a pained, disbelieving expression and declare loudly: 'I'm going back to bed out of yer way. Perhaps then I can have a bit of peace.'

At twelve o'clock on a wet, cold Sunday, silence would be restored and we would switch on the radio. At a quarter to two Mother would make us clear the table on which she spread out a clean white tablecloth. As she prepared to dish up, one of us would have to go and tell Dad his dinner was ready. The meal would be eaten in a pleasant enough atmosphere and by mid-afternoon, with the dishes cleared away, we would resume our activities at the table.

As the war became a distant memory Sundays took on a new meaning. We could expect a walk across the fields with the dogs until lunchtime, or a walk in the park followed by a glass of fizzy pop in the gardens of the Hen and Chickens pub. Sometimes we had the added pleasure of a visit to Dudley Zoo or a bus ride to a place we hadn't been to before.

The main purpose of these outings was to keep us out of the way while Mother got on with her work but, in reality, I think that Dad just liked our company on his jaunts. However, though these days were delightful, they were nothing when compared to the occasional pre-arranged Sunday trip when, on the day before, Dad would book seats on a train or coach to somewhere special.

From my early teens I remember two such outings. One was to Weston-super-Mare and the other to Blackpool. There was no cooked breakfast on those days, but Mother would be up at the crack of dawn making piles of sandwiches before we set off to join other families who were doing the same thing. Sometimes there might be a family on the trip that we knew and the men would address each other as Mr Brown, Mr Green and so on. It was very formal. The children had to read or talk quietly, or just sit and take in the view from the windows of the train or the coach.

When I started work many things changed, but the Sunday cooked breakfast did not. We still couldn't get up until we were called but, by then, after an evening out on the town the night before, we were in no hurry to get up anyway. If, after five minutes, you were not downstairs and seated, your breakfast was put on a tray and carried up to you. After that you were left in peace until noon. What a life.

However, I didn't always stay in bed. I would sometimes get up and go across the fields with Dad, Jim and the dogs.

The Sunday best and roast dinner have been disappearing gradually over a period of many years. Sunday best clothes seem to have gone forever and for many people the roast dinner has been replaced by something quick and convenient. I'm not suggesting this is a bad thing. For many women, including me, there is more to life than the kitchen. By the end of the twentieth century Sundays had changed in almost every respect. In my childhood the only shops that opened on a Sunday were corner newsagents, and then only until lunchtime. Now supermarkets and smaller shops are open for business until late afternoon.

Another Sunday tradition which has disappeared is the 'shortening' of babies. Shortening was the changeover from wearing long nightgowns all the time to wearing proper baby clothes during the day. This was very much dependent on the time of year; warm weather was preferred. If you were born in November or December you would not be shortened for many months. Because my brother Jim was born in August and the weather was very warm, he was shortened only three weeks after birth.

In those days nightclothes for a very young baby consisted of a warm vest, terry nappy, winceyette nightdress, knitted jacket and booties. These were worn by both boys and girls until they grew out of them. The shortening event would be announced a few days in advance. After its morning bath the baby would be dressed either in a little dress or a romper suit and would then be paraded, usually by a sibling but accompanied by the mother, around the neighbours' houses for everyone to see. If the morning was wet then the neighbours would take it in turns to see the baby at home. Older children loved this occasion. These days, or so it seems to me, babies wear baby grows for a couple of months and then they are unceremoniously plunged into whatever is fashionable. Or is it me just getting old?

Dad was a very keen cyclist. He could not resist the lure of the open road and we always had bikes. His favourite places were Bridgnorth, Ironbridge and Coalport so we ate our sandwiches in some beautiful places. However, by the time I was about nine or ten I had come to hate pedalling up those blasted hills. It was then that Dad hit on the idea of buying a tandem. He was very proud of that machine. To him it was on a par with a Rolls-Royce.

His reason for buying the tandem was that with four legs we could go faster and further. I did not quite see the logic. I still hated climbing the hills, while he looked upon them as a challenge. The minute I heard him say 'Right gel, put your back into it,' I would take my feet off the pedals and leave him to it. Halfway up the more strenuous climbs he would gasp 'Come on', to which I would whine, 'I'm doing my best'. Seconds later he would pull up and mutter: 'It's no good; we'll have to walk up.' I would say nothing, and I never did confess my actions to him. There were few cars on the roads, no motorways, and no lorries on Sundays. It was another world.

It was at about this time that Dad thought it would be a good idea if he taught Mother to ride a bike so that they could go out for short rides together. She soon got the hang of it but she was a bit wobbly and Dad thought she might feel more confident on a larger bike. So he bought her one with 28-inch wheels. This was commonly known as a 'sit up and beg'. One Sunday afternoon they set off for a test ride, the idea being that with everyone else indoors resting, no one would see them go.

Their parting words were that they would be back in about an hour and a half but Mother was back within five minutes, with a face like thunder. Dad came in a couple of minutes later. He opened his mouth to speak but Mother abruptly said: 'Before you start you can shut up and that's the end of it.'

We sat in silence for the rest of the afternoon and apart from the rustle of the newspapers you could have heard a pin drop. During tea we finally found out what had happened. As they had swung into a street further up the lane, Mother had fallen off, landed in a heap and become entangled with the bike. It was as simple as that. She was quick to add that she 'wouldn't have minded, but some silly old bugger had tried to help me up and he was only a frame of bones. You could have knocked him over with a feather.' Ted burst out laughing and in no time we were all having hysterics, Mother included. Needless to say, her cycling days were over and the bike went up for sale.

Long before we had the tandem, when I was still a novice confined to cycling in the street, Dad bought me a second-hand, but very shiny, bike. It was pale green and quite beautiful, with lots of impressive gleaming chrome. The following Sunday, having made sure it was roadworthy, Dad, Ted and I set off to see how I would cope with a longish journey. With my saddle set at its lowest position I could reach the pedals comfortably and the day went well. At about six o'clock in the evening we had to go down an extremely steep hill, which briefly levelled out at the bottom before climbing back up the other side. There were just one or two cars around, as well as some people who were out for a stroll, as we went over the brow. We didn't have to pedal but I had been told that it was important, as the bike gained momentum, to gently squeeze the back brake in order to keep control of the speed. It soon became apparent that I could not handle the speed that I was doing. Dad and Ted took up positions either side of me, even though riding three abreast was against the law, but catastrophe was looming.

I could not apply the brake no matter how I tried. A car pulled over to get out of our way as we overtook another. Dad shouted to Ted to get out in front and yell for all he was worth, which he did, and everyone scattered. My speed by this time was such that they had to pedal to keep up with me. Dad's unfastened jacket flapped in the breeze like a pair of wings. After what seemed like an eternity we finally came to a halt halfway up the hill on the other side. We dismounted and sat on the grass verge, glad to be off the road. After a few minutes Dad passed me a bottle of water and asked me what had gone wrong. I replied that the brakes wouldn't work. He replied, 'I don't understand that. They were all right when I checked it all.' He reached into his jacket pocket for a cigarette but his pockets were empty. No matches, no cigarettes and no money. He had lost everything when his jacket was flapping in the breeze. After a short rest we set off for home, with Dad beside me and Ted out in front.

The following evening after tea Dad did all the usual tests on the brakes. He knew it was not my fault and had only praise for the way I had kept a level head during the ordeal. It was only when he set the bike on blocks that he found the problem. He pedalled for all he was worth and the brake blocks simply wouldn't grip the very shiny wheel rims. He tried everything to overcome the problem but there was nothing he could do. Eventually he sold the bike but lost money on it, because he was honest enough to declare his reason for the sale. He was as sad to see it go as I was.

TELEVISION

At 3 pm on 7 June 1946 the BBC resumed its television service after the wartime suspension. For those fortunate enough to already own a TV set it must have been a wonderful moment, after looking at a blank screen for seven years. For us lesser mortals it would remain just a dream for some time to come.

The first working television we ever saw was through the window of the snooker hall in the lane. The hall had half a dozen full-size snooker tables, all properly equipped and lit. In full view from the window was an American style bar but as the owner didn't have a drinks licence he could only serve tea, coffee and soft drinks. The place was dimly lit and there, shining like a beacon in its place by the bar, was this magic box. With the keen eyesight of the young we would stand transfixed wishing we could hear what was being said. We had to do this 'on the sly' because if Mother had known about it we would have been in trouble. The snooker hall had the reputation of being a proper den of iniquity, supposedly frequented by hoodlums and spivs.

Ted came home one night at about nine o'clock. He was deathly pale and very quiet. He and another lad had been larking about outside the snooker hall when Ted was accidentally pushed against one of its big windows, cracking it. Mom and Dad were stunned, thinking that they would have to meet the cost of replacing it. The next morning Mom went to see the owner about what was to be done. He very generously said that he would not be pursuing the matter and that he would replace the glass. At this point he went up in Mother's estimation, and as she was leaving he asked her if her boy and all the other lads in the neighbourhood might be allowed onto his premises to play snooker and watch TV. It was clear that he and his establishment were not as disreputable as was generally believed. The outcome of this mishap was that for some months the chaps had a meeting place, a television set and, when they could afford it, a game of snooker.

In my last year at school I had the experience of being filmed for the programme *Children's Newsreel* which went out every Sunday at teatime. It had been arranged with the BBC that a camera crew would film a group of girls icing and decorating cakes in the cookery classroom. I was one of the girls chosen, although only my hands were seen in the bulletin that was screened. A few days before they were due to arrive, the headmistress received word that the BBC might have to cancel due to a problem with the crew that had been assigned to us. When she expressed her reluctance to break the news to the girls, who would be bitterly disappointed, Cyril Page stepped in and filled the gap. Cyril Page was the BBC's ace cameraman who filmed all the important world events and was seen as very dashing, which indeed he was. The words 'Filmed by Cyril Page' in the credits of a programme carried a great deal of prestige. We did not have a TV at the time and Mom made arrangements to take me to see the programme at the house of a friend who lived further up the lane.

As the years went by more and more TV sets were sold. When you visited friends or relatives for an evening's conversation they would say, more or less: 'Come in, sit down, shut up, it's on.' By 1953, with the Queen's coronation pending, there was a huge demand for TV sets. Pubs and cinemas nationwide became deserted. Thus began a style of living that allowed little or no conversation, as people eagerly consumed their weekly doses of Armand and Michaela Dennis, *Animal, Vegetable or Mineral, What's My Line?* and *Muffin the Mule.* However, we remained in the wilderness: Dad continued to insist that he couldn't afford a TV and on 2 June 1953 we had to be satisfied with listening to the coronation on the radio.

Dad finally succumbed and bought a 25" Ferguson in early November that same year. The television was a whopper for its time. He had only bought it because it had been announced that the Hungarian football team would be playing England at Wembley on 25 November with an evening kickoff, and the match was to be televised. It promised to be a good game because Hungary was on a run of 29 matches without defeat and England hadn't lost a match to a foreign team at home for 45 years. As it turned out, because of that game the names Puskás, Kocsis and Hidegkuti will be forever stamped on my memory.

The Hungarians gave a display of football the like of which we had never seen before. They left England standing. The picture quality was not good and we seemed to watch the entire match through a light snow shower, but the commentator kept us in the picture. At the final whistle the score was Hungary 6, England 3. Many felt that England had been lucky to get three goals. I don't think anyone minded that we had lost. Hungary was a great team.

Dad was very proud of his TV set but his pride was short-lived. The damned thing kept breaking down. Television sets were in their infancy and not very reliable. Ours seemed to be away for repair more than it was in the house. At the time, newspaper advertisements for Ferguson sets pictured a head-and-shoulders drawing of a man with a jutting chin and a smug, self-satisfied look on his face holding a pipe to his mouth at a carefree angle. In the cloud of smoke above his head were the words: 'Fine sets these Fergusons.'

Dad, a non-smoker by this time, bought himself a cheap pipe and would sit in the evenings in the same manner as the man in the advert, staring at the vacant space left by the TV. He would keep saying in sarcastic tones: 'Fine sets these Fergusons.' Mother would reply snappily, for she was missing the set more than any of us, 'Oh, for God's sake, give it a rest. Find something to do. Yoh'm getting on me nerves.'

For our first few months of TV ownership – that is, when the set was working – we lived like everyone else, sitting in a dimly lit room to make the poor quality picture look as sharp as possible. Dad was the first to get fed up. He limited his viewing to football and boxing. I quickly followed suit because when the TV was on and the light turned off I couldn't see to do my knitting and needlework. Ted and Jim always had better things to do anyway. Mother loved television and would watch it night after night, right through to the epilogue, the National Anthem and the white dot.

As the white dot disappeared from sight she would keep her eyes fixed on the blank screen. A disembodied voice would then give the warning: 'You won't forget to switch off your television set, will you? Good night.' Only then would she reluctantly switch it off. When Dad was in a bad mood he would snap at her: 'If they was to put a dollop of 'oss muck on you'd 'ave to sit and watch it in case it moved.' But nothing would move her and she remained a devotee.

I remember Colonel James Carne proudly leading the Gloucestershire Regiment through the streets of their city on a triumphant return to this country after their ordeal in Korea. They were to receive the freedom of the city. I also remember seeing film of the atrocities at Belsen and other wartime horrors, as historians began their attempts to interpret Hitler's state of mind, offering suggestions as to why he had done this or that. This speculation still goes on today. The historians live in hope that they can discover something which has so far been overlooked.

Who could forget the BBC's adaptation in 1954 of George Orwell's *Nineteen Eighty-Four*? It starred Peter Cushing, Yvonne Mitchell and Andre Morrell. Most of the country sat horrified as Big Brother did his worst. And what about all that brainwashing? Some older people actually thought it would involve a bowl of soapy water. Well, it was all just too much to cope with. Mother said, 'They hadn't ought to be allowed to put this sort of thing on the telly,' but she made no effort to leave the room or switch it off. The next day the newspapers were full of the previous evening's 'entertainment'.

In those days the BBC was the only channel. It put on a play every Sunday evening which would be repeated the following

Thursday evening. So what you watched on Sunday you would watch again on Thursday. All those poor souls (including Mom and me) who had been frightened witless the first time sat down and prepared themselves for another dose a few days later. Big Brother seems to have been watching us ever since.

It took us some time to get used to television after so many years of radio. I continued to do my knitting and needlework while listening to the TV and would glance at the screen only occasionally. Ted was always tinkering with bits of wire and switches and there wasn't much on TV to suit Jim.

Mother was blissfully contented. After seeing a group of completely naked men performing a tribal dance, she became a committed fan of this type of documentary. Dad remained very difficult to please. He was never happy with the moving picture, be it on the box or at the cinema. On many occasions he would jump out of his chair and, on leaving the room, his parting words would be: 'I can't watch any more of that. It's enough to give you the diarrhoea.'

In the circle, along with the hand of Malcolm Sargent, are some programmes and people that have been on television over the years that come easily to my mind. *The Sky at Night* has been going forever, along with nature programmes, outside broadcasts and sport. *The Saint, Inspector Morse, Prime Suspect, The Fugitive* and *The Avengers* are just five in a long list of whodunnits. The red orb represents the overpowering sun in *Tenko*. The blue and white flag is a Blue Peter, representing the children's programme. Also represented in the form of the Ministry of Funny Walks is *Monty Python*. The glasses are for Alan Wicker and the 6–5 is for *6–5 Special* which was, I believe, the first pop music programme aimed at teenagers.

We can also see a remote control and 'Bob'. This is Bob Warman, the anchorman for our local ITV news programme for

30 years, with whom I have a special bond. We are growing older together. In the circle we are now left with a rather fat man who was Landburgher Gessler from the series *The Adventures of William Tell*. This was a popular series of 39 episodes which were shown between 1958 and 1959. Landburgher was the man we loved to hate as he went about collecting exorbitant taxes from Swiss peasants; he was played by Willoughby Goddard. William Tell, the hero, was played by Conrad Phillips whose ultimate weapon, greatly admired by the viewers, was a state-of-the-art crossbow which made a terrific swooshing sound when it was fired.

These days there is more choice, due to an increasing number of channels. But most evenings there is nothing on worth watching because I live in one of those parts of the country where Freeview and Channel Five are still not available to those who do not wish to pay extra. While televisions might have got bigger the programmes are not better. Do-it-yourself and garden makeover shows have come and gone. Soaps occupy the largest number of hours with endless chapters in a never-ending ritual of births, marriages and deaths, and 'reality' programmes are nothing like reality. In the meantime, repeats of old programmes help to fill the gap while we continue to live in hope.

UNDER

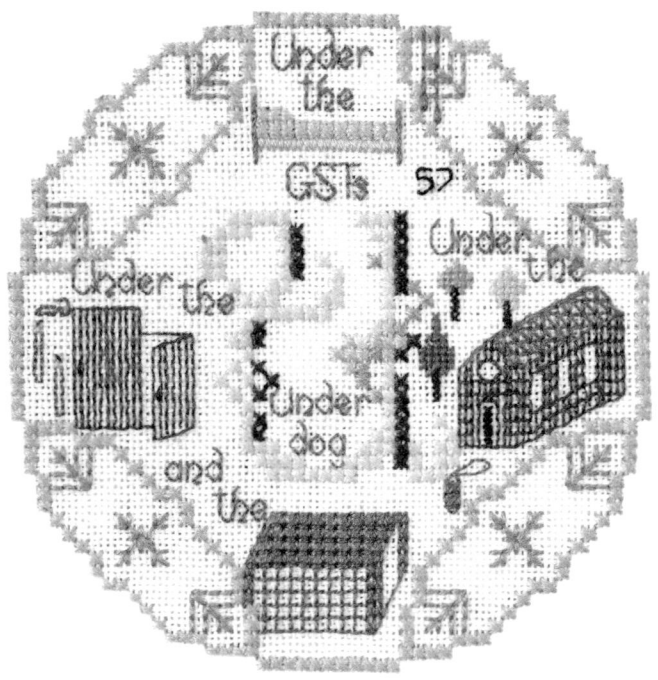

It seemed reasonable to use my memories of sheltering during air raid warnings as a subject for the circle containing the letter 'U'. I seem to have spent much of the early years of my life, whether hiding or otherwise, under something. Ted and I spent many evenings under the kitchen table pretending to be in a different world all of our own. The real world was in such a parlous state that it was often good to escape to the world under the table.

We did have an air raid shelter in the street. With its brick walls and flat concrete roof, it looked like all the other shelters that were springing up in many areas. Ours was built for residents and the many workers from the factories, but we only went to it once. Mother carried me in. It was very dimly lit and packed solid with people from the pubs in the lane and night shift workers. The smell was very unpleasant and the air was thick with cigarette smoke. One man reached out to take me from Mother but I would not go to him. Another suggested that she sit me on one of the bunks, but again I clung on.

When the 'all clear' sounded Mother carried me back to our house on one arm and held Ted's hand with the other, muttering: 'That's the last time we do that. If we're going to meet our maker we'll do it in better surroundings than that.' It was well known that some air raid shelters had received direct hits, with disastrous results. Mom may have seen the conditions in our shelter as a good reason not to return to it. Those who had cellars would take refuge in them, and we did spend one night in a neighbour's cellar, but it seemed that Mother now felt safe only in her own house.

The worst night for our town came in November 1940. Fifty-four people died, many of them in one area. People from one street were sheltering in their cellars when the street took a hit from a high-explosive bomb. As well as the untold damage this caused to buildings in this heavily populated area, it also ruptured the gas mains and the water mains. People were either drowned in their cellars or gassed while trying to escape from them. One young boy was awarded a bravery medal for holding his younger sister's head above water for several hours while they were trapped in one of the cellars. When help finally arrived, though, the girl was dead.

That night a local girl became a national heroine. She had been an ARP messenger since the age of fourteen. She had lied about her age, since in order to be an ARP messenger you had to be sixteen. She was one of seven messengers who took messages from one ARP post to another on a bicycle. Her uniform was a tin hat and an armband. On the night in question she was blown off her bike several times because of enemy action, and it is said that she threw three or four unexploded incendiary bombs over a wall away from a row of houses. Her name was Charity Bick and she was awarded the George Medal for bravery above and beyond the call of duty. The medal can be given only to people over the age of sixteen but since she was really only fifteen at the time of the incident, she will always be the youngest person ever to receive this award. A portrait of Charity and her bike is held by the Imperial War Museum. I am of the opinion now that the night in question was also the night when our own street had a visit from the Luftwaffe (see Circle 29).

On the left side of this circle are two doors. The door to the stairs is closed. The open door leads to the cupboard under the stairs. If an air raid warning sounded, we would crouch in the cupboard. Ted could always tell from the sound of the planes whether they were ours or not, and it was always a relief when he calmly said: 'They'm ours.' Sometimes we would hear German planes droning overhead and, after a period of silence, we would hear bombs going off in the distance. Mom would sigh and say, 'Somebody's getting it,' but, sensing our concern, would quickly add: 'But it's not us, not tonight.' A little time later the planes would return. This time the drone would sound somehow lighter. They had done their worst.

We spent many evenings like this. Mother would sit on a very low stool, and Ted and I would sit on old cushions. He would be in charge of the candle. Although we were not comfortable I believe we all felt safe. If we had an air raid warning when Dad was at home, he would never sit in this cupboard with us. In this confined space, with the door almost closed, we were never shut in and we could hear him pottering about in the kitchen. Sometimes he would softly hum the tune of an old song. A couple of times we heard planes coming that were particularly low, and on giving us the order 'Get your heads down,' he would crawl under the table until the danger had passed.

There was a point during the London blitz when all householders in our area were asked if they could take an occasional evacuee from the capital to give them a brief respite from the nightly bombing raids. Mother declined because we had no spare room. But one of the neighbours, who had no more space than we did, decided that not enough was being done. She volunteered to take 'one female', thinking that she would hear no more about it. However, she was taken aback a few days later when she received a letter saying that 'one female' would be arriving the following day. Clutching the letter she approached Mother with the words: 'You'll have to help me out Ann, I can't take her.'

As it happened, Dad was doing a period of fire-watching duty at the factory so Mother decided that she would have Ted and me in her bed, which left our room free for this 'one female'. Mom said she was only doing it this once, and it was up to the neighbour to explain when the evacuee arrived.

Trixie arrived the following afternoon. I vaguely remember her as being about sixteen or seventeen years old. She was very pretty, with longish dark hair. She and Mom got on well and her two-night stay was successful. I think that the two of them reached some sort of agreement that Trixie could come again when Dad was on fire-watching duty. A couple of times she brought her aunt Olive with her. Olive was buxom, loud and good fun. One night when they were both with us we had an air raid warning, and all of us managed to squeeze into the cupboard under the stairs. It was a tight fit and I remember that I had to sit on the floor between Mother's legs. The three women chatted away as if it was the most natural thing in the world to sit wedged under a staircase in an old house listening to bombs going off in the distance. This particular evening the conversation came to an abrupt halt when Mother had a bout of cramp in one of her legs. The only way she could get out was if we all got out first. It was then decided that we would take the risk and go back to bed. We had just settled down when the all clear sounded and we were left in peace for the rest of the night. Trixie continued to write to Mother but eventually we heard no more, and I have often wondered if she and Olive survived the war. I will probably never know.

Because the space under the stairs was inadequate Dad applied for a Morrison shelter. This was a table the size of a double bed. It was made of steel and a family of four or five could spend a night under it, lying on a mattress. It was erected in our front room. Although it filled the room, it was very useful. Ted and I slept under it most nights and if there was an air raid Mom and Dad, if he was at home, would creep in with us.

If there was an air raid warning while we were at school, we had been drilled to form a line calmly, in pairs, with our gas masks over our shoulders. Holding hands, we would walk out of the school, cross the road, go to the church hall (which is on the right of the circle), and take our seats in the cellars. I don't recall this happening very often. We looked upon it as an adventure and a means of escaping classes for a while. We would sometimes practise putting our gas masks on. Of necessity they were very tight, so that the lethal fumes from escaping gas would be prevented from entering. I hated putting mine on. It was very claustrophobic and I found it difficult to breathe when wearing it.

I hung onto every word that was spoken when something was

happening in the war. I could tell from the way the words were spoken whether I should be worried or not. Ted seemed to sense this and always spoke with reassuring authority. (In 1940 he was just eight years old.) He would explain everything to me. There were times when all of the adults would be looking worn and talking in whispers, and he would tell me why.

At the end of May 1940 I knew that there was something going on at a place called Dunkirk. Dad came in one dinnertime and said to Mom: 'Have you heard the news?' Mom nodded and sighed. Dad went on, 'It makes you wonder where this lot is going to end.' I don't pretend to remember the events at Dunkirk; I only knew that Mom and Dad were worried and so was everyone else around me, and Ted explained it all to me. However, Ted would sometimes take advantage of his role as my informer.

I would not go to bed at night until either Mom or Dad had taken me upstairs and assured me that there was nothing under my bed, for Ted had convinced me that my bed would be the likeliest place for a bunch of German storm troopers to hide. Dad, on his knees, would look me directly in the eye and tell me that there was no one there, but I would reply: 'You haven't looked properly. Where's your torch? I want to see for myself.' This ritual went on and on; coming face to face with a bunch of German storm troopers was the greatest fear of my early life. With their square helmets and their strutting 'goose step', which we saw on cinema newsreels, they didn't seem to me to be human.

VICTORY

The Second World War came to an end with the surrender of Japan. For a little while the euphoria was wonderful; now we would get back to normal. Normality had been promised enough times during the conflict.

But then I realised that I had no recollection of what a normal life was actually like. In the event, for the rest of the 1940s and into the 1950s, it turned out to be the life I had known but without the fighting and bombing. In celebration of the victories in Europe and Japan we had earlier had a VE party and a VJ party, and that was it.

Some houses had a Union Jack in the window along with a piece of cardboard with handwritten words such as 'Welcome Home Bill', which was nice but very sad for those women whose men would not be returning. For them, all that the future held was the continued struggle of being both mother and sole bread-winner. I have always thought that the wording on the tomb of the Unknown Soldier should read: 'The unknown soldier, and his wife and family.' There were millions of them all over the world and this had been the true cost of the war.

Many of the men who returned from abroad were not the same men who had left. Some repatriated servicemen were virtual strangers to their wives and families and vice versa. Some had been physically badly disfigured. Many of these had become members of the Guinea Pig Club which was part of the work of Archibald McIndoe, a plastic surgeon whose patients had suffered serious burns causing grave facial disfigurement. At the war's end his work continued.

Much of his genius lay in his recognition that these men also needed help with social reintegration. Some men who came home were broken in spirit and their problems were not so obvious. The 'FG' in the circle represents a man who had spent a long period of the war as a prisoner of the Japanese. I had been told what a nice man he was. He was married to a woman who lived in the lane, who had received word that he was back in Britain but would not be allowed to return home or have visitors for a while as he needed 'building up a bit'. This was just another example of understatement that, at that time, the working classes accepted without explanation.

However, the day dawned when he was expected home; we were on holiday from school. He was due to arrive in the late morning and we excitedly gathered at the top of the street as his wife waited on her doorstep. All of us could clearly see the bus stop further up the lane, but the buses came and went and there was no sign of him. At 12.30 we went home to have dinner, and when we took up our positions again afterwards there were just a few children and no adults. In time a bus pulled up and we saw a man in a khaki uniform get off and raise his kit bag up onto his shoulder. He was here! Some of us ran off to fetch our mothers and one went to tell FG's wife. It was a joyful scene. All of us were cheering and he looked so happy. He had the most beautiful face.

The next day he spent some time just standing on the doorstep looking around and speaking to people that he had known before the war. The day after that his wife had two black eyes and he had stopped smiling. And that was that. Like many other wives, his had become a punch bag as he struggled with his horrendously troubled mind. Some time later he died, never having recovered from his physical and mental experiences at the hands of the Japanese. His illness was such that nobody could understand what he was going through.

I have never forgotten FG. He comes to the surface of my mind now and again. Like so many others, his name never appeared on any roll of honour or memorial stone, for he had not died in a war.

Throughout my life I have watched men fighting in wars and battles on cinema newsreels and television. To sit and watch mankind's continual efforts to destroy his own species is heart-breaking when you remember those who, like FG, gave their all.

No other species on earth does this.

– CIRCLE 59 –

WARWICK

I arrived at my new home in Warwick at the end of September 1998. My husband Ray had died in 1996 and during the intervening two years I had tried very hard to make a life for myself, but I was just so desperately unhappy. I came to the conclusion that the only thing I could do was to move on, and Warwick seemed as good a place as any. Jim asked me what I would do if I didn't like it, and I told him I would just keep moving on until I found a place where I could be happy. Fortunately, I found it first time.

I didn't know anyone in Warwick when I went there; I had

health problems and I didn't much care about anything one way or the other. I was drifting from day to day and had no purpose in life. I had only been to Warwick once before, when Ray and I had visited it some fifteen years earlier. I had never forgotten that, as we took in its beauty, he had said, 'I could live here.' Ray's words were my only reason for moving there.

Early on I found getting up the hills to be a bit of a problem but I was in no doubt that I had found good neighbours, and thus began my process of settling in. Having registered with a doctor I asked him if he thought I had made a mistake by moving here, and he said that it would probably be the best decision I had ever made. He was right. Eventually I was taking the hills in my stride. I did a great deal of walking and discovered that Warwick has a surprise around almost every corner. I spent time in the castle and its grounds and I fell in love with St Mary's church, which has an atmosphere that is uniquely its own. I was also fascinated by the Lord Leycester Hospital, which probably dates from the sixteenth century. There have been buildings on the site for about three or four hundred years but in 1571 the Earl of Leicester, Robert Dudley, acquired them. There he founded the Hospital to house twelve retired or infirm soldiers or seamen, and it is still used for this purpose today. The buildings do not appear to have changed since they were first erected, and they are beautiful. Surrounded by all this grandeur and beauty, the most significant event for me, which happened just a few days after my arrival, was meeting Betty Warner.

I had found a most excellent needlework shop not far from home, and had popped in to get a feel for the place when another customer spoke to me. This was Betty. We chatted for a few minutes, and then I left. After going to other shops for food I popped into the curtain fabric shop for some hooks, and there she was again. We chatted for a while once more and exchanged phone numbers. I think we both knew then that this would be a lifelong friendship. She is one of those rare people who give consideration to others without thinking. Through Betty I found many new friends who make up a small craft group which meets every Friday morning at the Leek Wootton Sports Club.

Leek Wootton is a lovely village situated between Kenilworth and Warwick, and the sports club has a cricket field which, for me, sums up a perfect English summer's day. This is probably due to the pampering it gets from those who care for it. Even languishing in winter it still looks mollycoddled. It is one of my favourite views because it simply oozes peace and tranquillity.

No matter what the craft, there is always someone in the group who is capable of doing it. I filled a number of half-circles around the edge of the tapestry with depictions of some of the things that the 'Ladies of Leek Wootton' have made. These include embroidery, patchwork, dressmaking, knitting (socks tend to be popular as winter approaches), chenille work, restoring an altar cloth and making greetings cards for all occasions. One of these half-circles is a memorial to two friends who have died. Another celebrates a friend's love of music. One is a rather convoluted tribute to Richard Gere, of whom one of the ladies is very fond. Struggling to figure out how I could depict the American actor, I settled on allusions to *Pretty Woman* – Roy Orbison's dark glasses and a red dress (another one of Angela's brilliant ideas).

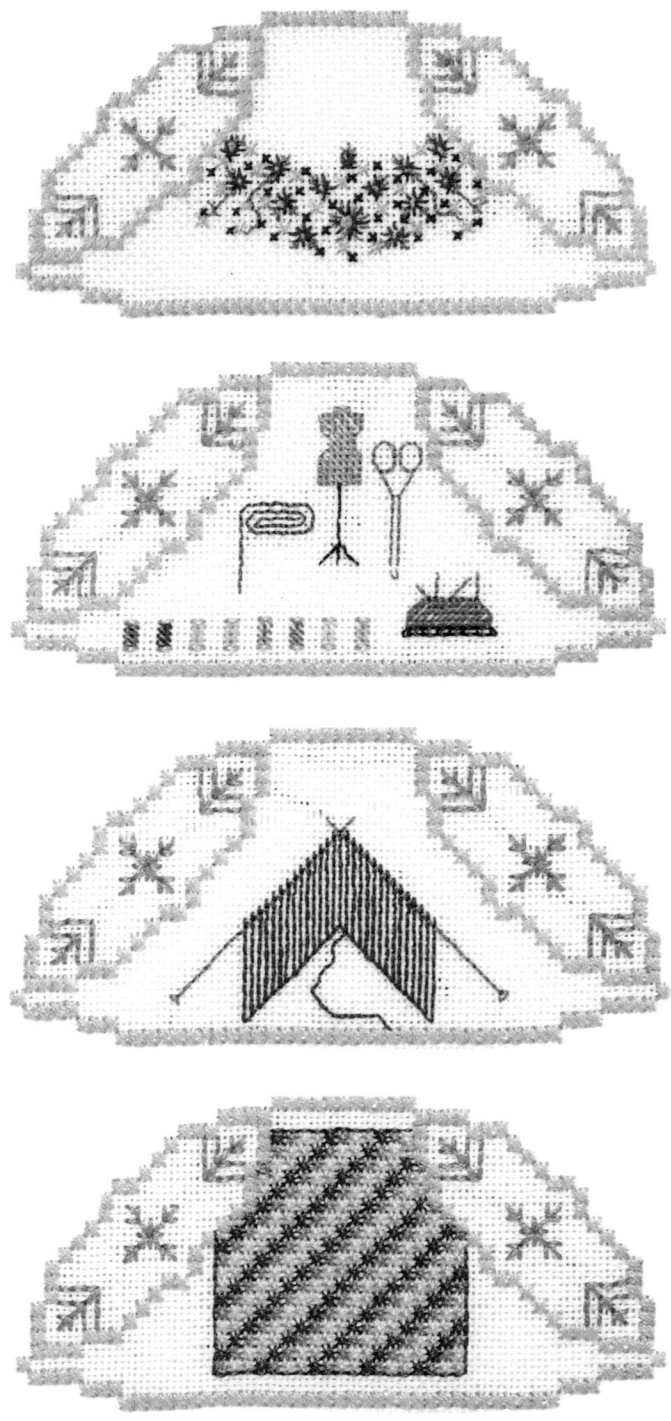

Having found my circle of new friends, I started to settle. I began to create the girl on the wall in cross-stitch, not realising at the time how important this work was going to prove. When it was finished, and having found Warwickshire College on one of my jaunts, I became aware that the world really was my oyster.

EXTREMES

It was difficult to find something interesting for the circle beginning with the letter 'X'. After much deliberation I decided to
cheat and use it to depict 'Extremes', interpreted as extreme
disasters. There have been many disasters in my lifetime, but
these are the ones I remember most clearly. Some are man-made
tragedies and others are acts of nature. Some are both.

Extreme weapons

We knew that atom bombs were in the making before America
dropped the bomb on the Japanese city of Hiroshima on 6

August 1945, from a B-29 bomber with the name Enola Gay. There was a buzz as the news went around the world. A second bomb was dropped on 9 August over Nagasaki and Japan formally gave its unconditional surrender six days later. In my eight-year-old mind I had naively envisaged that the damage would be similar to that inflicted on Coventry over a period of eleven hours, but this time it would be done with only one bomb. Like everyone else, I had not expected the mushroom cloud. When I first saw this in a cinema newsreel I realised that I had grossly underestimated its potential. As we celebrated the end of the war we could not appreciate the consequences of such a weapon. Pictures began appearing in newspapers of people suffering from radiation sickness and other horrors that had been unleashed by the bomb. It became obvious that the threat of this weapon would hang over us for evermore, and that it was something we would have to learn to live with.

Extreme terrorism
There have been terrorist acts of many kinds throughout my life-time. To me the Blitz was an example of prolonged terrorism. Many times such actions would shock the world. But the extreme ter-rorism seen on 11 September 2001 was of a different dimension. I have no need to go into detail: how can anyone who witnessed it ever forget it? While the death toll from that day hovers between 2,000 and 3,000, I am mindful of the fact that during the Second World War the average daily death toll for five and a half years (some 2,000 days) was much the same, and at no time during this period did my family or I become hardened to it.

Extreme disaster involving children
In October 1966 a slag heap consisting of millions of tons of black sludge slithered down a hillside at Aberfan in Wales,

engulfing a row of houses and a school to a depth of over 40 feet. Of the 147 killed, 116 of them were children. Heavy rain was blamed for the tragedy, but a tribunal came to the unanimous conclusion that the site for dumping the mine's waste was badly sited and revealed that an underground stream, swollen by the rain, had destabilised the foundations of the heap. Waste was being added to it at the very moment when the tip began to slide. The victims of this catastrophe drew sympathy from the whole world. As we watched the rescue efforts on television that night, knowing that there was little hope, I think every parent in the country looked at their own children and tried to imagine the agonies that the parents in Aberfan were going through. I don't think a nation ever felt as helpless as we did that night.

Extreme sporting disaster
The greatly anticipated football match at Hillsborough stadium on 15 April 1989 was an FA Cup semi-final between Liverpool and Nottingham Forest. What makes the memory of this tragedy so lasting is that the whole catastrophe, both inside the ground and out, was televised. The makings of an immense tragedy were already in place before the kickoff. When the referee blew the whistle to start the game there was a huge roar from the crowd which led to a massive surge forward by those outside still trying to get in which, in turn, swept along those already inside. The crush of people behind those spectators at the metal perimeter fence began the process which resulted in the deaths of 96 Liverpool supporters. It was one of those unbelievable tragedies that it was difficult to get to grips with.

Extreme storm
On the last day of January 1953 a spring tide, a tidal surge and northerly winds of over 100 miles an hour contributed to a wide-

spread disaster. Great waves hit the coast of Holland claiming the lives of 1,794 people, and in Belgium the death toll was 27. In Britain the flooding spread down the east coast from the Humber to the Thames estuary. Rivers in East Anglia broke their banks, and sea defences at Hunstanton, Heacham and Snettisham were unable to cope. King's Lynn was swept by a tidal surge, Canvey Island was devastated and the lighthouse in the harbour at Margate was destroyed. 307 people died that night in Britain, and many others lost everything as their homes were washed away. In response to distress calls, helicopters were put into action by the United States and Switzerland, lifting stranded people from rooftops. In the Irish Sea, MV *Princess Victoria* went down with 300 passengers and crew.

Extreme tornado
In America's Midwest, 324 people were killed in an eight-hour period during the night of 2–3 April 1974. The cause of so much death and destruction was not one tornado or even two, but 100 – reaching from Alabama to Ontario, just over the Canadian border. The death toll was highest in those areas that had had no experience of a tornado. Those used to these storms know when and where to take shelter as warnings are issued.

Extreme earthquake
The Armenian earthquake on 7 December 1988 measured nine on the Richter scale. Armenia was then part of the Soviet Union and the death toll was officially put at 50,000. The devastation was blamed on poor building construction. Within days the Soviet president, Mikhail Gorbachev, formally asked for humanitarian aid which was provided by several countries. This was the first such request since the start of the Cold War, which revealed just how bad the situation was.

Extreme tsunami

I have shown the Boxing Day tsunami of 2004 in the way it was described by those who witnessed it: as a wall of water. It has been suggested that the energy that created this tsunami was equivalent to that of thousands of atom bombs. The wave was caused by a mega-thrust earthquake, measuring 8.9 on the Richter scale, which occurred on the bed of the Indian Ocean. This triggered a massive sea upsurge that would speed across the ocean and devastate fourteen countries across two continents. The death toll was placed between 230,000 and 300,000.

However, if there is anything I have learned from these tragedies it is that the real death toll is often much higher than the estimates.

– CIRCLE 61 –

YANKS AND THE COOK SHOP

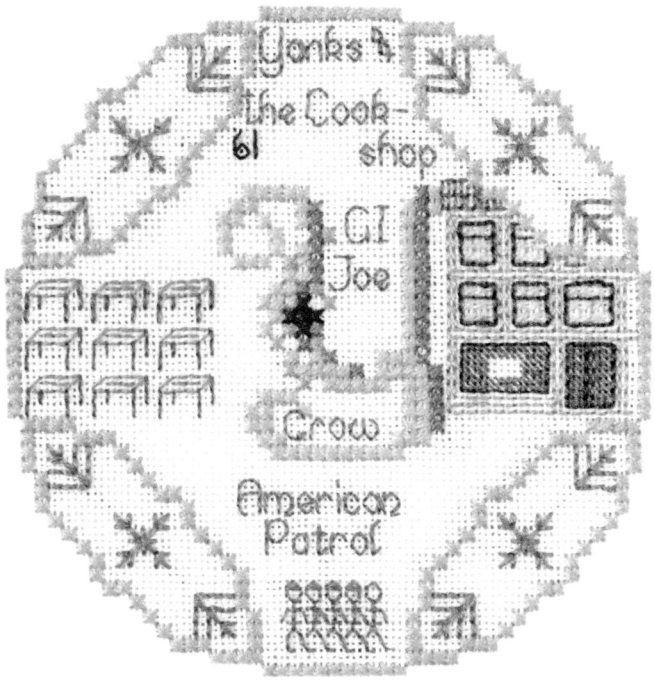

The Japanese attacked the major US naval base at Pearl Harbor in December 1941, leading America to declare war on Japan. Germany and Italy then declared war on America.

America was suddenly facing a war on two fronts. American servicemen were sent to the Pacific, and also began arriving in Britain in the spring of 1942. Those who were eventually billeted in our area would have worked at the Air Force signal supply depot in Smethwick. Its official name was USAAF Station 522 and it was situated in Beakes Road. It was in operation from August 1943 until the end of the war, supplying and repairing signal equipment required by American forces in Britain, and was also responsible for the supply of radio and radar equipment. Half a dozen men who worked there were billeted at the cook shop.

I don't remember the cook shop ever being open for business, though according to Mother before the war the shop had sold wonderful things like groaty pudding, faggots and peas and grey peas and bacon. We could look through the uncovered windows into a large room and see many tables and chairs in neat rows. On the right hand side there was a counter and, apart from a door which probably led to the kitchen, that was all there was to see. It was a large building with three floors. A woman lived there with her father. Her name was Rene, she may have been anywhere between 35 and 40 years old and she kept herself to herself. Her father (we never knew his name) was withdrawn and quiet, but was nevertheless quite a colourful character. He always wore richly embroidered hats with matching waistcoats. He also had a wooden leg, from just below the knee. This was very Long John Silver-like in style, ornately turned like a chair leg. We always called him 'Peg-leg'.

The servicemen billeted at the cook shop all seemed so handsome, clean and smart. They walked with such a jaunty swagger that they appeared to be from another planet. I found them awesome. It was reported that they had heaps of chocolate and ate butter, not margarine. They were also supposed to have endless supplies of sugar and pineapple chunks. Lucky blighters. All the teenage girls in the area paraded up and down the lane when they were about, hoping to catch their eye. Mother warned me to keep away from them 'because they have some very funny habits', but I couldn't resist standing in the lane with the other children in the hope that they might give us some chewing gum as they passed by.

How I envied those older girls. The Americans would take them to the cinema and they could have all the chocolate and chewing gum they wanted: all for nothing! Everything about the 'Yanks' was glamorous. The way they dressed, the way they talked, what they ate, everything. But as soon as the war in Europe was over they were gone, and that was that.

A few weeks after the war ended Mr and Mrs Trigger, who owned the local chip shop, joined forces with Rene and together they decided to give all the children in the neighbourhood a special treat. It was promised that, one Saturday afternoon when the necessary supplies of food could be arranged, the Triggers would give each child a fish-and-chip lunch. Rene would allow us to use her shop and would also supply mushy peas and bread and butter, together with a cup of tea and a piece of cake. It was quite unbelievable. Many of us knew the pleasures of a bag of chips but the poorer children would always have had to share a bag. There were not many of us who had savoured the delights of a whole fish with chips. A few children had a problem supplying their own crockery and cutlery, but other families rallied round and no child was left out.

On the great day we scrambled through the cook shop doors clutching our plates and grabbing the first available seat, our happy chatter adding to the excitement. As the Triggers and a couple of helpers brought in the food, the smell made every nose in the room twitch. To this day the smell of hot sizzling chips has an intense effect on me. Salt and vinegar was liberally sprinkled and the atmosphere was wonderful. Those who had made it all possible stood by the counter with their arms folded across their chests, flushed with success. Outside some of the mothers stood watching their children happily tucking in, probably wishing they could join them.

On a warm early July day, just after dinner, old Peg-leg died. I was eleven years old. Mother was asked if she would lay him out. She had been called on by others before to perform the same service. She washed the body and discovered that his wooden leg was a permanent fixture. She thought nothing of it, but when the undertaker arrived he refused to handle the body until the wooden leg had been removed. Mother had no alternative but to fetch one of Dad's saws and cut it off, leaving just a stump of wood. At first she had complained about having to do this, but when they increased the price they would pay for her services she shut up and got on with it.

That afternoon left me very disappointed because, while all this was going on, it was open day at my school. I sat waiting for her to show up since that year, as it was such an important one for me (see Circle 45), she had promised faithfully to come. I left the school that afternoon very downcast.

Back home Mother was busy at the table when I entered the kitchen. I gave her a withering look and, as I saw her hackles rise, I said: 'Why didn't you come?'

'Oh, don't start,' she replied.

'Well, you did promise,' I said, plaintively.

'I've been promised a lot of things in my life but I didn't get them.'

'Why didn't you come?' I asked again.

'Oh, shut up,' she said, as tears began stinging my eyes. She then proceeded to explain. I couldn't believe what I was hearing.

'Couldn't someone else have done it?' I asked. 'You're not the only woman who can deal with a dead body.'

'That's enough!' she snapped, and I knew that the conversation was at an end.

When I reflected on it later, it was just common sense that if she had had a choice between me and a one-legged corpse, and she was being paid for dealing with the corpse, then there could be little doubt as to who would get preferential treatment. What made it worse for me was knowing that we were not so hard up that Mother was desperate for the money.

ZAIRE

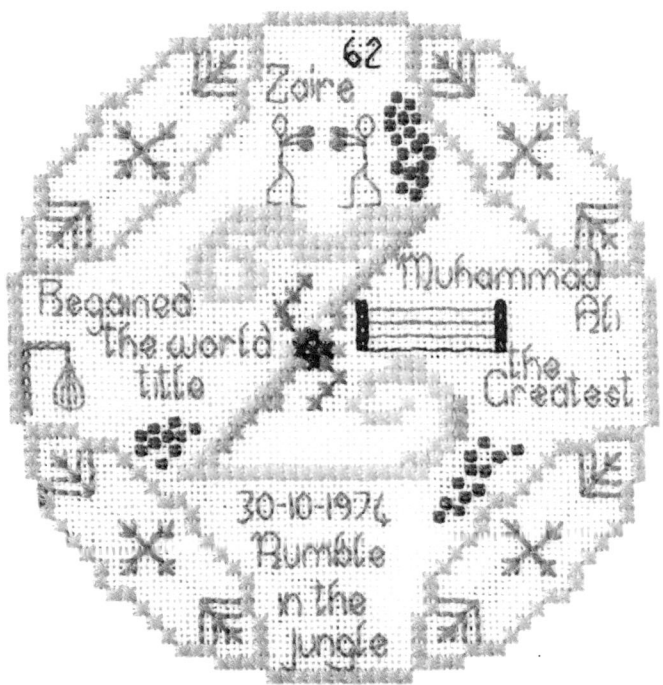

This is another slightly contrived title. The obvious choice for 'Z' would have been 'Zoo', but although I could have done embroidery and written a lengthy piece on the zoo in Dudley it might not have been very interesting. Angela, knowing of my admiration for Muhammad Ali, made the inspired suggestion of 'Zaire'.

Ali was born in Louisville, Kentucky on 17 January 1942. After winning the light heavyweight boxing gold medal at the 1960 Olympics in Rome he began his professional boxing career, using the name given to him at birth which was Cassius Clay. He declared to everyone that he was the greatest. Unfortunately he said it so many times and so loudly that he gained the nickname 'the Louisville Lip'.

I was among those who could see that this was the greatest publicity stunt ever devised; his antics were putting 'bums on seats'. At that point most people would have paid any amount of money to see him get a beating just to shut him up. Mother was one such person. She detested him. No matter how many times I told her why she was wrong, she could not see it.

When Ali beat the world champion, Sonny Liston, in February 1964, the Boxing Commission refused to accept it as a championship fight because of the way it ended. When the bell was sounded for the seventh round Liston refused to leave his corner and spat out his gum shield. Many thought that he had thrown the fight. The commissioners said it would have to be fought again and a return match was arranged. When they fought for the second time Ali knocked out Liston in the first round and it had to be accepted. Ali was declared world champion at the age of 22.

By 1967 two things dominated the headline news in America and in other parts of the world. One was the war in Vietnam, in which America was heavily involved, and for which it was being heavily criticised. The other was the civil rights movement under the leadership of Martin Luther King. Ali refused to enrol for active service when he was called up in March that year, claiming that the Vietnam War was America's way of making a return to colonialism.

Like King, he had the ability to hold the attention of a crowd. He made the point that, in exchange for the barest minimum of civil rights, blacks were expected to die for their country. He used phrases such as: 'Ain't no Viet Cong ever called me nigger'. In doing so he defined his own loyalties and came to represent those who, while having no quarrel with the Vietnamese, certainly had a grievance against the US government.

Having established his reasons for not going into the army, he became an inspiration to others who felt the same way. The New York State Athletic Commission suspended his licence and stripped him of his title in April 1967. Unfortunately for them, they had underestimated Ali's popularity. Robbing him of his right to continue boxing merely raised his profile throughout the world.

Joining the war in Vietnam was America's way of showing its military superiority over the communists, regardless of the loss of life and the degradation of the fighting men. Communism had always been a thorn in the side of America. This was apparent during the McCarthy era between 1950 and 1954, but was made even clearer by the fanatical way in which America's military leaders had tried to obliterate the communists in Vietnam. It was this fanaticism that made all those due for military service consider their own position, not simply black Americans. And it was Muhammad Ali who had made them realise that this was not just a civil rights protest: it was personal.

Black and white students began fighting for their own civil rights. In so doing, the civil rights movement also became the anti-Vietnam War movement. Throughout all of this, Ali kept his dignity while still keeping himself in trim. Eventually he did box again when his licence was restored but he was not given back his title, even though to millions he was still champion of the world.

By 1974 the world title belonged to George Foreman. Ali had done some boxing in the intervening years and in that year it was decided that he would try to retake the title. Foreman was a popular fighter. He and Ali were friends and Ali knew that Foreman was good. The fight was arranged for 30 October 1974 in Kinshasa, Zaire. The bout generated a great deal of publicity and hype. People talked about 'the rumble in the jungle' and 'the fight of the century'.

Against the odds, Ali regained his title and was back on top where he belonged. The war in Vietnam had come to an end with the signing of an agreement in Paris on 27 January 1973. The last of the American combat troops were pulled out two weeks later and the last of the US advisers were gone by April 1975.

At the end of the twentieth century a BBC viewers' poll voted Muhammad Ali the greatest sportsman of the twentieth century. This was repeated in polls taken in many other countries throughout the world. Few argued with these results. He still has the respect of millions.

THE SEVENTIES

In the seventies there was more human misery than this country could cope with at times, with ever-increasing unemployment and little improvement in living conditions for some. The workers were continually called out on strike by their trades unions and everyone was affected in some way by one strike or another.

In 1973 the miners' union brought down Edward Heath's Conservative government. This was a powerful display of union might, but the employment crisis deepened. To keep shareholders happy and in an effort to remain productive, efficient and competitive in world markets, industry bosses deployed more and more automation. This eventually led to fewer and fewer jobs. These situations were with us at the start of the decade and would continue right through to the end.

Under the circumstances it was not surprising that we had little interest in the launch of the Apollo 13 mission to the moon. Well, let's face it, we had seen it all before. Apollo 13 was launched on 11 April 1970, less than a year after Apollo 11's successful mission to the moon. Although the crew could not accomplish their mission, Apollo 13 still made history. It is remembered for the heroic recovery of Jim Lovell, Fred Haise and Jack Swigert from a desperate situation which they were not expected to survive. The phrase spoken by Lovell, 'Houston, we have a problem', became as familiar as Armstrong's 'giant leap'. Their plight gripped the world. On 17 April we sat glued to our television set on the evening when the astronauts were expected to re-enter earth's atmosphere. We experienced raw emotions yet again as we endured the period of nerve-racking silence from the command module. The radio eventually crack-led back into life. Relief.

It has been said that getting the three men back to earth safely was the greatest achievement of all the Apollo missions, while I think that Apollo 13 was a timely reminder that these missions were not the piece of cake that earlier flights had led us to believe.

A much-needed highlight of the sporting world in the seventies was afforded by Red Rum, the National Hunt racehorse. This magnificent horse had a distinct personality and he became a firm favourite with the British public. He won the Grand National in 1973, 1974 and 1977, and came second in the years 1975 and 1976.

In 1973 a wonderful book was published, and I got quite carried away when I was doing the circle for this decade. Illustrated by Alan Aldridge and written by William Plommer, *The Butterfly Ball* had 28 dazzlingly dressed insects and small animals ready for the summer ball.

How you remember the summer of 1976 depends very much on how you like your weather. When the heat wave began, many people were pleased and made the most of it, but it went on for too long. I was not happy with it and was constantly trying to stay in the shade. Standpipes appeared, accompanied by fraught nerves. Disease threatened. An occasional light shower would have been welcome, but we didn't see any rain at all and rivers and reservoirs began to dry up. There were forest and woodland fires. Before this summer began we had already been on drought alert, due to the previous dry summer followed by a dry spring. Warnings of crop failures had begun to spread, so I was relieved to wake one morning at the end of August to find it raining. I stood in the garden in my dressing gown, so glad of this small offering and praying that we would have more. There was relief all round even from me, much as I hated storms, when a series of thunderstorms began, followed by two months of rain. We were back to normal. But the misery of the decade did not go away.

By the end of the seventies we had seen a decade of unrivalled confrontations, strike action, disputes and unremitting rage. Because of industrial action during the Winter of Discontent in 1979 there was a breakdown of the basic functions of a supposedly civilised country. The dead were allowed to pile up in their coffins unburied, to the grief of their loved ones. Black bin bags of household waste and other rubbish clogged up the streets and rats had a field day as their numbers increased. When the Labour prime minister Jim Callaghan came back from abroad he was asked by a reporter what he was going to do about the crisis. He was reported to have replied: 'Crisis. What crisis?' This gave the Conservatives a massive popularity boost. In time the Conservatives issued posters showing long dole queues with the caption 'Labour isn't working', and Margaret Thatcher was installed in Downing Street by the beginning of May 1979.

The best and most appropriate description I have ever heard of this decade, which sums it up perfectly, is the observation that it was a hangover from the sixties. I have no idea who said it but, like everyone else, I was not sad to see the decade end.

I watched as the seventies went by. I threw myself into my roles as a wife and mother and, as all wives and mothers do, sacrificed much of my sense of identity and whatever ambition I might have had. I knew that if I was going to do anything else with my life it would have to wait until I had no responsibilities.

THE EIGHTIES

The eighties were a continuation of the strife and dire events of the seventies. There was simply no let-up. I just kept my head down and got on with life. Two things which were impossible to ignore dominated the first half of the eighties, and though they did not find their way into the circle they cannot be disregarded. The first was racial conflict and the second was unemployment in Britain. The unemployment figure for 1980 was 1,590,000. By 1981 it had jumped to 2,422,000. The numbers peaked in 1985 at 3,149,000. Racial conflict in the eighties began in April 1980 in the

St Paul's area of Bristol. Alarming skirmishes continued in various places throughout the country for a very long period before the 1985 riots at Broadwater Farm estate in Tottenham, London. I have no desire to go into the ins and outs of unemployment or racial violence but will say that, while they were happening, they dominated the lives of everyone, both black and white.

Women made their presence felt at the Greenham Common RAF air base in September 1981, when a group from Wales began protesting at the government's decision to base American nuclear missiles there. The Greenham Common Women's Peace Movement was formed and on 1 April 1983 a fourteen-mile chain of protestors stretched from the base to Aldermaston and beyond. The women were evicted one morning in April 1984 but had all returned by nightfall. Their vigil would last until the last missile left the base in 1991, and beyond.

On 2 April 1982 Argentina invaded the Falkland Islands. Within a matter of days a British task force had been assembled and set sail. On 25 April British forces recaptured South Georgia, and on 14 June Argentina surrendered. Nine hundred men had been killed in the conflict. It has been said that the military junta used the Falklands to divert attention from Argentina's domestic problems. If this is true, it was a very expensive diverson in terms of human lives.

The miners' strike of 1984 got under way in March and did not officially end until a year later, when the miners went back to work. This was a period of violent confrontation between the striking miners and the police. The mineworkers' union was possibly the most powerful union in Britain at that time and had been strong enough to bring down the Conservative government in 1974. But the 1984 strike gradually stripped away that power and the prolonged strike became a defining moment in British industrial relations.

The Live Aid concert of 13 July 1985 was one of those historic events that seem to emerge every now and then and unite the world with a sense of common purpose. On this occasion the purpose was to help the starving millions of Ethiopia. The event was held simultaneously at Wembley stadium, London, and the JFK stadium in Philadelphia. Eighty-two thousand people attended the concert in London and 99,000 attended in Philadelphia. There were other Live Aid concerts organised in other countries. Joining a worldwide TV audience of probably 400 million, I will never forget Queen's fantastic performance of 'Radio GaGa' or the images of the faces of the starving broadcast as we listened to 'Drive' by The Cars.

In the middle of 1985 dire news emerged of a new virus strain that could destroy or significantly impair the human immune system. HIV and AIDS soon became darkly resonant acronyms in America and Western Europe. For six years there had been a growing awareness of AIDS in African countries like Zambia, Rwanda and Zaire but by the end of 1986 it was found that there were one and a half million people with AIDS in America, and alarm swept through Europe and Australasia. The fear that this disease was spread through sexual promiscuity curbed, to some extent, the permissiveness that had become accepted in the previous twenty years.

At the end of April 1986 the Number 4 nuclear reactor malfunctioned at Chernobyl in Ukraine. The radioactive fallout from the accident which was carried around the world was hundreds of times more deadly than the fallout from the Hiroshima bomb. It was the world's worst nuclear power plant disaster, and its legacy is still being felt in the twenty-first century.

Twenty-two people died in England and France during the storm of 1987, which did immense damage. Initially it was thought that its effects would be confined to the south coast and the coast of France, but it eventually swept across much of England. It uprooted 15 million trees which disrupted road and rail traffic for days afterwards. Despite all this, as the years have gone by, this storm is best remembered for the flippant remarks made by BBC weatherman Michael Fish when he dismissed the worries of a concerned viewer the night before.

In 1989 a wind of change would blow through the Soviet Union. Early that year the Soviets withdrew their troops from Afghanistan. After ten years they had failed to win their war against the Mujahideen. By the spring of that year a process of profound political change had begun in the Soviet Union's Eastern European satellite states. Dissidents in Hungary and Poland, led by Václav Havel and Lech Walesa respectively, began campaigns to seize political control in a 'velvet revolution'. By November the Berlin Wall was being dismantled, literally brick by brick, and by December Czechoslovakia and Romania were no longer under direct control from Moscow. By the end of 1989 the 'velvet revolution' was almost complete. It had cut across a great swathe of Eastern Europe. The political repression that had been a staple of life under Soviet communist rule for over 40 years was ended.

The eighties had begun as a continuation of the seventies, but when the Berlin Wall came down it signified an ending. I think most people found a new hope that things could change for the better. Throughout my life I had heard the phrase 'we'll have to wait and see', so that is what I continued to do as my life chugged along in bottom gear.

CINEMA

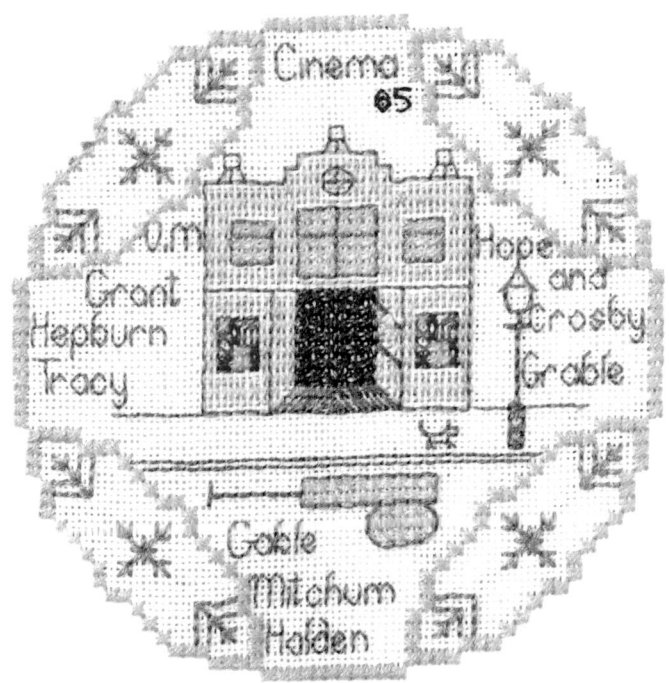

Although I couldn't go to the cinema every week when I was young, unless there was a serial running, I did go on a regular basis. Even the journey to the cinema in those days was a form of entertainment in itself. In our town we had six cinemas to choose from. If one was packed out we just moved on to another. If suitable films were available, most of them would screen a matinee for children on Saturday afternoons for 5d (2p). These cheap seats were always in the front stalls; you had to get there early and join the queue if you wanted to avoid sitting in the front row. The joke at the time was that if you sat in the front row to see a western, you would get dust in your eyes.

The queue would be absolute bedlam. There was much pushing and shoving and when the doors opened it was always a wonder that nobody was trampled to death as the great stampede began. Once inside, having jostled for a good seat, we would have to wait another half an hour for the show to start. The assistant manager would try to keep some sort of order, largely for the sake of those adults at the back who had been daft enough to pay good money to go to the movies on a Saturday afternoon. He would come around to the front and shout at the top of his voice for us to keep quiet, but we took no notice.

There would be a tremendous cheer as the heavy velvet curtains opened, the lights dimmed and the show began. The screenings always started with a newsreel followed by the supporting film. The peace would soon be shattered if the film contained long, boring bits. We would take the opportunity to start scrapping again and an adult at the back would shout: 'Put a bloody sock in it.' If the film broke, as it often did, there would be pandemonium, especially if we had just got to an exciting bit.

With almost a riot on his hands the assistant manager would come striding down the aisle carrying his ultimate weapon. Up would go the cry: 'He's coming!', and we would scramble back to our seats with lips firmly clamped together as we waited for the enveloping vapour. These under-managers all seemed to have a sadistic streak. With a pressure pump held firmly in his hands he would raise his arms to shoulder height and with a strong and purposeful action he would shower us all with a strong-smelling, evil-tasting liquid which, if you were mad enough to open your mouth, would sting the back of your throat and make you splutter.

No part of the front stalls was missed as he walked from one side to the other. He would then swagger back up the aisle with a fiendish grin on his face. The smile quickly turned to rage one afternoon when, as he was halfway up the aisle, an apple core caught him squarely on the back of his head. He marched to the centre of the front row and shouted angrily, 'You lot will sit quietly, even if I have to stand here all afternoon.'

And he did. And it was a boring film. We were glad to get out. We were sprayed in most of the cinemas in the town, sometimes two or three times per show, but we survived. I have no idea what was in these sprays. While it doesn't appear to have done us any harm, we didn't like it at all.

I tried never to miss a Betty Grable film. I thought she was the most beautiful creature on the planet. For me, her best film was *The Dolly Sisters* with June Haver. After seeing that film I spent hours practising my high kicks in the back yard where no one could see me.

Slapstick comedies were also very popular, as were westerns. Many weeks the cinema would feature a Roy Rogers, Gene Autry or Hopalong Cassidy 'B' movie. It was in a Hopalong Cassidy film called *Hoppy Serves a Writ* that I first set eyes on Robert Mitchum. I believe this was his first film. When I saw him again in a 1945 film called *West of the Pecos* I had found my all-time favourite leading man.

We enjoyed cartoon shorts. These were Bugs Bunny, Tom and Jerry and Donald Duck cartoons, which were used as fillers. If the complete show was considered too short they would put on a cartoon to make up the time. In those days large railway stations in cities would have a 'news theatre' close by. These showed nothing but continuous cartoons, newsreels and other shorts, each lasting no more than ten or fifteen minutes. These allowed anyone who had a long wait for their next train to be entertained without becoming involved with a lengthy film. There were only two feature-length cartoons in my early days, as this kind of movie-making was in its infancy. These feature-length films were *Bambi* and *Snow White*. They would be rescreened occasionally, always to packed houses.

Being a sentimental soul, I enjoyed a good 'weepie'. Among the first films to reduce me to floods of tears was *The Song of Bernadette*, with Jennifer Jones playing a young nun who had seen a vision of the Virgin Mary. After seeing this I went about for days in a bit of a dream, determined that, as soon as I was old enough, I would take the vows myself.

Sometimes a cinema would show a serial for a few weeks, and that meant going along every Saturday so that we would not miss an episode. These were absolute rubbish but it was always necessary, once you had seen the first episode, to consider the effects on your street credibility if you gave up. Each supposedly cliff-hanging episode would finish with our hero about to meet his end in some ghastly manner. The following week we would pick up the story in a completely different place to where we had left it. Our hero would be alive and well and there would be no clue as to how he had escaped from his ordeal. The best of all the serials were concerned with the adventures of Flash Gordon, a futuristic hero from the twenty-fifth century, starring Buster Crabbe.

Dad didn't like going to the cinema. He said it was the unhealthiest place you could sit; shut in, in the dark, exposed to other people's germs. He took Mother to see *San Francisco* before the war started and then, with some relief, volunteered to give up cinema-going for the duration. Mother used to talk wistfully of the film *San Francisco* and its stars Clark Gable, Spencer Tracy and Jeanette MacDonald and would explain how she used to enjoy going to the movies occasionally.

But Dad was mostly deaf to her pleading. In 1946 she managed to persuade him to take her to see *The Wicked Lady*. It was another year before she got him to go again. A film called *Frieda* was showing to full houses all over the country including our local high street cinema, the Palace (a name that should be taken with a pinch of salt). It was about a young airman returning to Britain at the end of the war, bringing with him a German bride. On one Thursday evening, after a hurried tea, Mom and Dad arrived at the cinema to find that it was standing room only. Dad wasn't impressed but, after they had been standing at the back for about twenty minutes, an usherette offered them two seats right in the centre of the audience which they took.

However, after half an hour Dad decided that he needed to go to the gents. Having struggled to find his way there in the dark he decided it was too much trouble to find his way back to Mother, so he left her there and went home. He had been at home for about half an hour and was comfortably settled with a pot of tea and the newspaper when Mother came storming in. No matter how much he protested, she was having none of it and the evening ended with him well and truly in the doghouse.

In the end, to appease her, they went back to the Palace on the Saturday afternoon. (There was no children's matinee that week.) They came home as happy as Larry, both having enjoyed the film immensely. Dad was particularly pleased with the supporting film which he thought was as good as, if not better than, *Frieda* itself. It was called *The Overlanders* and starred Chips Rafferty.

We accepted Dad's judgement unquestioningly, with him being such a 'film buff'. I don't think he went to the pictures again until about 1963 when he went to see *South Pacific* and then again in 1967 to see *The Sound of Music*. As far as I am aware he never went again after that.

A horror film would have us queuing for hours. How we loved them. There are too many of these films to mention all their titles, but the masters of horror at the time were Lon Chaney, Bella Lugosi and Boris Karloff. At the first sign of something nasty looming on the screen we would be out of our seats and down on the floor. One film that frightened the life out of me was *The Mummy's Hand*. I spent most of the performance on the floor with Ted's cap over my face and my fingers in my ears. Ted bravely sat and watched every minute.

Some horror films didn't have werewolves, vampires or other monsters. They didn't need them. One film, made in 1942, was called *The Night Has Eyes*. It starred James Mason and began with the disappearance of a young woman on a walking holiday on the moors. Her friend goes off in search of her and encounters a strange young man and his housekeeper living in a large, ivy-covered house. The house held a terrible secret. I shuddered for days after seeing this one, and when it was shown on TV years later it still gave me the jitters.

Years later when Ray and I were courting it was still very difficult to get into a cinema on Saturday evenings. One wet Saturday, on being turned away from all the other cinemas, we ended up going to the local 'flea pit'. We were told that there were only a few seats upstairs. When we got up there we could not believe our luck. There was a double seat empty on the back row. Perfect. We struggled along the tightly-packed row and quickly sat down.

The seat was empty because it was broken. Now, in those days I carried a little more timber than Ray. As we sat down, I went down and Ray went up. We sat there all evening like that. Occasionally I would look up at him and he would look down at me and we would have a fit of the giggles. To make matters worse, I couldn't see the screen. There was no point in moving, as there were no other seats.

Ray loved swashbuckling adventures and exciting, epic battles. He always knew the details of every film that was shown on television. He knew whether it was worth watching or not, what it was about and who was in it. He said he went to the movies seven nights a week as a child, and such was his knowledge of films that I never doubted him. It was all he ever really wanted by way of entertainment. To him, going out meant going to the pictures. He is the only person on the tapestry to have two circles devoted to him alone.

Nowadays, of course, going to the cinema is a different matter. I have to admit that my cinema-going gradually declined as we became more hi-tech at home with a video recorder. I went to see *Jaws* in 1975 and *E.T.* in 1982. At some point I saw one of the *Star Wars* films but did not venture to the cinema again until some twenty years later. This was to see *The Lord of the Rings: The Fellowship of the Ring*. I was gob-smacked. To say that film technology and sound reproduction had come on a bit since the days of *Flash Gordon's Trip to Mars* would probably be the understatement of all time. To cap it all, with my first sighting of Viggo Mortensen as Aragorn at the Inn of The Prancing Pony, sitting in the shadows with a hood concealing most of his face, I felt as I had done the first time I set eyes on Robert Mitchum 60 years earlier. I saw the whole *Lord of the Rings* trilogy and sat entranced through each film. What a pity Ray could not have been there to experience them with me. He would have enjoyed them so much.

– CIRCLE 66 –

THE NINETIES

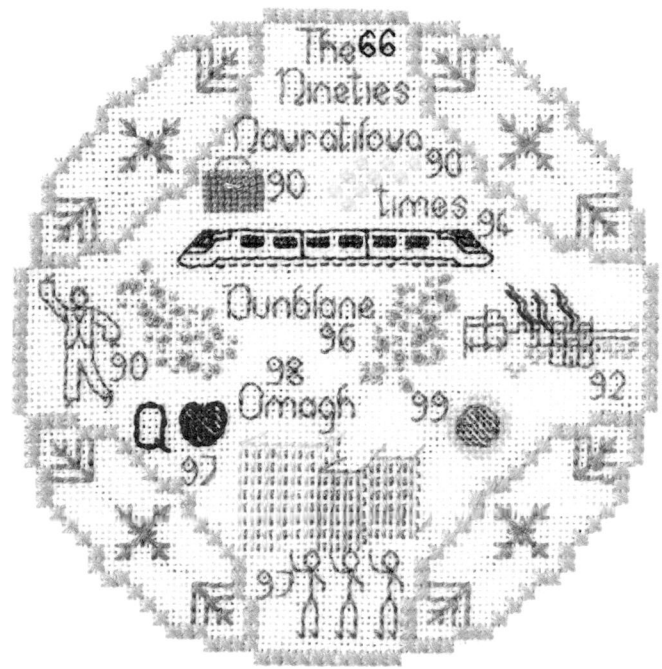

On 11 February 1990 Nelson Mandela was freed from the prison where he had become a symbol of the anti-apartheid movement. As a young politician and lawyer, in 1961 he had become the leader of the African National Congress's military wing. He was arrested by the South African authorities in 1962, after a tip-off from the CIA. He was held in prison for a total of 27 years. In July 1990 John Major replaced Geoffrey Howe as foreign secretary in Margaret Thatcher's Conservative government, and Howe became deputy prime minister. Howe's move back to

domestic politics was seen as a demotion. Howe resigned on 1 November, and Thatcher's fate was sealed the moment he finished his resignation speech in the House. While we had begun the year welcoming back Nelson Mandela, by the end of it we had said goodbye to Margaret Thatcher.

Martina Navratilova had been the world's most successful female tennis player throughout the eighties and in 1990 won her ninth singles title to great applause. In 1991 a significant law in favour of women's rights was passed. From then on it would be illegal for a man to rape his wife. It would have been interesting to know what Mother might have said about this.

In November 1992 a fire started in the Queen's private chapel at Windsor Castle and spread rapidly. It raged for many hours before being brought under control. Questions about who should meet the cost of rebuilding it raised, once again, the question of funding the monarchy. The Channel Tunnel was opened in 1994 having cost twice its initial estimate. It runs from Folkestone in Kent to Coquelles near Calais. I have no desire to use it; I have never been comfortable on the water, let alone under it.

In the nineties there were two tragedies which still do not bear thinking about. On 13 March 1996 a lone gunman entered a primary school in the small cathedral town of Dunblane in Scotland at half past nine in the morning. In cold blood he murdered sixteen children, all aged five or six, and their teacher. He then turned the gun on himself.

The Omagh bomb was detonated on Saturday 15 August 1998. It has become one of the blackest days in Ireland's troubled history and was widely condemned as the worst kind of indiscriminate killing. The town was busy with weekend shoppers. Among the dead were representatives of many age groups and religions. Of the 29 killed, one was a woman pregnant with twins and nine were children. This Real IRA bomb brought condemnation from many countries in the world, as well as from the IRA and the Irish people.

On 31 August 1997 Diana, Princess of Wales, was killed in a Paris car crash and Britain experienced a great outpouring of grief. Thousands of people placed flowers outside the royal palaces in London and many people across the world expressed deep sorrow.

Hong Kong was returned to China on 1 July 1997. The small Chinese colony had been passed to the British as part of the Treaty of Nanking in 1842. From 1898 it had been held on a 99-year lease. The acquisition of Hong Kong fitted in with China's commercial ambitions as the communist government continued to open up to world trade.

The expected total eclipse of the sun in 1999 had been well publicised. Everything would depend on the weather, of course. But in this instance it did not matter whether it was sunny or not, because this was a total eclipse and it would therefore become quite dark. On 11 August the sun shone. I had already decided that I would remain indoors. As the time approached I seated myself in the bay window and when the birds in the trees outside went very quiet I knew it was about to happen. It was quite eerie and I was glad when it started to brighten up again.

During the nineties I experienced every emotion that a human being can experience. I had, like most people, suffered anxieties and anger at man's inhumanity towards man as the world moved from one tragedy to another, and at home I had more than I could cope with at times. But, for me, things did get better, helped in no small way by two holidays with Jim, Judy and their children while they were living in Cape Town in South Africa. I have lovely memories of my granddaughter Emma's ballet class, and my grandson Tim's enthusiasm when

we went for a drive along the breathtaking Chapman's Peak. Judy and I had a lovely afternoon at Hout Bay and I still regularly use the world globe that Jim found for me at a market in Milnerton. When things are tough good memories can help you through, and I did get through. By the end of the nineties I had much to look forward to in the twenty-first century.

ILLNESS

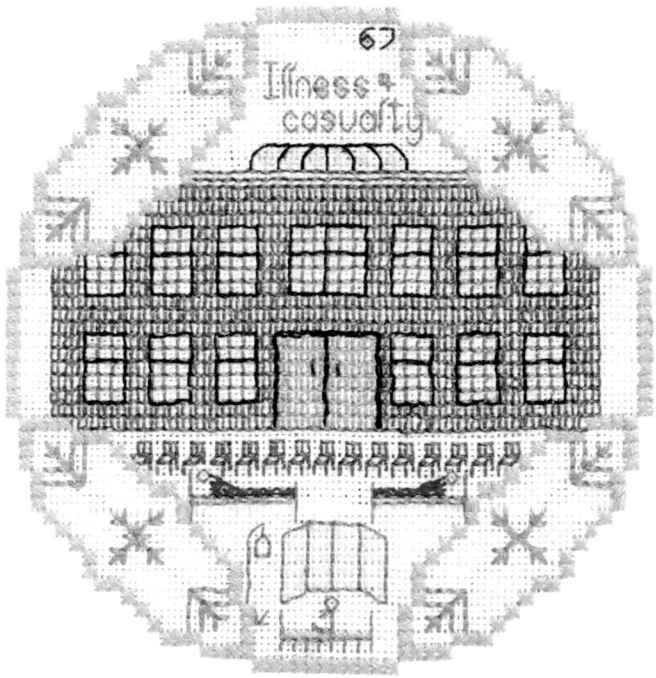

In my youth you had to pay to see a doctor. So, when you sent for him, he had no doubt that he was needed. If he thought it was necessary he would call in every day. In serious cases he would call twice a day. When he said that he need not call again, you knew the patient was better.

Aside from all the usual ailments, serious illness was quite common among children then, even among the better-off families. I can remember the deaths of four of my school friends, though not what caused them. Two of the four died suddenly.

They had been perfectly well one day and were dead the next. One girl was ill for a long time and when she died her family, in their grief, asked if some of the children from her class could stand outside the house as the coffin was carried out. I was one of them. Another one of my friends, a boy, died of gastroenteritis at the age of twelve. There were two children who had leg irons. Another periodically had convulsions.

Ted once had mastoids. He had had earache in both ears during the day at school and when he arrived home at teatime Mother took one look at him and rushed him to see the doctor. The receptionist looked at him and sent him straight into the surgery. The doctor looked at him, bundled him and Mother into his car and hurried to the district hospital, having phoned ahead with a request to prepare for an emergency double mastoid operation. The reason why they all knew that something was wrong was that both of Ted's ears were sticking out like jug handles. This, apparently, is the first sign that a mastoid is present. In Ted's case it was both ears. He made a quick recovery after the operation and was soon home again. In those days an operation was the only answer. These days it can be treated with antibiotics although it is still considered a serious illness.

I had scarlet fever when I was still a small child and apparently spent six weeks in the isolation hospital. As I was in isolation, Mom and Dad were only allowed to climb the fire escape and take a peep at me through the window while a nurse kept me occupied. I don't remember any of this but I do remember the day I was allowed to go home. As a nurse led me down the staircase I didn't recognise Mom and Dad, who were standing at the bottom. As the nurse let go of my hand and turned away I ran after her. She calmed me down and I was eventually persuaded to sit on Dad's lap on the bus. I clearly remember that he was wearing one of his trilbies. As I furtively looked up at him he looked down at me and smiled and I thought he looked all right, so that was OK. At home, on the hearth in the front room, was a lovely doll in its pram which had been offered to my parents by some kindly person for a few shillings. I loved it.

My brother Jim had more illness than any of us. When not much more than a baby he ended up in the children's hospital in Birmingham with a twisted gut. I did not realise until recently that there was only a 50–50 chance of surviving this ailment.

At one time he was ill in bed with measles and the doctor was making daily visits. When he called in on the Sunday morning before the August Bank Holiday, not only had the rash become rampant but, worryingly, Jim was also suffering a great deal of discomfort with stomach pains. The doctor immediately diagnosed appendicitis and there the problems really began.

Because it was a holiday weekend every hospital had only a skeleton staff, and there was also the problem of him having measles. An ambulance arrived. Mom and Dad went with Jim in the ambulance, the doctor followed in his car and they sped off for the district hospital. This hospital could isolate Jim by putting him in a private room, but they didn't have a surgeon. Another hospital had neither a surgeon nor spare isolation facilities. The isolation hospital did not have an operating theatre. The neurosurgery centre was the only hospital to have a surgeon and an operating theatre, but did not have isolation facilities.

At every hospital Mom and Dad remained in the ambulance with Jim while the doctor rushed inside to see if they could be of any help. But then Jim's illness took a serious turn when peritonitis set in. The urgency of the situation forced a compromise. The surgeon from the neurosurgery centre was rushed to the district hospital and Jim was saved.

On another occasion when Jim was very poorly, he was hot and feverish and the doctor was sent for. He left a prescription and gave strict instructions that Jim must be put to bed and not be allowed out of it. With a fire in the very small bedroom fireplace, Mother and I took turns sitting with him. He was asleep through all of this. In the evening two of the neighbours came to take turns watching over him while Mother got some rest. One of them had a little weep as she sat with him, and stayed on to comfort Mom when she returned to take over. Jim, now in a very deep sleep, was as white as a sheet and appeared to be totally unconscious. He remained this way for many hours, with no movement at all. I remember Mother being very worried.

Dad tried to get some sleep, for he had to go to work the next day. Mother didn't leave our room all night, and disturbed my slumbers a couple of times when she added more coal to the fire. The next thing I knew it was morning and Dad was bringing in a cup of tea for Mom. I was still half asleep. As Mom and Dad talked in whispers, Jim woke from his long sleep. He was as bright as a button and his temperature was down.

Mother wept.

SOUTHAMPTON WATER

I have already mentioned the village of Netley, where Ray and I lived (see Circle 38). The village is set on Southampton Water. This is a very busy stretch of water which links the Solent to Southampton docks and is used by all sorts of sea-going craft.

When we moved to live there I had not seen much of the sea during my life. To me, with my land-locked upbringing, watching great ocean liners coming and going was like looking into another world. During the couple of years that we lived in Netley I saw the liners *Queen Mary, Queen Elizabeth* and *United States* many times, and these were just three among many. However, no other sighting would equal the time I saw the *Queen Mary* sailing towards the docks, quite late on a summer's evening, lit up from stem to stern. Gliding gracefully, with her reflected lights shimmering on the water and a flotilla of tug boats in attendance, she looked outstandingly beautiful.

In the autumn of 1957 the magnificent aircraft carrier the USS *Forrestal*, pride of the American fleet, made a courtesy visit to Southampton which lasted for about three days. Commissioned on 1 October 1955, she was the first supercarrier built specifically for jet aircraft, and the first to have an angled flight deck and steam catapult. She carried 552 officers and 4,988 enlisted men. Her first deployment was with the 6th Fleet in January 1957.

Later that same year, after a NATO exercise in the North Sea, came her visit to Southampton. There was a civic reception for the captain and his staff, and this hospitality was returned the following night when the town's mayor and other dignitaries were wined and dined on the ship. Both of these events were reported extensively in the *Echo*, the local newspaper. There were also many accounts of what happens when a huge seaport town is taken over by 5,000 men with plenty of money to spend, particularly as the *Forrestal* was not the only military vessel in port at the time. It is enough to say that the visit was a great success and a wonderful time was had by all.

The ship left port at around noon on the Saturday and many spectators lined the shore to see it leave. I was among them that day and it was a sight I have never forgotten. The ship was festooned with flags and it seemed like most of the crew lined the decks; they were standing easy but in perfectly formed ranks. Below decks the hold doors were open on both sides of the vessel allowing a splendid through view of the many jet fighters inside, with their wings folded. I felt privileged to see it.

AIRCRAFT

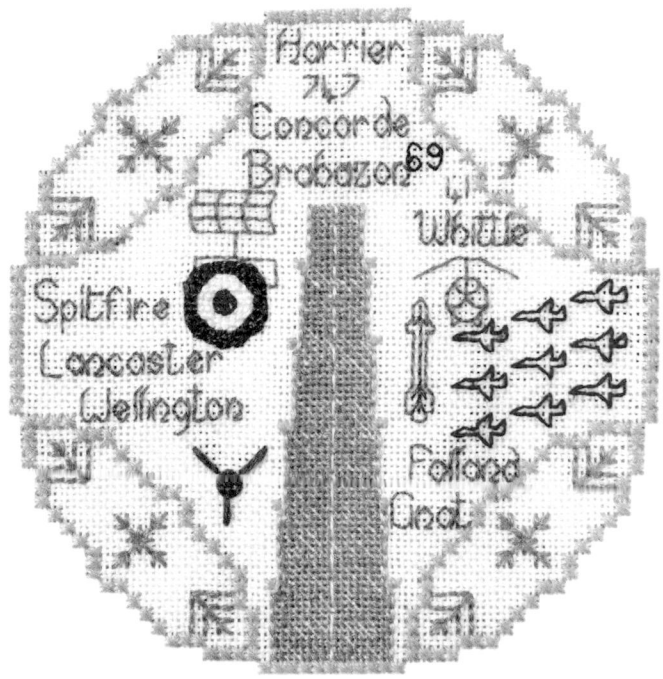

I have always loved aeroplanes. Not flying in them, but watching them. I was raised on daring tales of Spitfire and Hurricane pilots and the bravery of Lancaster crews, especially the plight of the 'tail-end Charlies'. While American bombers had a certain futuristic, glamorous look, Britain's Lancaster bomber was my favourite. It always looked so big and reliable. It was almost 70 feet long with a wingspan of 102 feet.

But this was eclipsed when the Bristol Brabazon transatlantic airliner completed a series of test flights in 1949. We saw it on cinema newsreels which gave us glimpses of its interior – it was awe-inspiring. I remember the aviation pioneer, Lord Brabazon of Tara, as one of those people who are often described as 'larger than life'. The aircraft which carried his name was ahead of its time and there is, as far as I know, still nothing to compare with it today. It was 177 feet long with a wingspan of 230 feet. It had eight engines with eight paired contra-rotating propellers in four nacelles. To get some idea of its size it is helpful to compare it with a Boeing 747 or 'Jumbo' jet, introduced nearly 30 years later, which is nearly 232 feet long with a wingspan of just over 211 feet.

While there is some similarity in the size of the two planes, the Boeing can carry 400 to 500 passengers and the Brabazon was designed to carry fewer than 100, but it would carry them in absolute luxury. The cabin was the last word in comfort. There would have been a bar, a restaurant and sleeping quarters for every passenger. Work began on it in 1947 and its first commercial flight was on 4 September 1949. Alas, there is sometimes a price to be paid for being ahead of the times. Designed with only very wealthy passengers in mind, it seemed to completely miss the idea that super-sized airliners might actually help to reduce the cost of international air travel and so it was declared too expensive to be commercially viable. The Bristol Brabazon was never developed past the prototype stage. Any future plans were abandoned in 1953 and the prototypes were broken up.

While on our way, by coach, to Weston-super-Mare for a day out in 1949 Mom, Dad, my brother Jim and I saw the Brabazon in the air. Its size seemed unbelievable. Jim and I still talk about it occasionally. On our way home we saw it parked in front of its hangar, and if we hadn't seen it in the air that morning we would have doubted that it could be flown. It was stunning.

The Folland Gnat, with a wingspan of just 24 feet, was tiny in comparison but no less amazing in my eyes. It was still being tested when Ray and I worked at the huge Folland Aircraft factory near Southampton Water. Ray worked on the shop floor, and I worked in one of the many small offices dotted around the factory which recorded the time that engineers spent working on various jobs.

The prototype Gnat came a cropper during one test flight and limped back into the factory a bit dented and scraped. I can remember going to have a look before they started work on it, and I seem to recall that one of its wings was a bit battered. It was a low-cost, compact aircraft which could be built without the need for special equipment. This made it attractive to other countries. A fleet of Gnats eventually went into service as training planes for RAF jet pilots. Because of its manoeuvrability and top speed of 636 mph at altitude, it later became the plane of choice for the Red Arrows display team which was formed in 1965. The Folland Gnat continued with its breathtaking aerobatic displays until it was replaced by the Hawk in 1979.

While the Gnat remains in service in other parts of the world one of my all-time favourite aircraft, Concorde, is now sadly a museum piece in Britain. I took little notice of all the exchanges between France and Britain through the years of Concorde's development, but in time the new supersonic plane was shown on television news coming in to land after a test flight. I was hooked. So was Ray. Concorde began its descent looking like a graceful, giant bird. As its feet (wheels) touched the runway its beak (nose cone) dipped down. It had all the grace and beauty of a swan landing on water.

Concorde could fly at roughly 1,350 miles an hour – twice the speed of sound – and eventually began commercial flights between London and New York in 1975. It could travel between these two cities in 2 hours and 22 minutes. It ceased operations in October 2003 and its retirement flight was on 26 November 2003. I have been on Concorde – but only to walk through it while it was on the tarmac at Duxford.

At the 2006 Fairford air show I was overwhelmed by the range, size and capabilities of modern aircraft and I spent most of the day transfixed. This was the first, and so far only, time I have been able to watch a Harrier jump jet being put through its paces. It has now been in service for over 40 years and was always Ray's favourite military aircraft. I was also greatly impressed, although I would not be exaggerating if I said mesmerised, by the capabilities of the Russian MiG. Fantastic.

Towards the end of that afternoon my curiosity was aroused when, during a brief lull between the quick-fire displays, a number of young men, all wearing the same style of outfit, began to gather in groups among the crowd. These were quite obviously the pilots of the modern aircraft we had seen in earlier displays. What had they come to see? A quick look in the programme confirmed that they were there to witness the fly-past of the Lancaster, the Spitfire and the Hurricane. After all those years these wartime planes still drew the attention of a crowd who showed great admiration and respect for their achievements of over 60 years earlier.

HOBBIES

You will not be surprised to know that I find it difficult to sit with idle hands. The reason for this is that Mother would never let us just sit and do nothing. At the first sign of a glazed look spreading across your face as you settled into the luxury of doing nothing, she would bring you out of your reverie with the words: 'Find something to do before you get too comfortable. The devil makes work for idle hands.'

Just precisely what uses the devil could have found for my small, idle hands was never established. The result of Mother's interventions was that Ted, Jim and I were always doing something. In fairness to Mom, I have to say that I don't ever remember her sitting with idle hands in those days either.

I began with scrapbooks. I had a scrapbook for film stars, of course, and books on flowers, cuddly animals and the royal family. I would fill the pages of any old book that was no longer wanted, sticking the pictures in with a mixture of flour and water. In our home the King, the Queen and the Princesses Elizabeth and Margaret Rose were always held in high esteem. I recall one cold, wet night when Dad came in from work. As he was hanging up his cap and coat, Mother said that there had been an earlier radio announcement that the Princess Margaret Rose had a severe chill. He replied that this was bad news, and said that it demonstrated just how ill she was that those in authority had seen fit to let us know. He meant every word.

As a child I always had a box containing old birthday cards and Christmas cards which had been passed on to me by elderly people I knew. These cards were not part of the enormous greetings cards industry that exists today, and they were consequently all the more treasured. I was given some very beautiful cards, and it is one of the very few regrets of my life that I do not still have them all. The most beautiful of these were the embroidered ones from France and other European countries involved in the First World War from soldiers to their wives, sweethearts or mothers. They had been kept and treasured for years but when they arrived in our house Mother would say 'They've come to their last home now', and I am ashamed to admit that they had. I always thought I could do something useful with them such as making them part of a small purse or handkerchief sachet, but each time I tried I was too ambitious.

I began knitting at an early age. I had spent some time trying to master the intricacies of this ancient skill but had had no luck.

I always dropped more stitches than I actually knitted. Mother had tried many times to show me but these little sessions would always end in the same way when she, in frustration, would push me aside and declare: 'Yoh'm 'opeless.'

At one of our frequent family gatherings I had been sitting in a corner trying to concentrate on my knitting, but it started to go wrong and I sensed that I was about to start 'grizzling'. Not wanting to let anyone see my frustration I began to make my way to the back yard. As I passed by Auntie Ria she asked: 'What's the matter with little Jeanie?'

I wailed my reply, 'I can't knit', whereupon she took control and showed me how to do it. I think the difference between Auntie Ria's teaching methods and Mother's could be put down to vibrations. Auntie Ria may have had a sip or two of alcohol and was therefore calm, while Mother would have been fully wound up and vibrating with impatience before she started, and I could sense it. Having got the hang of this age-old craft I, unfortunately, always tended to set my targets too high. For example, when Dad came in from work one evening I proudly showed him the scarf I had just started knitting for him. Two days later I had undone the scarf and started to knit him a tie. After that I undid the tie and started a small purse, and that was how it went. As the years went by I taught myself how to do crochet and tatting and spent many a happy evening making doilies or a new dressing table set, but these items are no longer in vogue and have become things of the past.

When I was a young mother I adapted the old wartime adage of 'make do and mend' to 'make a new one instead', and taught myself dressmaking. I became a serious 'sewist', as I called it, impressed as I was then with all things ending in 'ist'. For a period I was a numismatist and then I became a philatelist.

Philately led me on to the art of letter-writing, and with this hobby I decided to start at the top. I had been given some envelopes with old British stamps on them. Some of these had not required a stamp, because they had come from Buckingham Palace, but did have a postmark. The lady who had given them to me thought I might find them interesting. One of these Buckingham Palace envelopes was edged in black, meaning that the court was in mourning. Using the date of the postmark neither Ray nor I could work out for whom the court was in mourning so I wrote to the Queen. I was so thrilled with the response I received, and a further exchange of letters on this matter, that I became an avid letter-writer. As it turned out, the subject of the court's mourning was some obscure European royal.

I got into the habit of collecting china; a cup and saucer, a plate or a dish from places that I visited, as a memento of my day out. I found this very rewarding, as there is nothing nicer than enjoying a cup of tea while recalling a nice day out. It is particularly pleasant to do this in the winter months when I don't go too far from home.

This is a hobby that I would have happily continued, but I ran out of places where I could display the pieces I was collecting. This lack of space led me to take an interest in doll's houses. This kept me going for many years because not only could I buy many beautiful things in miniature, I could also make such items as rugs, bedcovers, cushions and tablecloths. As I began furnishing my fifth house I knew it was time for another hobby, and through my efforts to recreate miniature paintings I was drawn (so to speak) into art.

Luckily, in 1999 a new shop had opened in Smith Street, Warwick which met all the needs of the dedicated artist. I approached the shop tentatively, hoping that I would not be dismissed as a complete novice, but the people who own it, the Taylors, provided much encouragement and advice as I developed my own methods. I found it both a relaxing and rewarding hobby as I began looking at everything around me in a different way. Though I had to give up painting when I began my university education in 2003, I have always promised myself that I will take it up again one day.

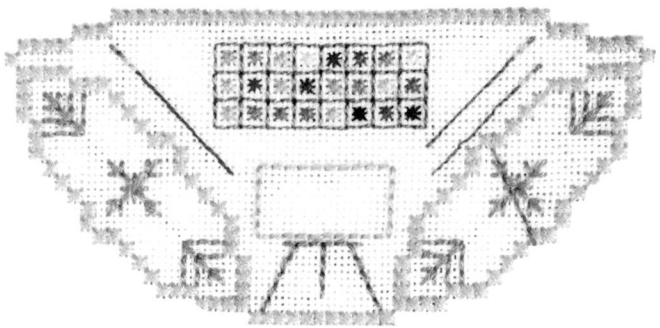

Having filled the space in this circle I became rather flummoxed when I realised that I had completely forgotten to add a representation of needlework. How could I have forgotten that? In the end the only thing I could do was squeeze in 'and needlework', which I'm afraid looks exactly like the afterthought it was.

POLITICIANS

It is never advisable to get me started on politicians. The way I see it, the whole British political system is outdated. By the time I was nine I had learned the hard way that politicians were not to be trusted. While the war was on, and for some time afterwards, politicians had promised me – I use the word 'me' advisedly – that when the hostilities ceased and everything was back to 'normal', the country would be overflowing with milk and honey, chocolate, sweets, bananas and nice clothes. Everything was going to be lovely.

It wasn't, and in the intervening years the parties in power have gone back on their word many times. Even the Trades Descriptions Act does not seem to apply to them.

Dad appeared to have more faith in the system. When he cast his vote he always felt that it was the best way of getting things done. He put his trust in the party of his choice.

In my early years, misdeeds and scandals among our political masters rarely appeared in the newspapers. Of course, there were rumours. The adults would mutter and tut when a new piece of gossip came their way, and I believe it was the Profumo scandal that blew the lid off the private lives of politicians. And what a pathetic lot some of them turned out to be. John Profumo was the Conservative secretary of state for war. He resigned in 1963 after lying to the House of Commons about his involvement with call girl Christine Keeler, who, at the time, was the mistress of a Soviet naval attaché. This case rocked the establishment when it became obvious that Profumo was only the tip of the iceberg. Along with stories involving the sordid world of another central figure in the scandal, Stephen Ward, which led to him committing suicide, much was made of the goings-on among our 'betters' at Cliveden, the stately home of the Astors where Profumo met Keeler.

Today hardly anything remains hidden for long. When a politician falls from grace the electorate feels let down. Politicians seem to forget that in a democratic society they owe their positions to the electorate, though many of them give me the impression that they think everyone should be eternally grateful to them for devoting their lives to working for our benefit.

THE NOUGHTIES

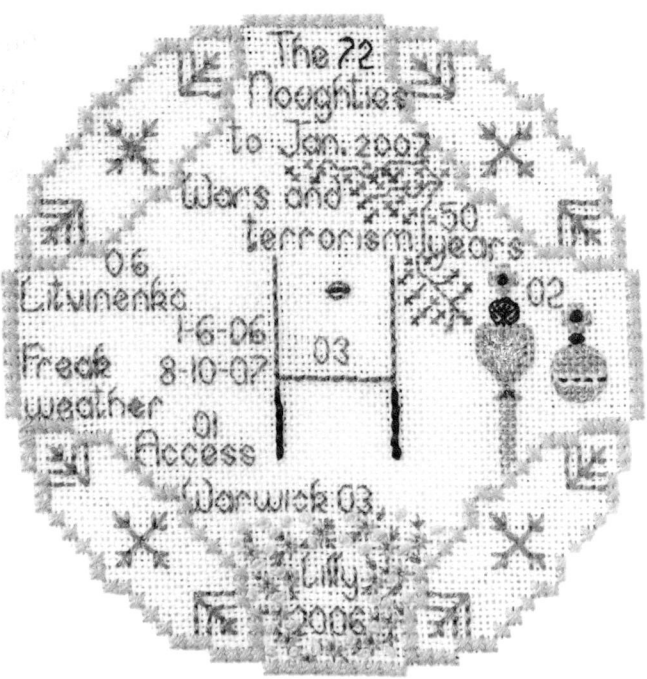

By the time I finished the tapestry at the end of 2007, the noughties had been dominated by acts of terrorism, wars and freak weather. We watched on television as the catastrophe of 9/11 unfolded in New York in 2001. We saw the devastation of the Boxing Day tsunami in 2004. The London bombings of 7 July 2005 were closer to home when, during the morning rush hour at 8.50 am, three suicide bombs were detonated in the underground system. A fourth exploded on a London bus in Tavistock Square at 9.47 am. Both Jim and Mark were in the city that morning. They were both fine, but I am rather glad I didn't know that they had been there until later.

Freak weather conditions have plagued us as weather patterns have changed. We have spells of mild weather in the winter months and wet and windy weather in the summer. In 2004, at the height of the tourist season, the river in the village of Boscastle in North Cornwall became a torrent and swept aside everything in its path, including cars and 60-foot trees. We are left with the feeling that these freak conditions could now happen anywhere and at any time.

Political intrigue between nations has always played a part in ensuring irreparable mistrust and non-cooperation. In the forties we had to rely on the likes of Humphrey Bogart to show us the existence of such scheming. By 2006 we had been living with it for donkeys' years via television news programmes. In that year came the slow death of Alexander Litvinenko, a former member of the Russian KGB (by now renamed the FSB), who was living in London as a political refugee. He suffered radiation poisoning from a small ingested dose of polonium-210. It took him three weeks to die. There was no satisfactory conclusion to this affair but again, through television, we were witness to his death.

On a lighter note, in 2002 we saw the Queen's jubilee, a celebration of her 50 years on the throne. In 1952, as head girl of my school, I had stood with a teacher listening to the Proclamation of the Queen's Accession speech. In the large crowd gathered outside the town hall we were representing the school. As I recalled these events, I began to wonder where the 50 years had gone. I expect the Queen felt much the same. It doesn't happen very often that the Queen and I share some thoughts. It could be a first.

England won the Rugby World Cup on 22 November 2003, in front of a crowd of nearly 83,000 people and millions more watching on television throughout the world. They had beaten Australia 20–17 at the Telstra stadium in Sydney, in a game that had had a nail-biting finish. The evenly-balanced match had gone into extra time. With only 21 seconds remaining, Jonny Wilkinson scored a drop-goal, at which point everyone went wild. The England side returned home on 8 December. An immense feeling of national pride swept the country as the team paraded the trophy through the streets of London on an open-topped bus. Mark was in the city again that day. As they pulled into Trafalgar Square the huge crowd sang 'Swing Low, Sweet Chariot'. Marvellous!

When I consider the news service in the forties and compare it with the technical achievements of today's media, I find it difficult to believe the changes that have taken place. When we view events now on our TV sets we are sometimes looking at something that is actually happening, in real time, on the other side of the world. In the forties, if a journalist wanted to send a photo from the other side of the world it had to come on the next available flight. The only alternative was a radio picture which would still take hours to arrive, and when it did it would be badly blurred.

In 2003 I began taking an annual holiday with Angela and her family, and all of these holidays have been special for me. With her husband Mark as our guide I have seen things that I never thought I would see, and all of them in the company of my grand-daughter Megan, together with Mark's two sons Brodie and Kurt. Megan has always been a thoughtful girl, but you need to spend some time in the company of Brodie and Kurt to realise just how easy and uncomplicated they are. All six of us have enjoyed everything that could be found in the Lake District, the Peak District and other places; but each time, at the end of the holiday, I have had to return to the reality of everyday living.

For me, this decade has been dominated by two things. The first was my university education which is still ongoing. It has been such a long time coming that I long ago accepted that it might never happen. However, anyone can do it if they put their mind to it. It opens up a new world and makes you see things differently. I removed any doubts I had about taking it on by telling myself that I was doing it for the girl on the wall, because I knew it was what she wanted. This turned out to be a wise decision.

There have been three occasions when I felt that I couldn't go on with it any longer. The first was when I got fed up with the journey to the Warwick University campus. While a crow could do it in five minutes, it takes me an hour and a half travelling by bus. The second was when I got a mark of 60 for an essay which I considered to be worth at least 75. When I read it again two years later I could see that it was worth about 52. On the third occasion I just felt that I had had enough. But you always have to keep in mind that, if you are struggling, the help is there if you seek it out. While it would have been regrettable to have let down my family by giving up, I found that I simply could not fail the girl on the wall. In other words, I could not let myself down.

These feelings show how important the girl on the wall has become to me: she is at the other end of the bridge that spans my life. This awareness of the other, earlier me has slowly developed into a form of self-respect, of which I had never had much during the twentieth century.

The second dominating factor of this period was my work on this tapestry. It began simply enough on 1 June 2006 as a work detailing the traumas and pleasures of a very ordinary working-class life. Then I realised that I had been fortunate to have witnessed so much in my lifetime that it was going to be very difficult to decide what to exclude. As the work developed I began to realise it had other possibilities. I could write about each circle. With that, the studies, the writing and the needlework became all-consuming passions while I continued to do everything in my power to please the girl on the wall.

WOMEN'S CLOTHING

You cannot write about female clothing without mentioning underwear and writing about girls and women in general. As a young child I wore a vest, liberty bodice and knickers. Vests haven't changed much and, in our house, were worn all year round, even in hot weather. Mother considered it indecent to leave off this garment. One very hot Sunday in the park she became very agitated when she realised that I was not wearing my vest under my best frock, and made me put my cardigan on.

Liberty bodices have now disappeared completely. These were

worn to keep your chest warm in the winter months and were dispensed with as one neared the age of ten or eleven. They were very snug and were made of thick, soft cotton, brushed on the inside and best remembered for their rubber buttons down the front.

Knickers had elasticated legs which came to just above the knee; or below, in the case of Mother who was very much on the short side. The grown-ups' version were known as 'directoire' knickers. For school we had to wear a dark colour such as navy blue or bottle green and on the right leg was a small pocket for keeping your hankie in. If you changed out of your shoes into pumps and tucked your dress inside your knickers, you were ready for games or drill. The mind boggles. Women could choose between directoire knickers, briefs or French panties. Briefs were favoured by younger women and were the same as knickers except that the leg was shorter. Mother said that French panties were only worn by women with low morals. She said this in a way that could only be interpreted as a warning, and I made a mental note never to buy any of these when I grew up or else I would likely feel the wrath of God.

Knickers and briefs were made of cotton interlock, a cotton jersey fabric, for everyday wear and celanese for best. They came in white or delicate shades of pink, blue and green. As celanese was a very soft, silky, finely-knitted rayon fabric, I suppose they could feel quite slinky. It was many years before Mother gave up wearing her directoire knickers, and the bigger she could get them the happier she was. We jokingly called them Mother's 'smalls'. My dark knickers stayed with me until I left school at fifteen, although the legs did get shorter and the elastic was replaced by a sort of ribbed cuff. These were known as briefs but I use the term 'briefs' very loosely. At the time Mother had doubts about these. She thought they were a bit racy.

And so to brassières, pronounced not as the French would say it but in the local idiom, in which it came out as 'brazzears' with the emphasis very much on the 'zears'. Some of the older women still preferred to call them 'bust bodices', but my contemporaries and I were happier with the term that was just creeping across the Atlantic – bra. I suppose I was approaching the age of twelve or thirteen when I developed alarmingly disproportionate protrusions on my chest. Mother wouldn't buy me a bra, even though I was cringing with embarrassment. It was only when one of the neighbours commented that I could do with a bit of support that she relented.

I remember that first bra well; it was tea rose broché with built-up shoulders. The colour tea rose was a sort of ghastly brownish pink, and broché was a fabric with self-coloured, raised, woven flowers. Very matronly. I hated it but at least I had stopped wobbling all over the place. In around 1950 someone came up with the idea for A, B and C cup bras, which meant a better fit. As was the way in our house, we soon changed that. These became E, B and C cups, standing for 'egg cup', 'breakfast cup' and 'challenge cup'. I, of course, went straight into the challenge cup size which only added to my embarrassment.

One Tuesday evening the family were sitting round the kitchen table. Nearby was the clothes horse holding all the ironing that Mom had done that afternoon. Ted took one look at my bra and remarked: 'I see you've found something to make your Christmas puddings in then, Mother.'

Nylon stockings had been around for quite some time before Mother could afford a pair, as they were ridiculously expensive. There was a man at the indoor market who sold nothing but stockings. There were several ranges. Lisle stockings were very thick and usually worn by elderly women. Rayon stockings were worn by most women for everyday use. Pure silk stockings were reserved for weekends and special occasions. All were available in 'ordinary' or 'fully fashioned' varieties. The fully fashioned stockings were much nicer but more expensive. With the shape of the heel block and the shaping in the stocking itself, there was no mistaking them especially when they were worn inside out. This was done to make the seam down the back stand out more. Mother always wore rayon but for special occasions she would buy a pair of pure silk, fully fashioned stockings.

Then along came nylons. The last word in 'oomph'. There were several methods recommended for storing nylons: the most popular and cheapest of these made use of a jam jar. If you kept each pair in a jar there was nothing for them to snag on. The older women stuck with what they were used to for a long time and would say, with a meaningful sniff, that nylons were for the young flibbertigibbets that had cotton wool for brains. I didn't quite understand this observation, because Mother did not strike me as a flibbertigibbet when Dad bought her her first pair in 1951.

Mother knew exactly which pair she wanted and I was promptly dispatched to the market. They were Bear Brand nylons and, at sixteen shillings, were by no means the most expensive pair. They weren't even fully fashioned but, even so, sixteen shillings (80p) was almost a king's ransom. I made my purchase and didn't have them wrapped. I displayed the precious packet all the way home and desperately hoped that everyone who saw them would think they were mine. To give some idea of the value of sixteen shillings in 1951 I would have to jump forward to when I started work in 1952: my first week's wage was 37 shillings and sixpence (£1.82). As time went by the prices tumbled and by 1954 a cheap pair of nylons could be bought for two shillings and eleven pence (15p), but it was wiser to pay three shillings and eleven pence (20p). These were harder wearing.

Mother hated suspenders and whenever she had a new corset she would immediately snip these off with a pair of scissors. Instead she used garters. That evening I watched spellbound as she drew these filmy stockings over her chunky knees and, with an expert double flick of the wrist, knotted them inside her garters. She did this with such a flourish, she could have knotted stockings into garters for England.

When she went off later that evening with Dad she had a very haughty expression on her face and an unmistakable 'knowing head-wobble'. But she returned three hours later in a fury. She grabbed the gleaming jar that she had left ready and waiting to receive its precious cargo and muttered: 'That can go in the dustbin!'

I looked down in horror. She had a ladder. The following morning she gave the stockings to me and, never having worn a pair of stockings before, I gently washed them so as not to make the ladder worse. I made myself a pair of garters. The next day I went off to school with a virtual tourniquet just above each knee, having concealed the ladder as best I could. It was not a good day. Everyone seemed to take delight in telling me I had a ladder. By the time I got home I could stand it no longer; I removed the garters and for the next hour was forced to massage my legs in order to restore the circulation. I vowed that it would be a long time before I wore stockings again. It was, and when I did I kept them up with suspenders.

When I was young, a baby was dressed like a baby and a girl was dressed like a girl. When the girl left school she dressed like her mother and that was the end of that. This, more than anything else, gives some indication of the time warp in which the working classes had been living for so long. But things would change. By 1945 many of the women who had worked in factories during the hostilities had experienced life outside the home for the first time in years. The woman of the house had had a job; perhaps only a part-time one, but still a job that gave her the company of other women and a pay packet at the end of the week. This is not to say that all women preferred to continue working. Many found fulfilment at home. But after the war women wanted the freedom to choose.

The wartime clothing trade had been ruled by the shortage of fabric. Only a certain amount of fabric could be used in each garment and the number of buttons was also strictly limited. In 1947 French couturier Christian Dior gave women the 'New Look'. It was more feminine than the styles women had been used to and consisted of a softer shoulder line, nipped in at the waist with a fuller, longer skirt. Those who could not buy new clothes and who had become skilled in 'make do and mend' now put their ingenuity to work yet again. One of the most popular ways of updating an old garment, which I can remember doing myself, was to cut six inches off the skirt of a dress or coat and put in a four- or five-inch strip of a contrasting but suitable fabric to create a longer skirt. There were many botched jobs, but the perpetrators wore their 'ingenuity' with pride. Through this new-found confidence, the fifties became the decade when young men and women forged ahead in their mass breakaway from parental control. By the end of the fifties young women were ready for the opportunities of the sixties, and they grabbed at them with great enthusiasm.

During this decade the clothing industry began catering mainly for the young. Carnaby Street and King's Road in London became the centre of the universe. We no longer had fashion shops, we had boutiques. Biba, started by Barbara Hulanicki, was one of the best. Mary Quant became the high priestess of fashion. Lesley Hornby and Jean Shrimpton were seen everywhere and known only as 'Twiggy' and 'The Shrimp'.

Skirts got shorter and shorter and it didn't seem to matter if you had thighs like an ostrich. They were at their shortest between 1967 and 1968, when they became known as 'belts'.

Fashions could change overnight and were marked out in 'periods'. For instance, the psychedelic period is remembered for its swirling, garish colours. In 1964 André Courrèges launched a 'Space Age' collection; this consisted of white boots and gloves worn with a trouser suit, and a kind of baby bonnet designed to look like a spaceman's helmet. To achieve the Gina Fratini look of 1968, you needed a willowy body dressed in a very short miniskirt and brief top, and it was necessary to have very long legs, long, straight hair and a baby-faced look. The baby-faced look was, in part, achieved by painting long lashes under the lower lids and freckles each side of the nose. This constant change brought down the smaller boutique owners and allowed in the larger stores: Chelsea Girl and Miss Selfridge became the places to be seen. By the end of that decade the fashion industry had changed forever.

In the seventies we saw the further development of fashions for babies, children, teenagers and women. Casual clothes became the in thing. T-shirts were used for advertising and carrying slogans or pictures, and were personalised using tie-die or batik. The fashion for jeans really took off. These had become popular in the fifties as part of the move away from adult styles. By the seventies jeans had to have a label. If they didn't have a label you were not 'with it', and a trend was established which is still with us.

During the rest of the century women started to dress to please themselves. Their attitude became: if it's fashionable, that's fine; if it isn't, who cares? In the forties young women had dressed like their mothers. At the start of the fifties there were still no shops for younger women. But in the sixties, mothers began to copy the way their daughters dressed.

By the end of the century there were no shops for mature women, and perhaps the most important development during my lifetime is that such women, at least as I remember them, seem to have disappeared forever. Seventy years ago the mature woman would have worn a tightly laced corset with busk front, drab-coloured dresses and coats, a hairnet, thick stockings and sensible shoes. In the forties a young woman who wore mascara was pushing the boundaries; today, many older women wouldn't be seen dead without it.

EPILOGUE

Through this work, I have become aware that my life seems to have been lived in stages. I have recalled with much satisfaction the happiness that we were able to find in childhood, when the world was in such a mess and times were hard because of the war. We survived despite everything that came our way. But then we realised that the planet would never be at peace. Very few lessons had been learned from five-and-a-half years of world misery which cost 57 million lives and ruined twice as many more.

However, we had the enjoyment of living in a time when the closeness of the extended family was simply a way of life, and this helped us through the forties and into the fifties. As I grew and married, with my own life willingly put on hold, I learned to appreciate the pride I have in my son and daughter, which I have never hidden and never will. As Mother used to say: 'If you can't take a pride in your own whose can you take a pride in?' She'd got room to talk. Then in the course of time I found delight in watching my grandchildren grow and achieve, although they grew too quickly.

With the deaths of Dad, Mom and Ted came a deep sadness, followed by my absolute despair when Ray died and I had to cope with the ordeal of learning to live without him. This was tinged with the gladness I felt that he had found me in the first place. In time I rediscovered my enthusiasm for living after whoever, or whatever, guided me in my despair to Warwick, where I found so many lovely people and an education. I found again that all-important sense of purpose as I began to take care of the girl on the wall.

I also found immense pleasure in working on the tapestry; each day my brain went into overdrive as the memories tumbled out. I recalled the dignity of the working men I used to see on a daily basis as they walked to and from the factories in the street, when expectations were lower and life at home was less demanding. I am immeasurably glad that I still have a brother with whom I can share some of the earliest of these memories.

I shall always be grateful for being born at such a time and in such a place, although I could have done without the twang. Finally, I am truly thankful that I am still here to talk about a life that has been unique – as is everybody's, although few seem to realise it.

Buy a large-scale print of Jean Baggott's tapestry – special offer for readers of *The Girl on the Wall*

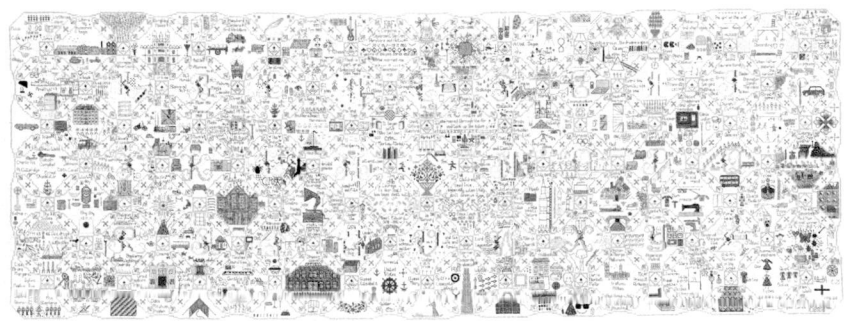

Jean Baggott's tapestry around which this book is based took sixteen months to sew and contains 36,992 stitches, sewn on 32-count evenweave linen.

It was designed to fit over a table in Jean's living room and measures 112 x 41cm.

To buy a high-quality, A1-sized print of the tapestry (which is just slightly smaller than the original) direct from Icon Books for only £6.99 including post and packing in the UK,* please:

- Visit www.thegirlonthewall.com/tapestry and follow the 'Buy the Tapestry' link

- Phone TBS Distribution on 01206 255800 quoting '*The Girl on the Wall* Tapestry Offer'

- Send a cheque, payable to Icon Books Ltd, or a letter including credit card details, to:

The Girl on the Wall Tapestry Offer
Icon Books Ltd
Omnibus Business Centre
39–41 North Road
London
N7 9DP

For postage outside the UK, please email info@iconbooks.co.uk for prices and availability.

The print measures 594 x 841mm and will be supplied in a rigid poster tube.

Interested in sewing your own life story as a tapestry? Jean Baggott has provided a useful guide on 'The Girl on the Wall' website. Please visit www.thegirlonthewall.com and click on 'Making Your Own Tapestry'.